AGEING AND DIVERSITY

Multiple pathways and cultural migrations

Edited by Svein Olav Daatland and Simon Biggs

First published in Great Britain in April 2006 by

The Policy Press
University of Bristol
Fourth Floor
Beacon House
Queen's Road
Bristol BS8 1QU
UK

Tel +44 (0)117 331 4054
Fax +44 (0)117 331 4093
e-mail tpp-info@bristol.ac.uk
www.policypress.org.uk

British Library Cataloguing in Publication Data
A catalogue record for this book is available from the British Library.

Library of Congress Cataloging-in-Publication Data
A catalog record for this book has been requested.

ISBN-10 1 86134 847 9 paperback
ISBN-13 978 186134 847 9

Svein Olav Daatland is Research Director for Ageing and Life Course Studies at Norwegian Social Research (NOVA). **Simon Biggs** is Professor and Director of Gerontology, Institute of Gerontology, King's College London.

Cover design by Qube Design Associates, Bristol.
Front cover: photograph supplied by kind permission of Dawn Rushen.
Printed and bound in Great Britain by MPG Books, Bodmin.

Contents

List of tables and figures   v

Notes on contributors   vi

one   Ageing and diversity: a critical introduction   1
       Simon Biggs and Svein Olav Daatland

Section I: Individual pathways

two   Ageing differently: potential and limits   13
       Jacqui Smith and Denis Gerstorf

three   The personal meaning of individuality and relatedness: 29
       gender differences in middle and late adulthood
       Gerben J. Westerhof and Christina Bode

four   Diversity, health and ageing   45
       Lars Andersson and Peter Öberg

five   Gender trajectories: how age and marital status influence patterns   61
       of gender inequality in later life
       Sara Arber

Section II: Social identifications

six   The search for ageing identities   79
       Andrew Blaikie

seven   New ageism: age imperialism, personal experience and ageing policy   95
       Simon Biggs

eight   Sexuality in gerontology: a heteronormative presence,   107
       a queer absence
       Ann Cronin

Section III: Migration and otherness

nine   Making sense of the construct of successful ageing: 125
       the migrant experience
       Sandra Torres

ten   Older foreign migrants in Europe: multiple pathways and   141
       welfare positions
       Tony Warnes

eleven   Transnational communities, migration and changing identities   157
       in later life: a new research agenda
       Chris Phillipson and Nilufar Ahmed

Section IV: Structure and agency

twelve   Societal trends and lifecourse events affecting diversity in later life   175
             Jenny De Jong Gierveld

thirteen   Quality of life and social inequality in old age   189
             Andreas Motel-Klingebiel

fourteen   Class, power and inequality in later life   207
             Paul Higgs and Chris Gilleard

fifteen   Ageing and diversity, what next?   223
             Svein Olav Daatland and Simon Biggs

Index   229

List of tables and figures

Tables

2.1   Ageing differently – nine subgroups with different psychosocial   23
profiles identified in BASE

3.1   Percentage mentioning personal concerns of individuality and   36
relatedness by age group and gender

3.2   Case studies (category numbers in brackets)   38

5.1   Income, material well-being and health by age and gender in Britain   65
(age 65+)

5.2   Odds ratios of income, material circumstances and health by gender   67
and marital status in Britain (age 65+)

10.1   Foreign citizens in selected European countries (1980-2001)   145

10.2   German social insurance pensioners receiving their old-age benefits   150
in foreign countries (1997)

12.1   Descriptive statistics of the respondents by sex and lifecourse types   181

12.2   Interconnectedness with children, and loneliness of older adults   183
with at least one child alive, corrected for differences in age ...

13.1   Quality of life – the WHOQOL-Bref instrument   195

13.2   Overall and domain-specific quality of life (OLS regression, all countries)   199

13.3   Overall and domain-specific quality of life (OLS regressions by country)   201

Figures

2.1   Three theses about patterns of intra-individual psychological change   17
from 70 to 100 years

3.1   Patterns of individuality and relatedness by age group and gender   34

4.1   Long-term illness after retirement   49

4.2   General health status after retirement   49

4.3   Physical disability after retirement   50

4.4   The discrepancy between chronological age and ideal age for   57
respondents in different age groups

4.5   The distribution of the discrepancy between chronological age and   58
ideal age for the same sample shown in Figure 4.4

5.1   Percentage living in a communal establishment ...   72

10.1   The average age of nationals and foreigners in Belgium (1930-2000)   146

10.2   The age structure of the immigrant and total populations of   147
Norway (2001)

13.1   Overall quality of life and age (all countries)   195

13.2   Means of domain scores of quality of life (all countries)   196

13.3   Coefficients of variance of domain scores of quality of life (all countries)   197

13.4   Overall and domain-specific quality of life (OLS regression, all countries)   198

Notes on contributors

Nilufar Ahmed is currently a Research Fellow at St George's Hospital Medical School, London. She was previously active in the voluntary sector where she deployed her skills in various community organisations and acquired expertise in working with Asian women before effecting a return to academia. She has worked on numerous academic projects primarily focusing on the British Bangladeshi community. Research interests include transnational migration, representations and identities of British Muslims and mental health.

Lars Andersson is Professor of Social Gerontology at ISAL (Institute for the Study of Ageing and Later life), Linköpings University, Sweden, and Associate Professor of Gerontology at the Karolinska Institute in Stockholm and Research Director at the Stockholm Gerontology Research Centre. He is President of the Swedish Gerontological Society, President of the Research Committee on Sociology of Aging of the International Sociological Association, President of the Nordic Gerontological Federation, Fellow of the Gerontological Society of America, and appointed member of the WHO Expert Advisory Panel on Ageing and Health. He has edited *Cultural gerontology* (Auburn House, 2002) and *Socialgerontologi* (Studentlitteratur, 2001), contributed chapters in several books, and published extensively in scholary journals.

Sara Arber is Professor of Sociology and Co-Director, Centre for Research on Ageing and Gender at the University of Surrey, UK. She is well known for her research on ageing and gender and on inequalities in health. Recent projects examine older men living alone, food in later life and the sociology of sleep. Her edited books include *Gender and ageing: Changing roles and relationships* (with Kate Davidson and Jay Ginn, 2003); *The myth of generational conflict: Family and state in ageing societies* (with Claudine Attias-Donfut, 2000), and *Connecting gender and ageing* (with Jay Ginn, 1995).

Simon Biggs is Professor of Gerontology and Director of the Institute of Gerontology, King's College London, and has previously worked at the Centre for Social Gerontology at Keele University, UK. He is currently on the Executive Committee of the European Masters Programme in Gerontology. He has published widely in the areas of social policy, critical theory, and emancipatory practice in health and social care. His research interests extend to the study of adult ageing, including: social policy and its effect on personal identity, interprofessional partnerships, participative research methods and practice, and attitudes toward ageing, particularly in relation to the psychotherapies. Recent publications include: *The need for theory: Critical approaches to social gerontology* (with Ariela Lowenstein and Jim Hendricks) and *Social policy, social theory and old age: Critical perspectives* (with Carol Estes and Chris Phillipson).

Andrew Blaikie is Professor of Historical Sociology at the University of Aberdeen, UK. While he has researched and published widely within social gerontology, his interests span demographic, social and cultural history and he has endeavoured to broaden the remit of ageing studies across these disciplines and in sociology. His current research focuses on cultural dimensions of ageing, as expressed particularly in visual and historical sources and through the dialogue between expert and popular perceptions. Most recent publications include: 'The secret world of subcultural ageing: what unites and what divides?', in L. Andersson (ed) *Cultural gerontology* (Auburn House, 2002); 'It's a wonderful life? Cultures of ageing', in E.B. Silva and T. Bennett (eds) *Contemporary culture and everyday life* (Sociology Press, 2004); and 'Imagined landscapes of age and identity', in G.J. Andrews and D.R. Phillips (eds) *Ageing and place* (Routledge, in press).

Christina Bode is a Post-doctoral Researcher at the Department of Health Psychology, University of Utrecht, the Netherlands. She was previously researcher for the German and Dutch Aging Surveys and recently published her dissertation on individuality and relatedness in middle and late adulthood, using data from both surveys. She is currently involved in a project on the role of proactive coping in the aging process. She designed a programme on goal-directed preparation for ageing and is evaluating its effects in a randomised clinical trial.

Ann Cronin is a Lecturer in Sociology at the University of Surrey, UK. She has published in the areas of sexuality and research methodology. Her research interests include sexuality and later life, gender and the social construction of social identities, the sociology of storytelling and managing vulnerabilities in everyday life. Her current research is a qualitative study on the experiences of older lesbian-identified women, which focuses on the interaction between gender, age and sexuality. Forthcoming publications include journal articles on the social capital of older lesbian networks and the erasure of sexuality in social gerontology.

Svein Olav Daatland is a Research Director at Norwegian Social Research (NOVA), and a former Director of the Norwegian Institute of Gerontology. He has been active in European studies on ageing and the welfare state, and has published extensively on ageing, intergenerational relationships and welfare policy both in the Nordic countries and internationally. Among the later publications are 'Time to pay back? Is there something for psychology and sociology in gerontology?', in L. Andersson (ed) *Cultural gerontology* (Auburn House, 2002); 'From variables to lives: inputs to a fresh agenda for psychological ageing research in Norway' (*European Psychologist*, 2003) and 'Lost solidarity or changed solidarity: a comparative European view of normative family solidarity' (*Ageing & Society*, 2003, with Katharina Herlofson).

Jenny De Jong Gierveld is Honorary Fellow at the Netherlands Interdisciplinary Demographic Institute (NIDI) in The Hague, and Professor of Sociology and Social Gerontology at the Vrije Universiteit, Amsterdam. From 1987 to 2000 she was director of NIDI; from 2000 to 2003 she worked as Permanent Fellow of the Netherlands Institute for Advanced Study in the Humanities and Social Sciences (NIAS) of the Royal Netherlands Academy of Arts and Sciences. She has published in the areas of social research methodology, including books about survey research design, questionnaire development and operationalisation of theoretical concepts. She developed a loneliness measuring instrument that is frequently used in empirical research among younger, middle-aged and older adults. Her current interest is the demographic and social aspects of ageing. Publications include *A review of loneliness, concept and definitions, determinants and consequences*; *Social integration and loneliness: A comparative study among older adults in the Netherlands and Tuscany, Italy* (with Theo Van Tilburg); *Remarriage, unmarried cohabitation, living apart together: Partner relationships following bereavement or divorce*; and (with Peter Uhlenberg) *Age-segregation in later life: An examination of personal networks*.

Denis Gerstorf is Doctoral Fellow at the Max Planck Institute for Human Development and a member of the Graduate Program 'Psychiatry and Psychology of Aging' at the Free University of Berlin. His research interests focus on psychological factors of survival and longevity, issues of selectivity in research on the oldest old, and person-oriented approaches to examining differential ageing.

Chris Gilleard is Director of Psychology for South West London and St George's Mental Health NHS Trust. He has been collaborating for some years with his co-author Paul Higgs on issues concerning age and ageing in contemporary society. Recent books include *Cultures of ageing: Self, citizen and the body* (Pearson Education, 2000). With Paul Higgs, he has completed another book *Contexts of ageing: Class, cohort and community*, to be published in 2005 by Polity Press.

Paul Higgs is Reader in Medical Sociology in the Centre for Behavioural and Social Sciences in Medicine at University College London. He is an editor of the journal *Social Theory and Health* and co-author, with Chris Gilleard, of *Cultures of ageing: Self, citizen and the body* (Pearson Education, 2000). His research interests include social theory, social policy and consumption. He is a member of the English Longitudinal Study of Ageing and has been funded to conduct a project into consumption in later life by the AHRB/ESRC. With Chris Gilleard, he has completed another book *Contexts of ageing: Class, cohort and community*, to be published in 2005 by Polity Press.

Andreas Motel-Klingebiel is Vice-Director of the German Centre of Gerontology (DZA). He is joint coordinator of the Research Network on Ageing in Europe of the European Sociological Association (ESA) and member of the board of the Section Ageing and Society in the German Sociological Association (DGS). His main research areas include: social security systems and ageing, national and international social policy, social inequality structures, families, intergenerational transfers and service systems.

Peter Öberg is Associate Professor in Sociology at Uppsala University, Sweden. He has been a researcher in the field of social gerontology since 1985 at Kuntokallio Gerontological Centre for Training and Research in Finland, where he was also responsible for courses in gerontology. The research concerned social contacts and loneliness among older people. He continued as a Research Assistant at the Academy of Finland in a Nordic biographical project, 'Ways of life, ageing and well-being'. In 1997 he defended his thesis 'Life as narrative. On biography and aging' at the Department of Sociology, Uppsala University, where he now works as a researcher. His latest projects have been on 'Ageing, body image and identity'.

Chris Phillipson has held the post of Professor of Applied Social Studies and Social Gerontology, at the University of Keele, since 1988. He is Pro Vice-Chancellor (Learning and Academic Development) for the University. Current research interests include problems relating to poverty and social exclusion in old age, the impact of urbanisation on older people, and family and community relationships in later life. Recent publications include: *The family and community life of older people* (Routledge, 2001, co-authored); *Women in transition: A study of the experiences of Bangladeshi women living in Tower Hamlets* (The Policy Press, 2003, co-authored); *Social theory, social policy and old age: A critical introduction* (Open University Press, 2003, co-authored).

Jacqui Smith is Professor of Psychology and Senior Research Scientist in the Center for Lifespan Psychology at the Max Planck Institute of Human Development in Berlin. Her research interests include the study of profiles of psychological functioning in the young old and oldest old, psychological mortality, and the application of intelligence and wisdom-related knowledge to everyday life.

Sandra Torres holds a Senior Lectureship in Sociology at Mälardalen University, Sweden and is an Affiliated Researcher to the Social Gerontology Group at Uppsala University, Sweden. Her research interest lie at the crossroad between the sociology of ageing and the sociology of migration and ethnic relations. Her publications have dealt, among others, with the lack of culture relevance in gerontology; the issues of late in life migration and culturally appropriate care; the effects of late in life migration upon elderly immigrants' explanatory models of illness; the implications of postmodernism and globalisation for ethnogerontology; the effects of migration upon cultural values; and the formulation and preliminary empirical testing of a culturally relevant theoretical framework for the study of successful ageing.

Tony Warnes is Professor of Social Gerontology and Director of the Sheffield Institute for Studies of Ageing, University of Sheffield, UK. From 1994 to 2000 he was Chair of the British Society of Gerontology, the association of social scientists with special interests in studies of older people, and he is Editor of *Ageing & Society* (Cambridge University Press). Tony has worked with numerous agencies concerned with the welfare and activities of older people, including local Age Concern organisations and the federal bodies for Yorkshire and for England, The King's Fund, and the Royal Surgical Aid Society (AgeCare). Among recent research projects have been ESRC-funded studies of the 'Retirement residential strategies of Londoners', 'British retirement to the Mediterranean', and 'The causes of homelessness among older people, a three-nation comparative study' (with Maureen Crane). He recently coordinated a European Science Foundation Network on the 'Wellbeing of older migrants'. His recent books include *Sunset lives* (with Russell King and Allan Williams), *Care services for older people: Transformations and critiques* (with Nolan and Warren), and *The homelessness factile* (with Maureen Crane, Ruby Fu and Naomi Whitehead).

Gerben J. Westerhof is Senior Lecturer at the Centre for Psychogerontology, University of Nijmegen, the Netherlands. His research and teaching focus on the cultural dynamics of the development of self and identity in middle and late adulthood. He is also interested in the epistemological grounds and the practical use of qualitative and quantitative methods. He was involved in three large-scale survey studies, the German and Dutch Aging Surveys and the Survey on Midlife Development in the United States (MIDUS), and has published on well-being and personal meaning and the experience of ageing, as well as on identities in work, health and social relations.

ONE

Ageing and diversity: a critical introduction

Simon Biggs and Svein Olav Daatland

Introduction

What does it mean to grow old under contemporary social conditions? What are the possibilities for diversity of culture, lifestyle and experience? What are the constraints placed upon us as we grow older and how are they negotiated?

This volume critically assesses notions of adult ageing as they affect older people's lives and their social and personal identities. Drawing on a wide range of theory, original research and empirical sources, the contributors to this volume examine the idea that to understand contemporary ageing it is necessary to recognise its diversity. To begin with, individual pathways are examined; then some of the social sources of identification available to adult ageing. Next, the key questions of global ageing, migration, transnational community and citizenship are used to sharpen key issues that are increasingly influencing contemporary ageing. Finally, we examine the tension between social structures and the possibilities for personal and social agency. In an increasingly complex world, multidisciplinary and international perspectives are an important means of capturing diversity.

Ageing and diversity

That there are more older adults around than at any other time in history is now well known. It is less well understood that, as the population ages, it becomes more diverse. In part, this is because individuals have had time to develop a more integrated and particular sense of self; in other words, who they believe themselves to be. Additionally, we are exposed to many more cultural pathways than preceding generations, making life appear richer and with substantially more options than has traditionally been the case. Diversity is also a consequence, however, of cumulative inequalities that have been accrued across a lifetime and now accentuate difference in later life. Each of these trends contributes to a widening variety of experiences of ageing in contemporary societies – for good and for bad.

While there is an increase in diversity among older people, this is not to say that the stereotyping of what it means to grow old has in any way abated. If increasing diversity requires us to recognise the heterogeneous nature of ageing, there are countervailing tendencies to render ageing more manageable, simplified and subject to control. Thus, as people age, they become subject to a series of social expectations that may or may not correspond to their actual circumstances or personal potential. And while the contents of stereotypes will change with different historical periods, their limiting influence on wider perceptions of what it means to 'age well' is nevertheless pervasive.

From this perspective, the history of old age can perhaps be thought of as a history of the tension between diversity and homogeneity. Older people become more integrated and individual at the same time as attempts are made, consciously or simply through accepted 'commonsense', to allocate them a socially legitimised place in their particular societies.

It is currently assumed, then, that the pathways available to people as they age are becoming increasingly varied, both as individuals and as social groupings. Older people are no longer a pre-modern and small minority leading to a mythical number of respected individuals who can exert personal power within fixed frameworks: the rare survivor, worthy of respect and a holder of traditions. The stripping away of accrued wisdom as social change heats up has often been linked to industrialisation, where, for the majority of the population, youthful physical strength became the criterion for social value. A minority of privileged older people could insulate themselves from this process through accumulated wealth and social position. However, for the majority, elders were at best ignored and at worst characterised as a burden, carried by other parts of the population. Such a view of contemporary history has identified ageism as existing at the intersection of gender, class and age, although the latter is very much the invisible guest at this gathering of inequalities. Recent arguments suggest that the current generation of older adults is experiencing something different to these modern and pre-modern templates, driven by lives that are healthier and longer (Fries, 1980). Many of the problems of later life, it is claimed, can now be modified or even reversed (Rowe and Kahn, 1998), while the growth of occupational pensions has allowed increasing lifestyle choice (Gilleard, 1996). Such observations have promised a possibility of not growing old, or at least not in the same way as previous generations.

One of the consequences of individual societies becoming more culturally diverse than they had been for the majority of the 20th century is that one has to adopt a stance toward cultures of ageing. It is easier to communicate locally and transnationally, to share similarities, but also to be more aware of otherness. Thus, as social experience becomes more heterogeneous, it also highlights awareness of people who are not 'like us'. We have others to help us define ourselves through comparison, and thereby make our own sense of who we are more defined and similar to members of our own particular in-group. Exposure to many different pathways to growing old can provide positive alternatives to traditional patterns, but also intimate fragmentation and a lack of solid ground on which to find security. A key question here becomes how the dominant culture accommodates diversity and generates a defining discourse, a legitimate reality that is so difficult to step out of. Age is as much a part of this process as other social classifications. Older adults may be encouraged to define themselves in terms of younger groups, identify with them, adopt this dominant group's values, or possibly withdraw from or react against the values of youth. The question of how far issues of ageing are self-defined therefore becomes increasingly problematic. A critical perspective would need to ask how these positions correspond with the circumstances and experiences of older adults. These circumstances and experiences are reflected in studies of the socio-structural position of particular groups of older adults, in the images depicted in policy and elsewhere and in the self-reports of older people themselves as social actors. In order to explore these and other issues, we have chosen the motif of multiple pathways and of cultural migrations in an attempt to capture something of the tension between the increasing complexity of contemporary ageing and the need to identify common patterns of flexibility and movement that are simultaneously tempered with dangers of rootlessness and risk.

Multiple pathways

Hence, 'multiple' has been used to convey a sense of contemporary ageing as an increasingly complex business. There is no single accepted route to travel. Social expectations may no longer be fixed, and while traditional roles to grow old by are more often than not characterised by restriction, at least people knew what they were arguing about. Now the very notion of ageing is subject to considerable uncertainty. The effects of globalisation, for example, are mixed. On the one hand, it could be argued that trends towards a global society are exposing older people to an increasingly diverse series of options. On the other, globalisation may be producing a trend toward a homogenised and standardised perspective on the meaning of success in ageing. Similarly, medico-technical advance may be used to maintain or enhance the ageing body, but is it psychologically advisable to see oneself as 'staying young', and how will access to these technologies be divided?

We chose 'pathways' in order to emphasise ageing as a process that, like a journey, involves a direction and a progression through time. One can look back at the pathway that has been trodden, and make decisions about the possibilities for new directions and destinations. It is not, in other words, a state of being that is fixed and unchanging, either as a social category or as a personal experience. Adult ageing involves a series of challenges and an increasing interdependence between the body, the psyche and the social. Being exposed to many different pathways and having the possibility of travelling on them are not necessarily the same, as the opportunity to develop personal potential is again structured by a variety of inequalities and life experiences. There is continuing pressure to reshape spontaneous patterns of adult ageing into clearly defined social groups and thereby to establish some control over which pathways are taken and where they might lead.

Cultural migrations

The term 'cultural' has been used to identify the social discourses and pre-existing patterns that direct ageing in certain directions rather than others. Culture represents a set of broad social allegiances and determinants of acceptable behaviour, which, when compared one to another, extend an understanding of different expectations of adult ageing. Understanding culture in this way also poses the question of whether there are different cultures for different ages. Perhaps, then, we might begin to speak not only of culture in terms of ethnicity and nationhood, but also of the comparative difference between different parts of the lifecourse. Age cohorts – that is, groups of people who have aged together through a particular series of historical events and developed a sense of collective identity – are to a certain extent cultural when compared with other cohorts.

'Migration' refers to the movement across boundaries, into different states of being as well as physical relocation. An awareness of the age dimension of migration sensitises us to movement over time as well as over space. It is a process of leaving things behind, experiencing the new and maintaining connections. Ageing in a second homeland, for example, raises questions of the degree to which one 'carries' one culture to another, adapts to new situations, or adopts entirely different approaches to social and personal ageing. Continuing change marks both sides of the boundary between cultures as cultures themselves maintain their own trajectories, so that return is not a return to something exactly as one has left it. Age highlights the temporal dimension as well as the spatial, when it comes to movement, and while at one level this is simply a part of experience, it has at another rarely been highlighted in the academic study of age, culture and migration.

Gerontological implications

Gerontology may be particularly vulnerable to the dynamics implied by diversity and culture. It has been suggested by Moody (2001) that gerontology has a tendency to perceive itself as an amalgam of science and advocacy. Here lies an assumption, often tacit, yet deeply held, that the notion of progress, built on the successes of western medical science, is universally valid and will 'solve the problem' of adult ageing. It also suggests engagement in the promotion of particular forms of change, and a close relationship to policy formation and development. While it is important not to argue that a desire for continued health is in some way culturally specific, it is quite another to uncritically and exclusively adopt one model and its associated cultural trajectory. Yet such a trajectory determines much of the empirical research on ageing, and distorts our knowledge base and the values that determine the future accumulation of information to the exclusion of alternatives. Gerontology, left in the grip of such a direction, runs the risk of simply collecting confirming cultural evidence in the sense of uncritically answering questions set within an existing framework and finding solutions to the way the problems are posed there. An awareness of diversity in ageing has the potential to provide a powerful antidote to such an assumptive reality.

Pathways and migrations imply that boundaries are crossed, that areas of uncertainty are encountered and that commonsense assumptions are challenged. In many ways the 'gap' (Hendricks, 2003) or the 'nomadic' (Katz, 2003) nature of a subdiscipline such as gerontology takes the possibility of openness and experiment beyond the fixed paradigm outlined earlier. As a result of the close interaction between social, psyche and soma in old age, gerontology is necessarily multidisciplinary at heart and as such it is particularly capable of destabilising fixed positions.

Theoretically speaking, there is one key tenet in gerontological thinking that is challenged more than any other by the study of multiplicity and diversity: that a 'good old age' rests on a platform of personal and social continuity. Much of the thinking that takes place about ageing assumes a model that success in ageing is marked by a continuity of experience; that change is bad; that discontinuity is in some way disadvantageous. The models that underpin this perspective are often culturally specific, based on stable communities that are themselves relatively culturally homogeneous (Marshall, 1999). However, as the chapters of this volume indicate, the experience of many older people is anything but continuous and discontinuity can be expected to increase if trends toward transnational relations and complexity of identity continue on their current trajectories. Recognising the positive value of discontinuity can have a radicalising effect on how we think about adult ageing (Estes et al, 2003). There can be advantages to discontinuity at the personal and at the social level. First, it challenges established patterns, subjecting them to critique. Second, it highlights their cultural specificity. Third, it creates options, a possibility of exploring alternative pathways to those followed during earlier parts of the lifecourse, laid down by a particular culture or expected by other generations. Fourth, it reintroduces the positive value of certain if not all forms of stability, while avoiding the trap of seeing adult ageing as static and including a fixed series of attributes. Stability, in the sense of maintaining bodily competencies, may be good, for example, while increasingly fluid definitions of appropriate ageing may also be good. The first may be closely related to one's capacity to engage in the second. An awareness of discontinuity thereby sensitises us to the need for a balance between stability and change, itself suggesting the study of the strategies older people use to achieve a desirable equilibrium.

So, this volume consists of a number of attempts to understand diversity in ageing, and to shed light on at least some of the issues raised above. Each chapter begins with four points that the authors consider to be key. At the end of each chapter, and in addition to the references themselves, up to four further background readings are suggested.

In Section I, 'Individual pathways', Jacqui Smith and Denis Gerstorf (Chapter Two) indicate that there are many pathways to old age and that the processes of old age are multifaceted. They explore the concept of differential ageing in order to highlight the heterogeneity observed in populations of older persons, to summarise the many varieties of ageing phenomena, and to point to individual differences in intra-individual change. Findings from the Berlin Aging Study (BASE) are used as to illustrate points. The authors recommend that, rather than being treated as an outcome, differential ageing should be used to generate specific hypotheses about similarity and difference in age-related trajectories across domains of functioning or between subgroups of older people.

Gerben Westerhof and Christina Bode (Chapter Three) explore the personal meaning of individuality and relatedness through the lens of gender differences in middle and late adulthood. Individuality here refers to the experience of oneself as a coherent whole clearly separate from others. Relatedness refers to the experience of the self in relation to others. The authors conclude that these two concepts are more the concern of midlife than of older age and that different patterns and meanings exist within age groups, part of which is explained by gender. They do not, however, find an interaction between gender and age, and they warn against using such categories to conceal complexity and diversity at the level of the individual.

Next, Lars Andersson and Peter Öberg (Chapter Four) discuss diversity from a realist and a constructivist perspective. They argue that heterogeneity in health status within an ageing population can increase, decrease, or be maintained depending on context. They also point out that results vary depending on the research perspective adopted by a particular study and the presentation of data. Thus relations between health and social class appear to remain constant, increase, or even vanish over time. It is argued that social categorisation of data can decrease evidence of diversity, while qualitative research emphasising human agency may increase it.

In the final chapter in Section I, Sara Arber (Chapter Five) examines how ageing and marital status influence patterns of gender inequality in later life. She finds that older married men are advantaged on key aspects of quality of life, and this privileged position is the norm for older men since nearly three quarters are married. Widows are financially and materially disadvantaged, and widowhood is the norm for older women. However, the group projected to grow most rapidly in western societies – that is, older divorced people of both genders – faces the greatest financial, material and health disadvantages. Older women's higher levels of disability and widowhood result in them being more likely to spend the final stage of their life in a residential setting.

In Section II of this volume, 'Social identifications', Andrew Blaikie (Chapter Six) has paid attention to the how identities are produced and reproduced, both in relation to the experience of ageing and the way that social theories shape the understanding of age and identity. He notes that, within modernist interpretations of ageing, socio-structural factors are seen as determining lifecourse categories. By contrast, postmodern, deconstructionist, interpretations suggest that identities should be seen as developed 'from the self up'. It is suggested that notions of difference, judgements of what people are not, are used to negotiate the relationship between individuals, social structures and cultural representations. However, even within such a reflexive framework, consciousness of age and selfhood is not straightforwardly amenable to communication.

Simon Biggs (Chapter Seven) argues that questions of identity and ageing need to be seen as reactions to wider social definitions, such as can be found in social policy. Policy on ageing appears to have moved from responses to particular problems to attempted definitions of what it is to 'age well'. This shift can easily restrict the pathways open to older people and could be conceived of as an attempt by a dominant generation to shape the behaviour of others in its own image. Under these conditions ageing identity has increasingly to be managed. It is suggested that social ageism changes its contents over time, which requires closer attention to the processes involved.

And finally, Ann Cronin (Chapter Eight) examines how sexuality has been represented in gerontology, with a lack of attention being given to sexual orientation. An awareness of diversity challenges this 'queer absence'. Here, age is examined as a factor in access and participation in lesbian communities. Three key issues are identified: relationship status; the length of time a woman had lived a lesbian lifestyle; and geographical location. The diversity of these relationships affects the degree to which individual lesbian women access and maintain involvement in lesbian networks. Women who have always lived a lesbian lifestyle and are currently in short-term relationships or single are most likely to be actively involved in social networks, whether they are local, dispersed, or electronic.

In Section III, 'Migration and otherness', Sandra Torres (Chapter Nine) argues that the experiences of international migrants are a source of theoretically fruitful information about the shaping and reformulation of 'successful ageing' through the lifecourse. The potential embedded in engaging with migrant populations and the destabilisation of lifecourse continuity inherent to it could greatly enhance gerontological perspectives. Empirical illustrations are used to challenge eurocentric conceptualisations of 'a good old age'. They also indicate that, while migration is often formulated as a negative and disorienting experience, it is often experienced positively and can extend the repertoire of roles open to elders who find themselves growing old in a second homeland.

Tony Warnes (Chapter Ten) examines north-south migration within a European context. Two groups of older migrants are increasing in number throughout western Europe: labour migrants who moved north in the 1950s and are now growing old and affluent northern Europeans who move south in retirement. 'Older migrants' are immensely diverse and engage in complex interchanges between countries. They include some of the most socially excluded, as well as those who are pursuing innovative, positive approaches to their own old age. Warnes argues that there should be more recognition of the economic roles that migrants play, and more supportive policies for those who become sick or frail.

Finally in this section, Chris Phillipson and Nilufar Ahmed (Chapter Eleven) explore the relevance of the concept of transnational communities for work in the field of ageing. They identify how such communities have been defined in the research literature, and the links with wider themes such as globalisation and migration. Drawing on the experiences of women now in middle age, who migrated as young adults from Bangladesh to London, they discuss the impact of migration on the adult lifecourse, as well as implications for social identity and social roles in the community. The authors examine issues for social policy and research arising from the changes represented by the growth of transnational communities.

In Section IV, 'Structure and agency', Jenny De Jong Gierveld (Chapter Twelve) looks at societal trends and lifecourse events affecting diversity in later life. She notes that developments in the second half of the 20th century have resulted in new values and behaviour among today's older adults and their children. In particular, 'standard' lifecourse biographies have been replaced by choice biographies involving diverse lifestyles and life strategies. She maintains that partner history as well as status affect the social integration of older adults as far as children and the broader family are concerned. Policy makers will need to take into account a diversity in support needs suggested by a resulting variety in social contacts.

Andreas Motel-Klingebiel (Chapter Thirteen) examines the relationship between quality of life and social inequality in old age. He finds that quality of life is generally lower and more disparate within populations of older people when compared with other parts of the lifecourse. Factors relevant to quality of life vary considerably between age groups, with a key element being a shift from the outside world to inner spheres of being with age. While physical health is proved as the most important single domain for overall quality of life in old age, inequality of access to social goods is a key factor that emerges across national boundaries, resulting in restricted life changes and well-being.

Finally in this section, Paul Higgs and Chris Gilleard (Chapter Fourteen) explore the relationship between class, power and inequality in later life. They challenge the representation of older people as members of a residual class dependent on the rest of society and defined by the processes of poverty. Instead, they propose that later life should be viewed as both fragmented and complex, fully connected to contemporary economic and cultural processes, rather than as reflecting previous class locations. The welfare state has both transformed ageing by creating novel expectations about how it should be spent and created dilemmas of its own, as policy success is represented as demographic crisis and is subjected to the forces of globalisation.

As De Beauvoir (1970) famously observed, societies can be judged by the roles they allot to their older citizens. There are few things more challenging to the cultural assumptions of any group, be it national, cultural, professional or generational, than an encounter with alternative pathways and the possibility of migration from the existing state of affairs to something different and therefore more challenging. We hope that readers of this volume will be encouraged to take up such a challenge and that the arguments pursued here will contribute to that process.

Acknowledgement

This book project started out from the 34th European Behavioural and Social Science Section of the International Association of Gerontology (EBSSRS) symposium in Bergen, Norway in August 2002. Several of the chapters had their first formulations tried out there. We would therefore like to thank the EBSSRS and the sponsors of the symposium, the Norwegian Research Council, Norwegian Social Research (NOVA), University of Bergen, and the Norwegian Gerontological Society.

References

De Beauvoir, S. (1970) *Old age*, London: Penguin.

Estes, C., Biggs, S. and Phillipson, C. (2003) *Social theory, social policy and ageing: A critical introduction*, Buckingham: Open University Press.

Fries, J.E. (1980) 'Aging, natural death and the compression of morbidity', *New England Journal of Medicine*, vol 303, no 3, pp 130-5.

Gilleard, C. (1996) 'Consumption and identity in later life', *Ageing and Society*, vol 16, pp 489-98.

Hendricks, J. (2003) 'Structure and identity – mind the gap: toward a personal resource model of successful ageing', in S. Biggs, A. Lowenstein and J. Hendricks (eds) *The need for theory: Critical approaches to gerontology*, Amityville, NY: Baywood, pp 63-90.

Katz, S. (2003) 'Critical gerontological theory: intellectual fieldwork and the nomadic life of ideas', in S. Biggs, A. Lowenstein and J. Hendricks (eds) *The need for theory: Critical approaches to gerontology*, Amityville, NY: Baywood, pp 15-32.

Marshall, V. (1999) 'Analysing theories of ageing', in V.L. Bengtson and K.W. Schaie (ed.) *Handbook of theories of ageing*, New York, NY: Springer, pp 163-75.

Moody, H.R. (2001) 'Productive ageing and the ideology of old age', in N. Morrow-Howell, J. Hinterlong and M. Sherraden (eds) *Productive ageing: Concepts and challenges*, Thousand Oaks, CA: Pine Forge Press, pp 175-96.

Rowe, J.W. and Kahn, R.L. (1998) *Successful ageing*, New York, NY: Random House.

Section 1:
Individual pathways

TWO

Ageing differently: potential and limits

Jacqui Smith and Denis Gerstorf

Key points

- Lifespan theories have long recognised that there are many pathways to old age. Some authors have gone so far as to suggest that ageing is highly individualised.
- The concept 'differential ageing' has been used to highlight the heterogeneity observed among older persons, and to point to individual differences in intra-individual change.
- This chapter reviews variable- and person-centred approaches to differential ageing in the psychological and gerontological literature. Findings from the Berlin Aging Study (BASE) are used as to illustrate these two perspectives.
- To date, 'differential ageing' has been applied primarily as a summary description of outcomes. Future efforts should be directed toward devising theoretical models about the potential and limits of differential ageing.

Key readings

Baltes, P.B. and Smith, J. (2003) 'New frontiers in the future of aging: from successful ageing of the young old to the dilemmas of the Fourth Age', *Gerontology: Behavioural Science Section/Review*, vol 49, pp 123-35.

Smith, J. (2001) 'Old age and centenarians', in N. Smelser and P.B. Baltes (eds) *International encyclopedia of the social and behavioral sciences*, Oxford: Elsevier, pp 10843-7.

Smith, J. and Baltes, M.M. (1998) 'The role of gender in very old age: profiles of functioning and everyday life patterns', *Psychology and Aging*, vol 13, pp 676-95.

Smith, J. and Baltes, P.B. (1997) 'Profiles of psychological functioning in the old and oldest old', *Psychology and Aging*, vol 12, pp 458-72.

Introduction

Just as young adults differ from one another, so older adults are also not all the same. There are substantial inter-individual differences for example, in levels of cognitive functioning, personality, social networks, lifestyle, beliefs, interests, personal goals and satisfaction with life. Although theory and cross-sectional studies have long illustrated this heterogeneity (for example, Birren, 1959; Baltes, 1987, 1997), the social stereotypes of old age have still to be updated. Adults older than 60 or 70 are portrayed often as a single social group. Little attention is paid to the different life histories and capacities that contributed to individuals reaching old age or to the functional and longevity differences between older adults.

In this chapter, we ask questions about the nature, sources and implications of observed heterogeneity in old age. Our specific focus is the concept of 'ageing differently', or as some call it, 'differential ageing'. That is, we focus on the processes of ageing that occur over time, and attempt to explicate differences in patterns or pathways of ageing. In addition, our review is restricted to examples of ageing differently in psychological domains of functioning and findings from the Berlin Aging Study (BASE) (Baltes and Mayer, 1999).

The concept of differential ageing

The terms 'differential' and 'ageing' each carry their own sets of meanings. 'Ageing', for example, implies the inclusion of a time dimension and the implication that a behaviour or attribute has been present and was potentially observable on multiple occasions over months or years. Empirically, chronological age is frequently used as a proxy for time and ageing processes. 'Differential' suggests a diversity of distinct levels or directions. Joined together, the term 'differential ageing' has many connotations. It implies, for example, that people may change on many dimensions simultaneously, that there may be multiple forms of functional change observed within a person, that dimensions and their associated change trajectories may or may not be interrelated, and that different people may show different patterns of change across domains.

Research that addresses questions about differential ageing has taken several routes. One prototype is the search for trajectories of normal ageing as compared with successful, modifiable, or pathological ageing (for example, Rowe and Kahn, 1987). In addition, there is a recognition that not all individuals of the same chronological age may progress along the ageing trajectory in synchrony. For example, some may begin to show increased functional decline in their 70s, whereas for others the same trajectory may be delayed until their mid-80s. This idea is analogous to observations of early versus late (delayed) development or growth that are a well-known characteristic of early life. To date, although some research implies the idea of early versus delayed senescence – for example, 'compression of morbidity' (Fries, 1980) – much more work is needed in the field of ageing to determine factors that influence the onset of senescence (decline) trajectories.

Heterogeneity observed between individuals at one point in time could be due to the expression of inherited dispositions or to the cumulative effects of interactions between heredity and environment over time. Gerontologists and lifespan theorists generally assume the latter position: differences are interpreted as the cumulative consequences of previous intra-individual changes that differed across individuals in earlier phases of their lives. This assumption opens a realm of questions about the distribution of inter-individual differences and whether this distribution remains stable, expands, contracts, or changes shape across the lifecourse. The various positions on these questions reflect different lenses on the forces of heterogeneity across the lifecourse.

One position argues that early adult life is a phase when within-cohort heterogeneity expands greatly and that the consequences of this expansion are maintained for the rest of life (adult stability model). Young adulthood, for example, is a life phase that stimulates the initiation of a wide range of lifecourses in terms of education, work, family and health behaviours (for example, Elder, 1998; Vaupel et al, 1998). Humans are very susceptible to influence in their early years, but are thought to become increasingly stable in important respects with age. Some theorists suggest, for example, that personality structures are malleable mainly in early life, but are 'set in plaster' by age 30 (for example, Costa and McCrae, 1980). Furthermore, the social and cultural opportunities for change linked to the lifecycle generally decline with age.

A second position on the distribution of individual differences suggests that inter-individual heterogeneity may increase with age (magnification model; for example, Dannefer, 1988). Various reasons are provided for this expectation. To begin, the combined effects of individuals' unique experiences over more years should produce increasing differences between them. Genetically-based differences would also have had more time to be expressed and to produce diversity. Moreover, older adults, somewhat freed from the constraints of social systems linked to education and work, might be more likely to select their own courses of action.

Counter to these two positions, however, are proposals regarding the effects of selective mortality, especially among the oldest old. The reduction in birth cohort size among the oldest old as a function of selective mortality is thought to contribute to a corresponding restriction in observed inter-individual heterogeneity, at least for those factors and aspects of functioning that predict mortality (for example, Berg, 1996). Because data on the non-surviving members of the cohorts are usually not accessible, however, it is difficult to determine whether the selection effects nullify, create or diminish the range of observed individual differences. The 'structural compositions' of older samples certainly differ because of age/cohort and gender differentials in survivorship and life expectancies. Changes in cohort membership are quite dramatic in the 30 years from age 70 to age 100. In the Berlin population, for example, 70-year-olds on average represent approximately 70% of their birth cohort whereas 90-year-olds represent 12% (*Statistisches Landesamt* [*State Statistical Archives*], 1992). Men who survive beyond age 70 represent a proportionately more select subgroup of their birth cohort than do women of the same age. Furthermore, at a very general level, increasing age is associated with greater risk of death and a shorter average life expectancy (residual lifetime). With each decade from age 70 onwards, the proportion of cohort survivors who are one year from death increases. This feature is likely to be confounded with sample selectivity in most studies, adding to the difficulty of making statements about heterogeneity.

Age is related both to functioning and to death in complex ways that can not be easily addressed in a single set of analyses. Contemporary efforts to grapple with the notion of differential ageing thus often make reference to general theories of complexity and entropy that have gained in popularity and definition across many disciplines (for example, Schroots and Yates, 1999). Complexity implies, on the one hand, that there is structure and a level of orderliness but, on the other hand, that there are also non-linear variations. The non-linear variations can arise from multiple interdependencies and interactions among components, from the dynamic properties of these interactions, and from the idea that (among other things) feedback systems, thresholds and cyclical oscillations play a role in the orchestration of the interdependencies and interactions over time.

Whereas the ideas of complexity, entropy, self-organisation and diversity are acknowledged at a general theoretical level by researchers in the field of ageing, most empirical models describe linear interactions between components and static representations of phenomena. Some theoretical models stress the inherent potential for humans to change and adapt to new circumstances, for example, living systems perspectives (Ford, 1987), holistic interactionist models (Magnusson, 1995), and Baltes' (1997) model of selection, optimisation and compensation (Baltes and Baltes, 1990; Baltes et al, 1998). These latter models also include mechanisms that set constraints on the number of possible different personal pathways in development and old age. They therefore point to the deep complexity, interrelationships and dynamism inherent in development and ageing as well as the limits to inter-individual and intra-individual differences in change. Research design strategies and non-linear analysis methods have yet to match the explanatory level of these theories.

Criteria of differential ageing: variable- and person-centred perspectives

One way to summarise findings about patterns of ageing differently is to consider the functional criteria devised by researchers to describe differences. These criteria apply to constructs (variables), subgroups and individuals. At a functional level, ageing differently has been defined in terms of *status* (high, average, low), *quality* (successful, desirable, robust, resilient), *direction* (increase, maintenance, decline), *rate* (fast, slow, fluctuating), *timing* (early, late, event-related), and *individual differences in longevity*. Another complementary way to bring order to the issues and associated research on differential ageing is to determine whether the prime focus is on a single domain of functioning (variable-centred focus) or on a more holistic view of the person (person-centred focus: Smith, 1999). After outlining these different approaches below, we describe findings from BASE to illustrate them.

The variable-centred approach

The *variable-centred approach* to differential ageing focuses on mapping differences in functional intra-individual change in specific domains and delineating the mechanisms underlying domain differences. Four issues characterise this approach:

- the cross-domain comparison of normative ageing and change trajectories;
- cross-domain comparisons of the range of interindividual heterogeneity;
- comparisons of the nature of structural change; and
- discussion of the impact of different mechanisms of change across domains.

Figure 2.1 summarises three theses about trajectories of intra-individual ageing manifested in central domains of psychological functioning; namely, intellectual functioning and self and personality (Smith, 1999). The first thesis, labelled 'dimension specificity' (left-hand graph of Figure 2.1), represents a strong argument for multidirectional intra-individual ageing trajectories and for differences within and between domains. Not only is a distinction made between the typical trajectories expected in the domain of intellectual functioning compared with the domain of self and personality, but there are also expectations that within domains, various dimensions may evince trajectories of decline, stability and possibly growth.

Compared with the first thesis, the second one, labelled 'loss-related decline' (middle graph in Figure 2.1), is a much weaker argument for the differential ageing of domains. On the one hand, this thesis acknowledges that there are likely to be different processes and sources of change associated with various domains and dimensions of psychological functioning (for example, biogenetic, disease and social context). On the other hand, underlying this thesis is the idea that losses and declines accumulate during old age and eventually have a generalised impact. In this sense, the second thesis is analogous to stochastic

Figure 2.1: Three theses about patterns of intra-individual psychological change from 70 to 100 years

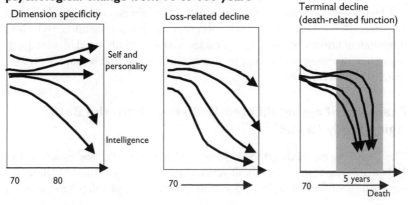

and cumulative stress models of biological ageing (for example, Finch and Seeman, 1999). Although there may be differences among domains in the timing of onset, rate of decline, and amount of decline, all aspects of psychological functioning are depicted as showing negative trajectories.

The final thesis, labelled 'terminal decline' (right-hand graph of Figure 2.1), illustrates the idea that psychological trajectories at the end of life may be better characterised as death-related than age-related. During a window of time before death in very old age (for example, 5-7 years), all domains of psychological functioning eventually show incremental negative trajectories characterised as 'terminal decline' or 'terminal drop' (see also Berg, 1996). Birren and Cunningham (1985) suggested that terminal decline involved a period of behavioural change that was larger and likely to be qualitatively different from normal age changes in behaviour. It is characterised by accelerated deterioration of performance in age-sensitive domains of functioning such as cognition as well as losses in domains of self-regulation that are usually regarded as age-insensitive. Indeed, Birren and Cunningham (1985, p 23) suggested that terminal decline represented the interaction of primary, secondary and tertiary ageing processes and the emergence of a "cascade of structural change".

The person-centred approach

The *person-centred approach* to differential ageing deals with differences among groups of people. The person is the main unit of observation. Key questions that characterise this approach concern the delineation of patterns (or profiles) of functioning that differ across individuals and among subgroups and the determination of antecedent conditions and processes that contributed to these differences. Central too, is the question whether or not the landscape of patterns of subgroup differences are qualitatively different among the young old (third age) and oldest old (fourth age) (see Laslett, 1991; Baltes and Smith, 2003).

The gerontology literature contains various descriptions of subgroup differences in patterns of ageing associated with differential survival, pathology and lifestyle. Researchers associated with the Kansas City, Duke and Bonn Studies played a prominent role in this research agenda (for example, Cumming and Henry, 1961; Williams and Wirths, 1965; Havighurst et al, 1968; Lehr and Thomae, 1987). Their ideas about successful and less successful lifestyles and subgroups of normal versus pathological agers have been advanced in subsequent research with representative samples (for example, Rowe and Kahn, 1987, 1997; Baltes and Mayer, 1999).

Examples of ageing differently: findings from the Berlin Aging Study (BASE)

The Berlin Aging Study (BASE) (Baltes and Mayer, 1999) was established in 1989 to investigate questions about very old age from the joint and collaborative perspectives of four disciplines: psychiatry, psychology, sociology and internal medicine. Distinguishing features of the first-wave cross-sectional BASE design are:

- a special focus on the very old (age range 70-100+: sample stratified by age and sex);
- sample heterogeneity achieved by local representativeness of the western districts of Berlin;
- intensive multidisciplinary data collection (involving 14 sessions and data from each individual collected over three to five months).

Descriptions of the study design, procedure, sample representativeness, and sample selectivity of the initial cross-sectional sample (*n*=516) and longitudinal samples have been published elsewhere and so are described here only briefly (Baltes and Smith, 1997; Baltes and Mayer, 1999; Smith et al, 2002; Smith and Delius, 2003).

The cross-sectional BASE sample consisted of six age/cohort groups (age 70-74, born 1922-15; age 75-79, born 1917-10; age 80-84, born 1913-05; age 85-89, born 1908-1900; age 90-94, born 1902-1896, age 95-105, born 1897-83). There were equal numbers of men and women in each group (*n*=43 respectively). Four longitudinal follow-ups of the survivors from the cross-sectional sample have since been completed at approximately two-yearly intervals. These follow-ups have involved different amounts of assessment. In addition, we regularly receive updated information regarding the mortality of the entire BASE sample from the City Register (in mid-2000, 70% were deceased).

Demographically speaking, the elderly population of the western districts of Berlin is more similar to that in other large cities of former West Germany than one might expect from West Berlin's post-Second World War history of enclosure. There are, however, some demographic differences. Economically and educationally, the older adults of the western districts of Berlin were somewhat better off than their West German counterparts. On a continuum of social stratification, participants in BASE were distributed as follows: lower class (7%), lower middle class (20%), middle class (31%), upper middle class (30%) to higher class (11%).

How about historical and culture-specific cohort effects? Study participants have lived in the midst of many historical events. The oldest participants were born in 1886 and the youngest in 1920. The oldest birth cohorts were aged in their 20s at the time of the First World War and the youngest were born during or shortly after that war. All participants experienced the Second World War, although at different points in their lives. These cohort-specific experiences of course had an impact on the educational and occupational opportunities, health experiences and family lives of the individuals (Baltes and Mayer, 1999).

Our research efforts in BASE focus on the investigation of age and death-related changes in psychological functioning from age 70 to 100+ from both the variable- and person-centred approaches. In addition, we search for psychological evidence regarding a transition from the third (young old) to the fourth (oldest old) age.

Trajectories of decline in intellectual functioning

Intellectual functioning in BASE was assessed using a computerised battery of 14 subtests covering five abilities: perceptual speed, memory, reasoning, fluency and knowledge (Lindenberger and Baltes, 1997). Cross-sectional analyses of BASE data revealed substantial negative age differences in indicators of all abilities between 70 and 100+ years, representing a 1.8 SD (standard deviation) difference in performance level and 35% of the interindividual variance (see Lindenberger and Baltes, 1997). These cross-sectional findings have now been extended by several longitudinal analyses. Singer et al (2003), for example, reported change trajectories for a longitudinal sample (*n*=132) examined over six years. Due to sample attrition and mortality this longitudinal sample represented a positive selection of the original cross-sectional BASE sample: their performance level at baseline was generally higher. Over time, considerable decline was observed in markers of the fluid mechanics (perceptual speed, memory, fluency), whereas the strongest marker of crystallised/pragmatic intelligence (knowledge) remained relatively stable for all participants, except those over age 95. The rate of change in intellectual efficacy over time was similar for persons above or below the mean on life-history variables, such as education, prestige, social class, or income.

Physical and functional health play a key role in the maintenance of cognitive functioning in old age. Verhaeghen et al (2003) found that five diagnoses were negatively correlated with cognition in BASE: congestive heart failure, stroke, coronary heart disease, myocardial infarction and diabetes mellitus. The presence of one or more of these diagnoses was linked to lower performance in general, but there was no differential cognitive decline over four years. This suggests that the impact of these diseases on cognitive decline in very old age may be smaller than in younger adults, not because of decreased vulnerability, but because the disease process adds little to the cumulative changes in brain physiology that have occurred over the course of a very long life. Specific cardiovascular risk factors (smoking, alcohol consumption, HDL-cholesterol levels) were associated, however, with both lower functional levels and greater decline in cognition.

The very old self: is adaptive potential maintained in very old age?

Measures of the motivational aspects of the self (for example, control beliefs, future-oriented goals) and overall subjective well-being (for example, life satisfaction, a sense of happiness and contentment) are considered to be important indicators of psychological adaptation and adjustment. It is generally expected that psychological processes operate to protect or 'immunise' the self against a loss of efficacy and well-being, even in conditions of poor health and chronic impairment. Individuals adjust their aspiration levels and comparison targets so as to achieve and maintain a sense of control over their life. These psychological processes contribute to a positive aura of well-being and to seemingly paradoxical observations that, after a period of adjustment, individuals report satisfaction in contexts of high stress and strain. A central question examined in BASE is whether or not these self-regulatory systems remain intact and efficient in both the young old and the oldest old (Smith and Baltes, 1999).

Longitudinal analyses of hopes and fears about the future self (possible selves) have revealed that this motivational system is relatively intact in old age (Smith and Freund, 2002). The possible selves of adults aged 70-103 years were highly personalised and varied. Contrary to suggestions that late adulthood is a period of disengagement from future planning in favour of life review and a focus on the present, participants in BASE reported desires to achieve new aspects of hoped-for selves especially in relation to identity (personal characteristics), health and relationships with others (friends and family). Furthermore, the profile of possible selves was dynamic over time. For example, 72% of participants added new hopes about personal projects over a four-year period and 27% added highly elaborated possible self-images (that is, ideas about the future self that were both positive and negative).

Kunzmann et al (2002) examined longitudinal changes in personal and external control beliefs and their relation to emotional well-being. Whereas beliefs about personal (internal) control over positive and negative aspects of life were stable over time, the belief that others play a significant role in determining the events in one's life (external control) increased. Stability in perceived personal control over desirable outcomes was associated with high emotional well-being. Perceiving that other people have control over one's personal affairs, in contrast, was shown to be associated with high negative affect and low positive affect. Although feelings of social dependency may lead to low emotional well-being, confidence in being able to use powerful others for one's own ends might have emotional benefits.

A sense of physical dependence on others together with accumulated chronic health and life strains play critical roles in the reduction of the potential to experience the positive side of life (Smith, 2001; Smith et al, 2002). Although the majority of BASE participants were typically satisfied with their present life conditions, those in the third age (70-84 years) reported significantly higher positive well-being, and higher satisfaction with life in general compared with those in the fourth age (85-100+). Considerable individual difference variance in well-being was accounted for by physical illness and functional impairment (for example, vision, hearing, mobility, strength). On average, reported satisfaction with ageing, life satisfaction and experience of positive emotions decreased after age 80. We have also found that reported personal well-being is associated with an increased mortality risk after statistical controls for age, sociodemographic characteristics and health measures (for example, Maier and Smith, 1999). Every one standard deviation decrease in personal well-being was associated with a 1.36 times higher relative risk of death. The multimorbid life contexts of the oldest old highlight the salience of issues of physical dependency and the psychological 'cost' of ageing.

Age-related trends in personality attributes

Cross-sectional age gradients (age 70-100+) found in BASE for the personality traits extraversion, openness and neuroticism, measured using items from the NEO scale, were in line with those found by McCrae et al (1999). In very old age, extraversion and openness appear to have small but significant negative ageing trajectories (age correlations were $r=-0.19$ and -0.20 respectively), while neuroticism showed no relation to age (Smith and Baltes, 1999). Initial longitudinal analyses of these dimensions have revealed similar change patterns. Estimated average t-score changes over 30 years (in SD units) are as follows: extraversion -1.2 SD; openness -0.9 SD. These estimated rates of change appear to be faster than found in younger ages (-0.5 SD) (McCrae et al, 1999). On average, neuroticism appears to increase (estimated 4.2 t-score units over 10 years) and this increase is explained by individual differences in changes in functional health and distance from death rather than by age per se.

Desirable and less desirable profiles of functioning: systemic loss in the fourth age

So far in this chapter, we have presented information about age-related differences and change in separate psychological domains. In this section, we summarise findings about subgroup differences in profiles of functioning *across* the domains of intelligence, self and personality, and social relationships (Smith and Baltes, 1997; Smith and Baltes, 1998; Gerstorf, 2004). A focus on subgroup differences in profiles exemplifies a person-centred approach to differential ageing.

Our work in BASE with regard to profiles of functioning had three main goals. To begin, we wondered how many subgroups would be revealed in the BASE data by cluster analysis and how the psychological profiles of these groups would differ in terms of overall level and shape (pattern of high and low scores across the domains included in the analyses). Twelve constructs selected to broadly represent the central psychological dimensions considered in the research literature on old age were entered in cluster analyses: perceptual speed, memory, knowledge, neuroticism, extraversion, life investment, internal and external control, social and emotional loneliness, reported number of close confidants, and perceived support.

Nine subgroups of individuals, four of which reflected different patterns of desirable functioning or successful ageing (47% of the sample) and five less desirable functioning (53%), were identified at baseline (Table 2.1). Individuals in one subgroup with a desirable profile, for example, were characterised by their high levels of cognitive performance, many personal goals, interests and

Table 2.1: Ageing differently – nine subgroups with different psychological profiles identified in BASE

Rank	Subgroup profile	n	%	Age	% women/ men
1	Cognitively very fit, vitally involved	50	9.8	77.9	48/52
2	Socially oriented and engaged	29	5.7	82.5	45/55
3	Cognitively fit, well-balanced easing through life	119	23.3	81.1	37/63
4	Cognitively fit, reserved loner	42	8.2	81.1	55/45
5	Fearful, lonely but supported	75	14.7	88.0	68/32
6	Anxious, lonely, holding on to control	44	8.6	84.7	50/50
7	Dependent but well-balanced	64	12.5	91.2	53/47
8	Cognitively impaired, disengaged but content	55	10.7	88.5	36/64
9	Cognitive impairment, withdrawn, in despair	32	6.2	91.2	69/31

Source: Adapted from Smith and Baltes (1997)

hobbies, but rather small social network. Another subgroup in this category was distinguished by their very large social networks, average cognitive functioning, and disposition to enjoy life. Less desirable profiles were distinguished by increasing levels of cognitive impairment, loneliness, psychological dependence on others, and a lower sense of well-being. Subgroups differed in aspects of life history, health risks and present life circumstances. The relative risk of membership in the less desirable profile groups was 2.5 times higher for the oldest old than for the 70- to 84-year-olds. Women were more prevalent in the less functional profile groups.

The outcome is clear. Risk of membership in the less desirable clusters was larger for the oldest old compared with the young old. The oldest old, and especially older women, are at a much higher risk for dysfunctionality than the young old. Whereas women live longer than men, their functional status is less desirable, and this disadvantage increases with age (Smith and Baltes, 1998). This pattern of a major increase in risk for the fourth age is even more remarkable because the sole focus was on psychological measures such as intelligence, the self, personality and social behaviour. Psychologically speaking, advanced old age appears to be a situation of great challenge and a period characterised by chronic stress (Baltes and Smith, 2003; Smith, 2003). Advanced old age, the fourth age, is a kind of testing-the-limits situation for psychological resilience.

In subsequent analyses, we have examined the long-term consequences of these profiles of psychological functioning in terms of survival (Smith, 2003; Gerstorf, 2004). Cluster membership indeed predicted survival over eight years (Smith, 2003). At the mid-2000 mortality update, 25% of the 516 sample was registered as alive. Cox proportional hazards models and survival curve analyses indicated that the nine clusters showed different survival curves that reflect our classification as desirable or less desirable. Whereas 60% of participants with desirable profiles of functioning survived, the large majority of members of less desirable profile groups had died. A unique effect for cluster categorisation remained after controls are added to the analyses for age, gender, socioeconomic status, physical health and functional capacity. Among individuals aged 85+ (where fewer than 15% survived to mid-2000), the finding was highly significant: individuals aged 85+ in the desirable clusters lived on average at least two years longer than individuals in the less desirable clusters. The maintenance of even a limited positive balance of gains over losses in very old age appears to have some survival advantages.

Conclusions

Our findings from BASE illustrate differential ageing from both the variable- and person-centred perspectives. Change trajectories differ by psychological domain (for example, intellectual functioning versus self-related functioning), and subgroups of the young old and oldest old show profiles of functioning that suggest differential vulnerability to dysfunctional change (that is, desirable versus less desirable profiles). At the present time, however, the concept of differential ageing is applied primarily as a summary description of an outcome, rather than as a generator of specific hypotheses about expected differences and similarities in age-related trajectories across domains of functioning or differences between individuals and subgroups in old age. Indeed, there is little consensus in the gerontological literature about what should be explained by models of differential ageing (for example, successful old age, longevity, life quality, active life expectancy, or residual life expectancy).

More thought needs to be given to questions about the potential range of variability and the relative limits to this variability as a function of age-related changes, life history, cohort survivorship, and closeness to death. In addition, we propose that future theoretical work should address questions regarding those phases of the lifecourse in which sources of differential ageing (biogenetic, social, environmental, and idiographic) are turned on, added to, multiplied, or diminished.

Acknowledgement

The Berlin Aging Study (BASE) was financially supported by two German federal departments: the Department of Research and Technology (13 TA 011: 1988-91) and the Department of Family and Senior Citizens (1991-98). Since 1999, BASE has been funded by the Max Planck Institute for Human Development, Berlin, where the study is located. Members of the Steering Committee are P.B. Baltes and J. Smith (psychology); K.U. Mayer (sociology); E. Steinhagen-Thiessen and M. Borchelt (internal medicine and geriatrics); H. Helmchen and F. Reischies (psychiatry). Field research was coordinated at various phases by R. Nuthmann, M. Neher and K. Fröhlich. Correspondence concerning this chapter should be addressed to Jacqui Smith, Centre for Lifespan Psychology, Max Planck Institute for Human Development, Lentzeallee 94, 14195 Berlin, Germany. E-mail: Smith@mpib-berlin.mpg.de

---

References

Baltes, P.B. (1987) 'Theoretical propositions of life-span developmental psychology: on the dynamics between growth and decline', *Developmental Psychology*, vol 23, pp 611-26.

Baltes, P.B. (1997) 'On the incomplete architecture of human ontogeny: selection, optimization, and compensation as foundation of developmental theory', *American Psychologist*, vol 52, pp 366-80.

Baltes, P.B. and Baltes, M.M. (1990) 'Psychological perspectives on successful aging: the model of selective optimization with compensation', in P.B. Baltes and M.M. Baltes (eds) *Successful aging: Perspectives from the behavioral sciences*, New York, NY: Cambridge University Press, pp 1-34.

Baltes, P.B., Lindenberger, U. and Staudinger, U.M. (1998) 'Life-span theory in developmental psychology', in R.M. Lerner (ed) *Handbook of child psychology: Vol 1. Theoretical models of human development*, New York, NY: Wiley, pp 1029-143.

Baltes, P.B. and Mayer, K.U. (eds) (1999) *The Berlin Aging Study: Aging from 70 to 100*, New York, NY: Cambridge University Press.

Baltes, P.B. and Smith, J. (1997) 'A systemic-wholistic view of psychological functioning in very old age: introduction to a collection of articles from the Berlin Aging Study', *Psychology and Aging*, vol 12, pp 395-409.

Baltes, P.B. and Smith, J. (2003) 'New frontiers in the future of aging: from successful ageing of the young old to the dilemmas of the Fourth Age', *Gerontology: Behavioural Science Section/Review*, vol 49, pp 123-35.

Berg, S. (1996) 'Aging, behaviour, and terminal decline', in J.E. Birren and K.W. Schaie (eds) *Handbook of the psychology of aging*, San Diego, CA: Academic Press, pp 323-37.

Birren, J.E. (1959) 'Principles of research on aging', in J.E. Birren (ed) *Handbook of aging and the individual: Psychological and biological aspects*, Chicago, IL: University of Chicago Press, pp 3-42.

Birren, J.E. and Cunningham, W. (1985) 'Research on the psychology of aging: principles, concepts, and theory', in J.J.E. Birren and K.W. Schaie (eds) *Handbook of the psychology of aging*, New York, NY: Van Nostrand Reinhold, pp 3-34.

Costa, P.T. Jr. and McCrae, R.R. (1980) 'Still stable after all these years: personality as a key to some issues in adulthood and old age', in P.B. Baltes and O.G. Brim Jr. (eds) *Life-span development and behavior*, New York, NY: Academic Press, pp 65-102.

Cumming, E. and Henry, W.E. (1961) *Growing old*, New York, NY: Basic Books.

Dannefer, D. (1988) 'Differential gerontology and the stratified life course: conceptual and methodological issues', *Annual Review of Gerontology and Geriatrics*, vol 8, pp 3-36.

Elder, G.H. (1998) 'The life course and human development', in R.M. Lerner (ed) *Handbook of child psychology*, New York, NY: Wiley and Sons, pp 939-1028.

Finch, C.E. and Seeman, T.E. (1999) 'Stress theories of aging', in V.L. Bengtson and K.W. Schaie (eds) *Handbook of theories of aging*, New York, NY: Springer, pp 81-97.

Ford, D.H. (1987) *Humans as self-constructing living systems: A developmental perspective on behavior and personality*, Hillsdale, NJ: Erlbaum.

Fries, J.F. (1980) 'Aging, natural death, and the compression of morbidity', *New England Medical Journal*, vol 303, pp 130-5.

Gerstorf, D. (2004) 'Heterogeneity and differential development in old age: the sample case of the systemic-wholistic approach', Unpublished dissertation, Freie Universität, Berlin.

Havighurst, R.J., Neugarten, B.L. and Tobin, S.S. (1968) 'Disengagement and patterns of aging', in B.L. Neugarten (ed) *Middle age and aging*, Chicago, IL: Chicago University Press, pp 161-72.

Kunzmann, U., Little, T. and Smith, J. (2000) 'Perceiving control: a double-edged sword in old age', *Journals of Gerontology Series B-Psychological Sciences and Social Sciences*, vol 57, pp P484-P491.

Laslett, P. (1991) *A fresh map of life: The emergence of the Third Age*, Cambridge, MA: Harvard University Press.

Lehr, U. and Thomae, H. (eds) (1987) *Formen seelischen Alterns: Ergebnisse der Bonner Gerontologischen Längsschnittstudie (BOLSA)*, Stuttgart: Enke.

Lindenberger, U. and Baltes, P.B. (1997) 'Intellectual functioning in old and very old age: cross-sectional results from the Berlin Aging Study', *Psychology and Aging*, vol 12, pp 410-32.

Magnusson, D. (1995) 'Individual development: a holistic, integrated model', in P. Moen, G.H. Elder Jr. and K. Lüscher (eds) *Examining lives in context: Perspectives on the ecology of human development*, Washington, DC: American Psychological Association, pp 19-60.

Maier, H. and Smith, J. (1999) 'Psychological predictors of mortality in old age', *Journals of Gerontology: Psychological Sciences*, vol 54B, pp P44-P54.

McCrae, R.R. Jr., Costa, P.T. Jr., de Lima, M., Simoes, A., Ostendorf, F., Angleitner, A., Marusic, I., Bratko, D., Caprara, G.V., Barbaranelli, C. and Chae, J-H. (1999) 'Age differences in personality across the adult life span: parallels in five cultures', *Developmental Psychology*, vol 35, pp 466-77.

Rowe, J.W. and Kahn, R.L. (1987) 'Human aging: usual and successful', *Science*, vol 237, pp 143-9.

Rowe, J.W. and Kahn, R.L. (1997) 'Successful aging', *The Gerontologist*, vol 37, pp 433-40.

Schroots, J.J.F. and Yates, F.E. (1999) 'On the dynamics of development and aging', in V.L. Bengtson and K.W. Schaie (eds) *Handbook of theories of ageing*, New York, NY: Springer, pp 417-33.

Singer, T., Verhaeghen, P., Ghisletta, P., Lindenberger, U. and Baltes, P.B. (2003) 'The fate of cognition in very old age: six-year longitudinal findings from the Berlin Aging Study (BASE)', *Psychology and Aging*, vol 18, pp 318-31.

Smith, J. (1999) *Differential psychological aging: Towards clarifying a longstanding concept*, Habilitationschrift (Psychology), Free University Berlin, Germany.

Smith, J. (2001) 'Well-being and health from age 70 to 100 years: findings from the Berlin Aging Study', *European Review*, vol 9, pp 461-77.

Smith, J. (2003) 'Stress and aging: theoretical and empirical challenges for interdisciplinary research', *Neurobiology of Aging*, vol 24(S1), S77-80.

Smith, J. and Baltes, M.M. (1998) 'The role of gender in very old age: profiles of functioning and everyday life patterns', *Psychology and Aging*, vol 13, pp 676-95.

Smith, J. and Baltes, P.B. (1997) 'Profiles of psychological functioning in the old and oldest old', *Psychology and Aging*, vol 12, pp 458-72.

Smith, J. and Baltes, P.B. (1999) 'Trends and profiles of psychological functioning in very old age', in P.B. Baltes and K.U. Mayer (eds) *The Berlin Aging Study: Aging from 70 to 100*, New York, NY: Cambridge University Press, pp 197-226.

Smith, J., Borchelt, M., Maier, H. and Jopp, D. (2002) 'Health and wellbeing in old age', *Journal of Social Issues*, vol 58, pp 715-32.

Smith, J. and Delius, J. (2003) 'Die längsschnittlichen Erhebungen der Berliner Altersstudie (BASE): Design, Stichproben und Schwerpunkte 1990–2002' [The longitudinal assessments in the Berlin Aging Study (BASE): design, samples, and topics 1990-2002], in F. Karl (ed) *Sozial-und verhaltenswissenschaftliche Gerontologie: Alter und Altern als gesellschaftliches Problem und individuelles Thema*, Weinheim: Juventa, pp 225-49.

Smith, J. and Freund, A.F. (2002) 'The dynamics of possible selves in old age', *Journals of Gerontology: Psychological Sciences*, vol 57B, P492-P500.

Smith, J., Maas, I., Mayer, K.U., Helmchen, H., Steinhagen-Thiessen, E. and Baltes, P.B. (2002) 'Two-wave longitudinal findings from the Berlin Aging Study: introduction to a collection of papers', *Journal of Gerontology: Psychological Sciences*, vol 57B, P471-3.

Statistisches Landesamt [State Statistical Archives] (1992) *Sterbetafel 1987/1989 für Berlin (West)* [Life tables for Berlin (West)], Berlin.

Vaupel, J.W., Carey, J.R., Christensen, K., Johnson, T.E., Yashin, A.I., Holm, N.V., Iachine, I.A., Kannisto, V., Khazaeli, A.A., Liedo, P., Longo, V.D., Zeng, Y., Manton, K.G. and Curtsinger, J.W. (1998) 'Biodemographic trajectories of longevity', *Science*, vol 280, pp 855-60.

Verhaeghen, P., Borchelt, M. and Smith, J. (2003) 'The relation between cardiovascular and metabolic disease and cognition in very old age: cross-sectional and longitudinal findings from the Berlin Aging Study', *Health Psychology*, vol 22, pp 559-69.

Williams, R.H. and Wirths, C.G. (1965) *Lives through the years: Styles of life and successful aging*, New York, NY: Atherton Press.

THREE

The personal meaning of individuality and relatedness: gender differences in middle and late adulthood

Gerben J. Westerhof and Christina Bode

Key points

- Individuality and relatedness are less central orientations in older than in middle-aged adults.
- Different patterns and meanings of individuality and relatedness exist within age groups.
- Part of the variation within age groups is explained by gender, but there is no age by gender interaction.
- Content analysis and further statistical analysis reveal age and gender differences at the expense of concealing complexity and diversity at the individual level.

Key readings

Guisinger, S. and Blatt, S.J. (1994) 'Individuality and relatedness. Evolution of a fundamental dialectic', *American Psychologist*, vol 49, pp 104-11.

Ryff, C.D. (1989) 'In the eye of the beholder: views of psychological well-being among middle-aged and older adults', *Psychology and Aging*, vol 4, pp 195-210.

Sinnott, J.D. and Shifren, K. (2001) 'Gender and aging: gender differences and gender roles', in J.E. Birren and K.W. Schaie (eds) *Handbook of the psychology of aging*, San Diego, CA: Academic Press, pp 454-76.

Westerhof, G.J., Dittmann-Kohli, F. and Katzko, M.W. (2000) 'Individualism and collectivism in the personal meaning system of elderly adults: the United States and Congo/Zaire as an example', *Journal of Cross-Cultural Psychology*, vol 31, pp 649-76.

Introduction

In this chapter, we focus on gender differences in individuality and relatedness in the second half of life. 'Individuality' broadly refers to the experience of the own person as a coherent whole clearly separate from other persons and 'relatedness' refers to the experience of the own person in relation to other persons (Guisinger and Blatt, 1994; Bode, 2003).

Personality psychologists have used a number of concepts similar to individuality and relatedness, such as agency and communion (Bakan, 1966; McAdams, 1988), self and other motives (Hermans and Hermans-Jansen, 1995) and independent and interdependent selves (Markus and Kitayama, 1991). Although subtle differences in the meanings of these concepts exist, they all refer to the aspects of self and identity mentioned earlier. They are seen as basic motives in human functioning that are not stable personality traits, but aspects of flexible, socially and culturally constructed identities. These basic motives are expressed in the self-concepts of ageing persons. Individuals may differ in the degree to which individuality and relatedness are important in their self-concepts as well as in the different meanings that they give to their own person as well as to their relations with others. In this chapter, individuality and relatedness are studied from this perspective, which represents the point of view of ageing persons themselves.

We here address the individual meanings of individuality and relatedness for women and men in the second half of life. The focus lies on age differences between middle-aged and older adults (aged 40-85 years) and on the role of gender in creating diversity within age groups. Besides using a quantitative nomothetic (variable-centred) approach to individuality and relatedness, we also make use of qualitative idiographic (person-centred) case studies which will further shed light on the diversity in ageing. Before we turn to the empirical examination of this question, we first review the literature on ageing and gender with regard to individuality and relatedness.

Psychological ageing theories

Schneewind (1994) describes individuality and relatedness as lifelong developmental tasks, which have to be balanced constantly in relation to age-related changes in personal and environmental characteristics. Yet, psychological ageing theories have focused more on individuality than on relatedness. Older theories describe a shift towards individuality in old age (Bühler, 1933; Jung, 1972; Erikson, 1973). Ryff's (1995) theory on psychological well-being, which was derived from a thorough review of humanistic lifespan theories, includes a number of different aspects of individuality (environmental mastery, autonomy, personal growth, self-acceptance, purpose in life), but only one aspect of relatedness (good relations). Recent psychological theories on successful ageing focus on individuality as well. The main standards of success in later life are the attainment of individual goals, control or individual well-being (Schulz and Heckhausen, 1996; Baltes, 1997; Brandtstädter, 1999; Westerhof et al, 2001).

Our own research has shown that *both* individuality *and* relatedness are important topics for meaning giving by middle-aged and older adults (Bode et al, 2001; Bode, 2003). Both themes are significantly less central in self-descriptions of older than middle-aged groups. As the age differences for individuality are larger than for relatedness, we observed a reversal in the centrality of individuality and relatedness around the age of 58. Individuality is more central than relatedness for individuals younger than 58 years, and the reverse is true for older persons. These findings are in agreement with other studies on self-conceptions over the life course (Dittmann-Kohli, 1995) and studies on lay conceptions of well-being (Ryff, 1989; Thomas and Chambers, 1989; Westerhof et al, 2001). They also resonate with efforts to combine individuality and relatedness in lifespan models (Gilligan, 1982; Franz and White, 1985; Bar-Yam Hassan and Bar-Yam, 1987). Hence, this study found no support for a shift to individuality as a major concern in later life.

Gender issues

Psychological research on ageing has been criticised for its lack of theoretical consideration of gender issues (Sinnott and Shifren, 2001). Similarly, psychological research on gender has been criticised for its lack of a lifespan perspective (Ashmore, 1990; Deaux and Stewart, 2001). It is often assumed that once a gender identity is achieved in early adulthood, it remains stable for the rest of one's life.

Research has typically shown that women are more oriented towards relatedness, men towards individuality. Our previous studies (Bode, 2003) clearly support earlier findings that women's construction of identity involves relatedness more strongly than men's, also in the second half of life. Surprisingly in the light of earlier findings, middle-aged and older women disclose orientations toward individuality more often than men do (Bode, 2003). Yet, this finding is in line with research by Twenge (1997), which has shown that women's scores on masculinity scales have increased between 1973 and 1993, so that women and men are nowadays rather similar on this individuality-related orientation. Men's scores on femininity did not differ and the gender differences on this orientation stayed the same over these 20 years. The finding may also be related to differences in methodology as well as to subtle differences in the definition of individuality and relatedness from other similar concepts used in the gender literature, such as masculinity and femininity (Bem, 1981), instrumentality and expressiveness (Spence and Helmreich, 1980), separateness and connectedness (Lang-Takac and Osterweil, 1992).

We could not find support for the hypothesis that women become more oriented towards individuality and men become more oriented towards relatedness as they age (Gutmann, 1987; Sinnott and Shifren, 2001). The age differences described earlier were found for men and women in the Netherlands and East and West Germany (Bode, 2003), showing that individuality and relatedness are less central to both older men and women.

Beyond dichotomies

Individuality and relatedness are often seen as two sides of the same coin. This implies that a person who is more oriented towards individuality will be less oriented towards relatedness. In other words, one cannot be both focused on individuality *and* on relatedness. Our studies have shown, however, that at least on a group level, younger adults and women are more oriented towards relatedness *and* individuality than older adults and men. Other studies have found that both orientations are statistically independent (Lenney, 1991; Singelis, 1994).

In this chapter, we try to get away from simple dichotomies. First, we will address the age and gender differences in how individuals combine individuality and relatedness. The literature on gender differences has often focused on androgynous persons who combine values of masculinity and femininity, in contrast to persons who favour masculinity over femininity or otherwise (Lenney, 1991). Similarly, we will distinguish persons for whom both individuality and relatedness are central from those who place a more exclusive value of one over the other and persons for whom both are not central.

Second, there may be diversity not only in these different patterns of individuality and relatedness, but also in the meanings attached to the motives. In everyday life, individuality and relatedness are not explicated in terms of abstract motives. Rather, they will become manifest in self-descriptions of individuals (Hermans and Hermans-Jansen, 1995). In other words, individuality and relatedness only acquire substantive meaning when people use them in relation to tangible personal concerns (Potter and Wetherell, 1987; Westerhof et al, 2000). Some personal concerns related to individuality and relatedness may be more relevant to some age and gender groups, whereas others may be more relevant to other groups. Hence, we want to uncover the more complex meanings of individuality and relatedness for men and women in middle and late adulthood.

Last, we present case studies that allow us to analyse in more detail how individuality and relatedness are expressed in individual descriptions of oneself and one's life. Here, we explore the idiosyncratic meanings of individuality and relatedness as well as the different ways in which these two latent motives become manifest in the self-descriptions of ageing persons.

Method

Participants

The participants of the Dutch Aging Survey (*n*=948) were identified through a random sampling of population registers of 77 Dutch municipalities (Steverink et al, 2001). The sample was stratified according to age groups (ages 40-54; 55-69; 70-85), gender and area of residence. Rate of participation was 44%

(age 40-54: 48%, age 55-69: 48%, age 70-85: 37%; no significant gender differences in response rate). All participants were community dwelling.

Material

All participants were asked to fill out the SELE instrument, a sentence completion instrument that asked for descriptions of self and life (SE=Self, LE=Life [*Leben*]) (Dittmann-Kohli, 1995; Dittmann-Kohli and Westerhof, 1997). It is designed to probe self and life conceptions in a non-directive manner by inviting comments on personal abilities, weaknesses, feelings, evaluations and beliefs as well as plans, future expectations, fears and anxieties. The subjects were asked to complete the sentence stems by expressing what they considered to be true and important about themselves.

In order to make the qualitative data available for quantitative analyses, the sentence completions were scored using a two-phase coding procedure (Bode, 1999). Responses were first coded on the basis of an inductive strategy. They were grouped together in 13 categories that are relatively close to the semantic features of the sentence completions. These 13 categories refer to the personal concerns expressed in the sentence completions. The second phase consisted of a further classification of these 13 categories on the basis of theoretical definitions: 'individuality' refers to the inner core of one's own person without reference to other persons or to boundaries between self and other, whereas 'relatedness' refers to the self in relation to other persons. Six subcategories were classified as individuality: well-being, control, achievement, independence, self-reflection, own projects. Seven subcategories referred to relatedness: social competency, society, transpersonal (that is, concerns about other persons), contact, behaviour of others, joint projects and quality of relationships. On the first level of coding (*orientations*) and on the second level of coding (*personal concerns*), inter-coder reliability was high: Cohen's Kappa (a statistic of the agreement between different persons coding the same data) was 0.83 and 0.81, respectively.

Analyses

In order to assess the patterns of individuality and relatedness, sum scores for the corresponding self-descriptions were calculated for each individual. The scores are normally distributed for individuality (M=6.2 [M=mean]; SD=2.9 [SD=standard deviation]; range: 0-18 descriptions) and relatedness (M=6.5; SD=3.0; range: 0-18 descriptions). A median split was made for both variables on the basis of the whole sample. Those with a score of <=5 on individuality were considered 'low' (44.6%) and those with a score of >=6 were considered 'high' (55.4%). On relatedness, the cut-off point was 7: those who scored <7 were considered 'low' (52.3%) and those who scored >=7 were considered 'high' (47.7%). Four groups were made on the basis of this categorisation: low on both ($I_{low}R_{low}$; 24.5%), low on individuality and high on relatedness ($I_{low}R_{high}$; 20.1%), high on individuality and low on relatedness ($I_{high}R_{low}$; 27.8%) and high on both ($I_{high}R_{high}$; 27.5%). We also computed a pattern on the basis of the tertiles of the individuality and relatedness scores. These showed the same age and gender differences as the pattern based on the median split presented here.

On the level of personal concerns, a variable was computed for each of the six individuality and seven relatedness subcategories. These variables indicate whether or not a person mentioned a particular category in at least one of the 28 sentence stems.

Chi^2-square analysis, loglinear analysis and logistic regression were used to assess the differences between the age groups and between men and women as well as the interaction between both.

Results

Patterns of individuality and relatedness

First, the age and gender differences with regard to individuality and relatedness were assessed. Figure 3.1 illustrates these differences. The age groups differ significantly on the patterns of individuality and relatedness in a bivariate analysis ($chi^2(6)=73.6; p<0.001$). The gender differences are also significant in a bivariate analysis ($chi^2(3)=33.8; p<0.001$). A loglinear analysis shows that a design with main effects of age group and gender is not significant ($chi^2(2)=4.0; p=0.134$). Hence, it is not necessary to introduce an interaction effect in predicting the categories of the individuality-relatedness patterns. It can be concluded that there is no interaction between age group and gender.

The age differences can be summarised as follows. The categories where individuality is low are found more often in the older age groups and the categories where individuality is high are found more often in the younger age

Figure 3.1: Patterns of individuality and relatedness by age group and gender

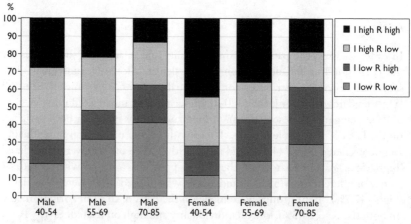

Note: n=948.

groups. Of those with a pattern where one orientation is dominant, the $I_{high}R_{low}$ category is found more often in younger groups and the $I_{low}R_{high}$ category is found more often in the older groups. The category low on both is found more often in the older age groups, whereas the category high on both is found more often in younger age groups.

The categories including high on relatedness are found more often in women than in men, whereas the categories low on relatedness are found more often in men than in women. More men are found in the $I_{low}R_{low}$ category, whereas more women are found in the $I_{high}R_{high}$ category. Men are more often predominantly focused on individuality $(I_{high}R_{low})$, whereas women are more often focused on relatedness $(I_{low}R_{high})$.

As there is no age-by-gender interaction, the age differences apply to men as well as women and the gender differences apply to all age groups. To conclude, both older men and women are more often low on individuality and high on relatedness compared with younger men and women, yet men of all ages are more often predominantly focused on individuality and women on relatedness.

Meanings of individuality and relatedness

Besides the general orientations on individuality and relatedness, we studied the more specific meanings of these orientations to men and women in the second half of life. At the level of personal concerns (the second level of coding), six subcategories of individuality and seven subcategories of relatedness were distinguished. Table 3.1 shows the proportion of men and women in the three age groups that mentioned a particular subcategory in at least one of their sentence completions.

In order to test the main effects of age group and gender as well as their interaction, 13 logistic regression analyses were carried out, for each of the 13 personal concerns separately. Four of the six personal concerns with regard to individuality and four out of seven personal concerns with regard to relatedness show significant age differences. Three out of six individuality-related concerns show significant gender differences. Men and women also differ on five concerns that show an orientation to relatedness. No interaction effects between age and gender were found in these analyses. Hence, the age differences exist for men and women and the gender differences exist in all age groups.

'Control', 'achievement', 'self-reflection' and 'own projects' are found less often in the older than in the younger age groups. 'Well-being' and 'independence', however, are not found less often in the older groups. Whereas individuality is in general less prominent in older adults, well-being and independence are equally important concerns for the older and for the younger groups. 'Social competency', 'society' and 'quality of relations' are found less often in older groups than in younger groups, whereas the opposite is true for 'contact'. The categories 'transpersonal' and 'behaviour of others' do not show significant age differences. With regard to social relations, older individuals appear to be focused more on the availability of contact per se, and younger

Table 3.1: Percentage mentioning personal concerns of individuality and relatedness by age group and gender

Column %	Age groups			$\chi^2(2)$		Gender			Total
	40-54	55-69	70-85		Male	Female	$\chi^2(1)$		
Individuality									
Well-being	93.1	91.0	91.3	1.1	91.4	92.3	0.7		91.9
Control	75.8	67.4	54.4	33.1***	65.3	68.0	0.6		66.7
Achievement	65.8	56.1	49.5	18.1***	61.4	54.2	4.8*		57.8
Independence	48.3	44.9	41.1	3.4	40.3	49.9	8.8**		45.0
Self-reflection	44.4	32.9	30.0	16.7***	33.6	39.2	3.0		36.4
Own projects	23.1	14.3	12.5	14.6***	14.4	19.8	4.5*		17.1
Relatedness									
Social competency	84.2	78.7	73.2	11.7**	73.3	85.1	19.3***		79.1
Society	76.1	73.1	66.2	7.9*	76.4	67.8	8.3**		72.2
Transpersonal	68.9	65.4	64.8	1.4	58.0	75.3	30.8***		66.6
Contact	49.4	51.5	58.9	6.1*	46.1	59.9	17.5***		53.0
Behaviour of others	40.0	47.5	41.8	4.0	39.9	46.1	3.4		42.9
Joint projects	37.8	38.2	36.6	0.2	39.0	36.0	0.2		37.6
Quality of relationships	23.3	20.6	15.0	7.3*	16.9	23.0	5.2*		19.9

Notes: * *p*<0.05; ** *p*<0.01; ***p <0.001; *n*=948.

adults more on the quality of contact and their own part in this. It can be concluded that individuality and relatedness have different meanings for different age groups.

With regard to the subcategories of individuality, women mention 'own projects' and 'independence' more often, whereas men mention 'achievement' more often. 'Well-being', 'control' and 'self-reflection' are found equally often among men and women. Whereas men are more 'agentic' in the sense of focusing on achievement and goal setting, women are more oriented towards drawing boundaries between self and others than men. With regard to the subcategories of relatedness, women mention the categories 'social competency', 'transpersonal', 'contact' and 'quality of relations' more often, and men mention the category 'society' more often. There are no significant differences for 'joint projects' and 'behaviour of others'. Relatedness has more society-oriented meanings for men and more relationship-oriented meanings for women. Again, besides the finding that men and women differ with regard to the patterns of individuality and relatedness, they also differ in the more specific meaning attached to them.

Case studies

In order to illustrate the different patterns of individuality and relatedness, we present four case studies. These were randomly chosen out of the category that was most often found in men and women in the youngest and oldest age group. For the men aged 40-54, a person was chosen from the $I_{high}R_{low}$ category;

for the women in this age group a person from the $I_{high}R_{high}$ category; for the men aged 70-85, a person from the the $I_{low}R_{low}$ category; and for the older women, a person from the $I_{low}R_{high}$ category. The findings are presented in Table 3.2.

The man chosen from the youngest age group scores high on individuality and low on relatedness. His individuality answers are focused on 'achievements', 'well-being', 'control' and 'self-reflection'. His relatedness answers concern 'social competency' and 'society'. The woman in the youngest group scores high on individuality and relatedness. She has the same subcategories with regard to individuality as the man from the preceding case, completed with an answer on 'independence'. However, the meanings attached to these personal concerns are rather different. Whereas the man shows a concern about success and control, the woman is concerned in particular with choices and involvements in different life domains. On the relatedness side, she mentions 'contacts', 'social competency', the 'quality of relations', the 'behaviour of other persons' and 'societal concerns'. Interestingly for each person, some relatedness concerns point in the same direction as the individuality concerns. The man describes his impatience as a weakness, yet he also mentions being impatient with other persons. The concerns about choice that characterise the individuality answers of the woman are also found in her concerns about social contacts and the feeling that others determine her life. For the woman, love and societal concerns are also important. These concerns can be seen as a complement rather than a contradiction to her individuality concerns.

The older man mentions 'well-being', 'self-reflection' and 'independence' as concerns around individuality. He mentions 'contacts', 'behaviour of others' and 'transpersonal concerns'. These concerns about relatedness are characterised by a balance between contact and loneliness. The individuality answers and relatedness answers show a shifting balance being built around autonomy and support: from a need to take care of himself to the possibility of accepting help from his daughter in case he would lose competencies in the future.

The older woman mentions the subcategories 'well-being' and 'achievements' as individuality concerns. 'Joint projects', 'social competency', 'behaviour of others' and 'transpersonal concerns' are found among her relatedness answers. The mutual support within the family which she describes from different angles appears to be her main concern.

On the basis of these four case studies, it can be concluded that individuality and relatedness are not contradictory orientations. Rather, they complement each other. Sometimes they are even formulated around the same themes, or they show a shifting balance. Furthermore, idiosyncratic meanings of individuality and relatedness for these four persons stand out.

Discussion

In this chapter, we have moved away from the simple dichotomy of individuality and relatedness. We found clear age and gender differences in the patterns of

Table 3.2: Case studies (category numbers in brackets)

Man, 54 years	Woman, 41 years
Individuality	*Individuality*
When I think about myself ... I am not unsatisfied; I often feel ... rather satisfied; In comparison to others ... I am not unsatisfied (11)	I often feel ... (too) busy; In comparison to others ... I am satisfied (11)
My weaknesses are ... impatience; What's been bothering me recently ... to get a grip on the situation in my job (12)	It is difficult for me ... to make choices; What's been bothering me recently ... how I can best divide my time; When I'm no longer capable of doing certain things ... I hope to be able to concentrate on other things (12)
Compared to the past ... I am more certain of myself; I feel rather miserable when ... I am occupied with myself too much (13)	I think that I ... can discover unknown aspects in myself (13)
I am proud that ... I have achieved a lot; Most important for me is ... achieving; I feel really good ... when I have success; It would be nice if ... could realise my intentions; I have noticed that I ... function well (16)	What I don't like about getting older ... is becoming dependent on others in case of physical and mental decline (14)
Relatedness	My weaknesses are ... wanting too much at the same time; I am afraid that I ... have much more plans than I can ever realise; When I look at my past life, I regret ... that I did not complete higher vocational education (16)
It is difficult for me ... to listen to someone for a long time (24)	*Relatedness*
It annoys me ... that others need much time (27)	Later, when I'm older ... I hope not to become lonely (21)
	I intend to ... make time for social contacts (22)
	I am proud that ... I have a good relationship; Most important for me is ... love (23)
	When I think about myself ... I am lived too much by others sometimes (25)
	It annoys me ... that there is much meaningless violence, intimidation and war; It would be nice if ... if there would be less crime and human mentality improves; I fear that ... the respect for other people declines very much (27)
Man, 78 years	**Woman, 82 years**
Individuality	*Individuality*
When I think about myself ... I am rather satisfied; I think that I ... am satisfied (11)	I often feel ... fine (11); I plan to ... nothing anymore (16)
It would be nice if ... I would stay the same as I am now (13)	*Relatedness*
I am quite good at ... managing for myself; Later, when I'm older ... I hope I will also get along by myself (14)	Compared to the past ... we are doing well (22)
Relatedness	I would like to ... take care of the family; When I think about myself ... I am sometimes difficult; I think that I ... have done well with the children (24)
I am proud that ... I have seven children; I often feel ... lonely (21)	When I'm no longer capable of doing certain things ... another person has to help me (25)
When I'm no longer capable of doing certain things ... my daughter helps me (25)	I am proud that ... the children are doing well; What's been bothering me recently ... illness of husband (26)
When I look at my past life, I regret ... my wife is no longer there (26)	

Codes: Well-being (11); Control (12); Self-reflection (13); Independence (14); Own projects (15); Achievement (16); Contact (21); Joint projects (22); Quality of relationships (23); Social competency (24); Behaviour of others (25); Transpersonal (26); Society (27) individuality and relatedness in the self-descriptions of the participants of the Dutch Aging Survey. More persons in the younger age group were found in the category of high scores on both fronts, and in the category favouring individuality over relatedness, whereas the older age group scored low and favoured relatedness over individuality.

The age differences might be caused by cohort differences or by development. There are arguments for both. As the middle-aged persons had their formative years in the 1960s and 1970s, a time when historically individual values came more to the fore, they might have incorporated more of an orientation towards individuality than the older adults. This cohort interpretation is supported by the finding in a comparable German study that East Germans did not show age differences in individuality as much as West Germans or the Dutch considered here (Bode, 2003).

From a developmental perspective, the finding that younger adults were focused more on individuality and older adults on relatedness is in sharp contrast to psychological ageing theories that expect an increasing focus on the own person in the later years. Our study leaves open the possibility that individuals are becoming more of an individual in the sense of a more integrated personality as described by theorists like Erikson or Jung. What was found here is that there is no shift towards individuality at the level of self-conceptions; that is, in the perspective of ageing persons themselves.

It might be argued that the age differences in individuality and relatedness are caused by the changing life contexts of ageing individuals. Individuality might be strongly related to work experiences and relatedness to responsibilities within the family. Bode (2001) has shown that relatedness is indeed associated with the composition of social networks. The findings that both individuality and relatedness are less central in older groups might thus be related to the experience of role losses in both domains. Furthermore, in this chapter we did not consider other orientations that might be stronger in the older groups. In particular, older persons were found to be more oriented towards psychophysical functioning, which is in turn related to the higher incidence of health problems in older adults (Westerhof et al, 1998). This developmental trajectory might also explain the higher proportion of older adults who scored low in both categories.

At the level of personal concerns, we found that individuality and relatedness have different meanings for different age groups. Although individuality is in general less prominent in older adults, no differences were found with regard to 'well-being' and 'independence'. The more specific meaning of relatedness in older age groups concerns the availability of contact per se, whereas for younger adults the quality of contact and societal issues are more important. These findings point to adaptation to age-related life contexts and preparation for age-related events. The younger age groups that are more involved in work and family responsibilities focus more on 'control', 'achievement' and their 'own projects' and on the quality of their relations. The older age groups focus more on remaining autonomous and maintaining contacts, anticipating losses in these aspects of life. It is important to stress here that the interpretations and expectations of ageing individuals make the difference. A cross-cultural comparison showed for example that Congolese elderly are not concerned about the maintenance of autonomy in the case of illness, but about getting support from their partners and children (Westerhof et al, 2000).

At both levels of analysis, we could reveal diversity in ageing. We found all four patterns of individuality and relatedness in each age group. Furthermore, some persons mentioned a particular concern whereas others did not. Part of this diversity is explained by gender differences. We found no evidence of interactions between gender and age or of an increase in the category high on both, which could be interpreted in terms of androgyny. Hence, there is no support for theories on gender crossover (Gutmann, 1987) or androgyny of later life (Sinott and Shifren, 2001). Yet, the patterns of individuality and relatedness differed systematically for men and women.

The fact that women are found more often in the category with a focus on relatedness and men in the category with a focus on individuality fits more traditional gender differences. In line with previous research, men are also found to be more 'agentic', in the sense of focusing on achievement and goal setting. The finding that relatedness has more society-oriented meanings for men and more relationship-oriented meanings for women fits in with more traditional roles of men in public and women in private domains. However, the finding that women are high on both individuality and relatedness is less expected, as is the finding that women focus more on drawing boundaries between self and others than men. These findings may be explained in terms of the historical changes in gender roles that were observed in the meta-analysis of Twenge (1997). From a generational perspective, these historical changes would have had a stronger effect on the younger cohorts than on the older cohorts. In our study, we did not find this kind of interaction. Apparently, older women have also adapted to cultural changes, in particular with regard to living an independent life in view of possible age-related declines in health and functioning.

At the level of the case studies, we could show that individuality and relatedness are not contradictory orientations. Besides the statistical independence that has been found in other studies (Singelis, 1994), our study also documents that individuality and relatedness have independent rather than contradictory meanings. Individuality and relatedness complemented each other; they are woven around the same concerns, or they show a shifting balance. Furthermore, individual differences in the meaning of individuality and relatedness were found even within the subcategories of personal concerns. The case studies show how individuals actively give meaning to their life contexts and how this results in diversity in ageing at this level of analysis.

By studying individuality and relatedness beyond the simple dichotomies, our study makes a clear case for diversity and ageing. At the lowest level of analysis, that of the case studies, we could show how individuals invoke the motives of individuality and relatedness in idiosyncratic ways in their self-descriptions. We found large individual differences at this level, as well as at the level of personal concerns and meanings. It is only by categorising the self-descriptions in terms of personal concerns that systematic differences between age and gender groups could be found. When further categorising the personal concerns in terms of individuality and relatedness at the first level of our coding scheme, and studying the pattern of these two motives across individuals, we could find diversity in ageing, which is partly explained by gender. It is only by aggregating the data by content analysis and by statistical analysis that systematic differences can be studied. Yet, these procedures conceal the complexity and diversity that idiographic research on individual self-descriptions makes visible. We hope that our way of analysing the data at hierarchically different levels combines some of the advantages of both in showing the diversity in ageing.

References

Ashmore, R.D. (1990) 'Sex, gender, and the individual', in L.A. Pervin (ed) *Handbook of personality: Theory and research*, New York, NY: Guilford Press, pp 486-526.

Bakan, D. (1966) *The duality of human existence*, Chicago, IL: Rand McNally and Company.

Baltes, P.B. (1997) 'On the incomplete architecture of human ontogeny: selection, optimisation, and compensation as foundation of developmental theory', *American Psychologist*, vol 52, pp 366-80.

Bar-Yam Hassan, A. and Bar-Yam, M. (1987) 'Interpersonal development across the life span: communication and its interaction with agency in psychosocial development', *Contributions to Human Development*, vol 18, pp 102-28.

Bem, S.L. (1981) 'Gender schema theory: a cognitive account of sex typing', *Psychological Review*, vol 88, pp 354-64.

Bode, C. (1999) *Coding scheme for independent und interdependent self-descriptions*, Research Report, Nijmegen: Department of Psychogerontology, University of Nijmegen.

Bode, C. (2001) 'Das soziale Selbst' ['The social self'], in F. Dittmann-Kohli, C. Bode and G.J. Westerhof (eds) *Die zweite Lebenshälfte – Psychologische Perspektiven. Ergebnisse des Alters-Survey* [*The second half of life – Psychological perspectives: Findings from the German Aging Survey*], Stuttgart: Kohlhammer, pp 279-342.

Bode, C. (2003) *Individuality and relatedness in middle and late adulthood: A study of women and men in the Netherlands, East- and West-Germany*, Enschede: PPI.

Bode, C., Westerhof, G.J. and Dittmann-Kohli, F. (2001) 'Selbstvorstellungen über Individualität und Verbundenheit in der zweiten Lebenshälfte' ['Self-conceptions: individuality and communion in the second half of life'], *Zeitschrift für Gerontologie und Geriatrie*, vol 34, pp 365-75.

Brandtstädter, J. (1999) 'The self in action and development', in J. Brandtstädter and R.M. Lerner (eds) *Action and self-development. Theory and research through the life span*, Thousand Oaks, CA: Sage Publications, pp 37-65.

Bühler, C. (1933) *Der menschliche Lebenslauf als psychologisches Problem*, Leipzig: Hirzel.

Deaux, K. and Stewart, A.J. (2001) 'Framing gendered identities', in R.K. Unger (ed) *Handbook of the psychology of women and gender*, New York, NY: John Wiley, pp 84-97.

Dittmann-Kohli, F. (1995) *Das persönliche Sinnsystem. Ein Vergleich zwischen frühem und spätem Erwachsenenalter*, Göttingen: Hogrefe.

Dittmann-Kohli, F. and Westerhof, G.J. (1997) 'The SELE sentence completion questionnaire: a new instrument for the assessment of personal meaning in research on aging', *Anuario de Psicologica*, vol 2, pp 7-18.

Erikson, E.H. (1973) *Identität und Lebenszyklus*, Frankfurt: Suhrkamp.

Franz, C.E. and White, K.M. (1985) 'Individuation and attachment in personality development: expanding Erikson's theory', *Journal of Personality*, vol 53, pp 224-56.

Gilligan, C. (1982) *In a different voice*, Cambridge, MA: Harvard University Press.

Guisinger, S. and Blatt, S.J. (1994) 'Individuality and relatedness. Evolution of a fundamental dialectic', *American Psychologist*, vol 49, pp 104-11.

Gutmann, D. (1987) *Reclaimed powers. Toward a new psychology of men and women in later life*, New York, NY: Basic Books.

Hermans, H.J.M. and Hermans-Jansen, E. (1995) *Self-narratives. The construction of meaning in psychotherapy*, New York, NY: Guilford Press.

Jung, C.G. (1972) *The structure and dynamics of the psyche*, London: Routledge and Kegan Paul.

Lang-Takac, E. and Osterweil, Z. (1992) 'Separateness and connectedness: differences between the genders', *Sex Roles*, vol 27, pp 277-89.

Lenney, E. (1991) 'Sex roles: the measurement of masculinity, femininity, and androgyny', in J.P Robinson, P.R. Shaver and L.S. Wrightsman (eds) *Measures of personality and social psychological attitudes: Measures of social psychological attitudes: Vol 1*, San Diego, CA: Academic Press.

McAdams, D.P (1988) 'Personal needs and personal relationships', in S.W. Duck (ed) *Handbook of personal relationships*, New York, NY: Wiley, pp 7-22.

Markus, H.R. and Kitayama, S. (1991) 'Culture and the self: implications for cognition, emotion, and motivation', *Psychological Review*, vol 98, pp 224-53.

Potter, J. and Wetherell, M. (1987) *Discourse and social psychology: Beyond attitudes and behaviour*, Beverly Hills, CA: Sage Publications.

Ryff, C.D. (1989) 'In the eye of the beholder: views of psychological well-being among middle-aged and older adults', *Psychology and Aging*, vol 4, pp 195-210.

Ryff, C.D. (1995) 'Psychological well-being in adult life', *Current Directions in Psychological Science*, vol 4, pp 99-104.

Schneewind, K.A. (1994) 'Persönlichkeitsentwicklung im Kontext von Erziehung und Sozialisation' ['Personality development in the context of education and socialization'], in K.A. Schneewind (ed) *Psychologie der Erziehung und Sozialisation. Enzyklopädie der Psychologie, Serie Pädagogische Psychologie* [*Psychology of education and socialization: Encyclopedia of Psychology, Series Pedagogical Psychology*], Band 1, Göttingen: Hogrefe.

Schulz, R. and Heckhausen, J. (1996) 'A life span model of successful aging', *American Psychologist*, vol 51, pp 702-14.

Singelis, T.M. (1994) 'The measurement of independent and interdependent self-construals', *Personality and Social Psychology Bulletin*, vol 20, pp 580-91.

Sinnott, J.D. and Shifren, K. (2001) 'Gender and aging: gender differences and gender roles', in J.E. Birren and K.W. Schaie (eds) *Handbook of the psychology of aging*, San Diego, CA: Academic Press, pp 454-76.

Spence, J.T. and Helmreich, R.L. (1980) 'Masculine instrumentality and feminine expressiveness: their relationships with sex role attitudes and behaviors', *Psychology of Women Quarterly*, vol 5, pp 147-63.

Steverink, N., Westerhof, G.J., Bode, C. and Dittmann-Kohli, F. (2001) *Dutch Aging Survey: Onderzoeksdesign en Instrumente* [*Dutch Aging Survey: Research design and research instruments*], Nijmegen: Department of Psychogerontology, University of Nijmegen.

Thomas, L.E. and Chambers, K.O. (1989) 'Phenomenology of life satisfaction among elderly men: quantitative and qualitative views', *Psychology and Aging*, vol 4, pp 284-9.

Twenge, J.M. (1997) 'Changes in masculine and feminine traits over time: a meta-analysis', *Sex Roles*, vol 36, pp 305-25.

Westerhof, G.J., Dittmann-Kohli, F. and Katzko, M.W. (2000) 'Individualism and collectivism in the personal meaning system of elderly adults: the United States and Congo/Zaire as an example', *Journal of Cross-Cultural Psychology*, vol 31, pp 649-76.

Westerhof, G.J., Dittmann-Kohli, F. and Thissen, T. (2001) 'Beyond life satisfaction: qualitative and quantitative approaches to judgments about the quality of life', *Social Indicators Research*, vol 56, pp 179-203.

Westerhof, G.J., Kuin, Y. and Dittmann-Kohli, F. (1998) 'Gesundheit als Lebensthema', *Zeitschrift für Klinische Psychologie*, vol 27, pp 136-42.

FOUR

Diversity, health and ageing

Lars Andersson and Peter Öberg

Key points

- Diversity may be illuminated by the phenomenon of latency in health status.
- Relationships between social class and health status can unfold, remain constant or vanish over time.
- Gerontological research can contribute to the process of constructing increased or decreased diversity, depending on the study perspective and the way of presenting the data.
- Decreased diversity can be constructed by collective identities and social categorisations, while increased diversity can be constructed by an agency perspective, and by qualitative research.

Key readings

Evans, R.G., Barer, M.L. and Marmor, T.R. (eds) (1994) *Why are some people healthy and others not? The determinants of health of populations*, New York, NY: Aldine de Gruyter.
Mortimer, J.T. and Shanahan, M.J. (eds) (2003) *Handbook of the life course*, New York, NY: Kluwer Academic.

Introduction

In this chapter, we discuss diversity from a realist and a constructivist perspective. In the former case, three positions about ageing and human development are illustrated:

- an increased heterogeneity;
- a decreased heterogeneity; and
- a maintained heterogeneity.

Smith and Gerstorf (Chapter Two of this volume) express this trichotomy in the following terms: (a) "the combined effects of individuals' unique experiences over more years should produce *increasing* differences between them"; (b) "the reduction in birth cohort size among the oldest old as a function of selective mortality is thought to contribute to a corresponding *reduction* in observed inter-individual heterogeneity"; and (c) "humans are very susceptible to influence in their early years, but are thought to become increasingly *stable* in important respects with age". In addition to the realist perspective, we also discuss the construction of diversity depending on research perspective.

According to Burgess and Bengtson (2001), the purpose of future theory building in social gerontology is to focus on theories of the middle range and to challenge linear models of age and ageing. The positions above suggesting increasing heterogeneity, decreasing heterogeneity or stability are, at least partly, based on assumptions of linearity. Furthermore, it is reasonable to assume that new understandings and explanations of ageing of the middle range – attempting to interpret and explain *elements* of the ageing process – will probably verify all three positions outlined earlier, depending on the context, the object of study and the research perspective.

Burgess and Bengtson (2001, p 1017) list several questions that theories in social gerontology need to address. One of them concerns "what social factors account for the considerable variability between individuals and groups in later-life trajectories and experiences". They continue:

> Although social gerontology has long acknowledged heterogeneity and new statistical procedures are able to capture a more dynamic portrait of ageing, few theories of ageing have been successful in addressing this complexity. (2001, pp 1018-19)

Our intent in this chapter is not to suggest a new theory, but critically to discuss the construction of diversity in ageing research generally and in ageing research about health especially.

Diversity in health

Generally, diversity in health is discussed in terms of social inequalities; that is, a comparison of groups, not individuals. As noted by Hertzman et al (1994), diversity in health is not just a result of every individual being different. They agree that individual variations can be cancelled out by aggregation, but "there are also significant differences between entire populations, or among subgroups of the same population" (1994, p 67). One such basic division, with policy implications, is the diversity in health based on socioeconomic status.

Inequalities in health

Swedish register data (that is, administrative records on national, regional and local level) highlight various types of inequalities in health based on socioeconomic status (*Folkhälsorapport*, 2001). One such type is socioeconomic differences in mortality, which remain through the lifecourse but are less pronounced among retirees than among the gainfully employed. Both average length of life and causes of death differ between housing areas with different socioeconomic characteristics. In 1993-97, remaining average length of life for men aged 65 was 5.7 years longer in areas with the highest mean income compared with areas with the lowest mean income. For women the difference was 5.2 years. The differences have increased from the years 1981-85. For men, the remaining average length of life in the wealthiest areas increased 2.1 years in this period, while the increase in the poorest areas was 0.7 years.

With regard to morbidity, the register data of married people born in Sweden show that among men belonging to the lowest income quintile, severe ill health is four times more common than among men in the highest income quintile. Among women in the lowest income quintile, severe ill health is three times as common as among women in the highest income quintile. For example, among men aged 65-69 the proportion with severe ill health is 12% in the lowest income group and 3% in the highest income group. For women, the corresponding figures are 13% and 4%.

Another illustration of this difference is to conclude that the proportion of men aged 80-84 in the highest income quintile with severe ill health is lower than for men aged 65-69 in the lowest income quintile − 7% and 12% respectively. The same is true for women. One way of expressing this is that there are more than 15 years of health difference between the highest income group and the lowest income group.

According to Statistics Sweden's Health Index, the probability for severe ill health is highest for those aged 80-84, who are single, were born abroad, and have an income in the lowest income quintile. The proportion with severe ill health in this group is 36% among men and 42% among women. The lowest proportion of severe ill health is found in the group aged 65-69, married, born in Sweden, and with an income in the highest income quintile − 3% among men and 4% among women.

Trajectories

The diversity in health described earlier shows health status at a particular point in time. We assume that the relationship between social class and health unfold over time, but we cannot generally specify the time lag. Nor do we know the social class history up until the point of measurement; that is, people may have changed social class either ways. Barrett's (2000) US Health Survey of disaggregated marital trajectories has highlighted the loss of information as a consequence of an aggregation.

Barrett examined the effects of marital status and marital history on mental health outcomes. She pointed out that the use of current marital status in studies of mental health leaves unmeasured heterogeneity with regard to marital history for everyone but the never married. She studied a number of trajectories:

Among the currently married:
1. one marriage;
2. marriage–divorce–marriage;
3. marriage–widowhood–marriage;
4. marriage–divorce–marriage–divorce–marriage.

Among the currently widowed:
1. married–widowed;
2. married–widowed–married–widowed;
3. married–divorced–married–widowed.

Among the currently divorced:
1. married–divorced;
2. married–divorced–married–divorced.

Results indicated that marital history matters; that there are significant differences in mental health among persons in the same current marital state, but whose marital histories differ. She also demonstrated that duration in a given marital state explained additional variance. The use of disaggregated trajectories will thus yield important information about distinctive patterns of change.

In the same vein, we can assume that several trajectories will unfold *after* the point of measurement. In some cases, it is pertinent to follow the study group until all are deceased.

A Norwegian study where people aged 80+ were followed to the end of their life showed that, although there were six main trajectories of Activities of Daily Living (ADL) limitations, the total number was 25. Thus, although the trajectories can be summarised in a simplified manner, on an individual level they are complex (Romøren and Blekeseaune, 2003).

It can be laborious to decide what exactly causes a change (in health) between individuals or groups over time. One possibility is to follow up the impact of an event shared by (almost) everybody. One such event is retirement, and different pathways following it can be identified.

Andersson (2002) has taken a closer look at subjective health around retirement. The original data set is based on interviews with 18,134 individuals aged 45-84. With regard to work–life issues, one can identify three pathways for the phenomenon of latency with regard to social class (here measured by occupation). The first could be called 'catch up', where the health status, measured as reported problems, among white-collar workers after retirement is getting closer to the level of blue-collar workers (Figure 4.1). Keeping in mind that mortality is somewhat higher in the blue-collar group, it is still evident how white-collar workers after retirement 'catch up' with surviving blue-collar workers to some extent and for some types of problems (here exemplified by long-term illness).

Figure 4.1: Long-term illness after retirement

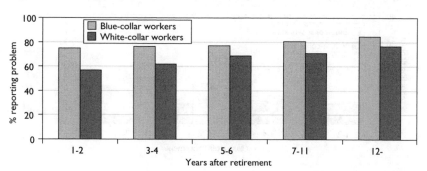

The second pathway is 'business as usual', where the differences between the groups remain the same after retirement, here exemplified by general health status (Figure 4.2).

Figure 4.2: General health status after retirement

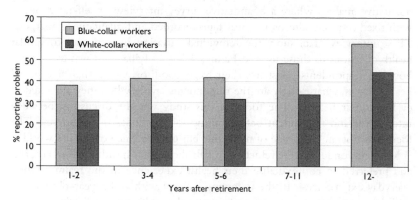

The third pathway, 'delayed effects', is exemplified by physical disability, where differences between the groups expand long after retirement (Figure 4.3).

Work life is one of several determinants of the diversity in deterioration of health with age. Although there is a stable difference between (social) groups on an aggregated level, as shown in the first part of this section, differences for various diseases or pains may vary over time.

Figure 4.3: Physical disability after retirement

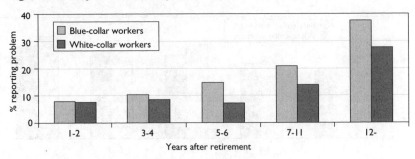

The impact on diversity by choice of measurement method

Gerontological studies with an 'inner perspective' (Birren et al, 1996), or studies of older peoples' everyday life and everyday experiences, have paved the way for showing the great variability among older people. One attempt to grasp this inner or emic perspective of ageing concerning health is Jylhä's (1994) qualitative analysis where a quantitative survey interview of self-rated health with fixed response alternatives was tape-recorded and qualitatively analysed. These interview data show the individual variation in responses to similar health questions to those used in Figures 4.1-4.3. Jylhä's aim was to find out how the respondents construct their 'very good' or 'worse than age peers' health; that is, what exactly are the respondents saying when they are asked to evaluate their health? The focus in this study was the discussion between interviewer and respondent before opting for the codes in the survey. The focus was not on 'the voice of medicine' but on 'the voice of the life world'.

Many respondents were reluctant to talk about their health in abstract terms and preferred to contextualise their health experience in the realm of their everyday experiences. In the following excerpt with an 85-year-old woman with leg prosthesis, it becomes obvious that 'health' is not a one-dimensional, decontextualised variable as is often used in surveys:

Q: *I would now like to ask you a few questions about your health. How would you rate your present health? Do you feel healthy?*

A: Well, yes, I'm more or less healthy, but I've got this leg prosthesis and you know what it's like. I had it cut off from here down. But it doesn't ache really; and generally it doesn't cause any troubles. But, of course, it's quite difficult.

Q: *How would you evaluate your present health status? Is it very good, good, average, rather bad or bad?*

A: Well I would have to say it's pretty good, because I've got no other pains and I can eat almost anything.

Q: *If you compare your health with that of other persons you know of your own age, is your health better, about the same or worse?*

A: Well, the only problem I can think of is this, but I mean surely you understand what it's like when they've taken one leg away, you can't really say you're healthy, but I've never been, never really been ill in my whole life.

Q: *Is it difficult for you to compare your own health with that of other people of your own age? Is it …*

A: Well, most of them are dead, aren't they? (Jylhä 1994, pp 987-8)

Jylhä's qualitative study reveals an obvious tension between the logic of everyday conversation with its vide diversity and the logic of a survey interview relying on an abstract health concept with, for example, five fixed response alternatives. The logic of the survey requires unambiguous and absolute answers to often very abstract questions, while the logic of everyday conversation is characterised by contextualisations, comparisons, accounts and narratives.

Up to this point, we have illustrated diversity from the three positions of increasing heterogeneity, decreasing heterogeneity and stability. In the next section, our focus shifts to how researchers in gerontology, by choice of research perspective and methods, contribute in producing images of ageing with reduced or increased diversity.

Constructing reduced diversity

It is reasonable to assume that diversity is less of an issue in relation to older people's collective identity than their self-identity. In this section, we are searching for issues of reduced diversity and we start with issues of collective identities, social categorisations, social roles and images and stereotypes ascribed to older people by researchers in gerontology. In the section that follows, we continue with the issue of self-identity, reflecting personal interpretations of the ageing process and personal experiences of health. As a part of self-identity, we also examine how diversity in age identity can be constructed in gerontological research.

In order to perceive any structure in an almost infinite variety of stimuli, we need categorisation. Consequently, it would be impossible to understand anything of the social structure if we did not group together people or situations that show some similarities (Tornstam, 1982). Examples of social gerontological categorisations are concepts such as 'young old/old old', 'third age/fourth age', 'generation', 'age stratification' and 'the institutionalisation of the life course'. A categorisation may contain a substantial number of categories. Where there are just a few categories describing a large group such as older people, there is a considerable risk of stereotyping older people (for example, as frail and ill).

In Neugarten's (1974) article, 'Age groups in American society and the rise of the young-old', Americans were divided into two groups – 'young-old' (55-74 years) and 'old-old' (75+) – in order to show that people at the beginning of their seventh decade showed great similarities with people at the end of their fifth decade. Ironically, Neugarten's intention of counteracting stereotypes of older people became a new popular stereotype, describing 65- to 74-year-old people as healthy 'young old' and people aged 75+ as poor and sick 'old old' (Binstock, 2002). In this sense, we can see how an intention of showing diversity between old people in fact may create new homogenising stereotypes. This, in fact, is an inherent problem in social gerontology. We create new stereotypes in research when trying to balance between the Scylla of the unique descriptions and the Charybdis of the large-scale generalisations.

A parallel can be drawn with Laslett's (1989) theory of the third age. According to Laslett, the 'first age' is about dependency, socialisation, immaturity and education; the 'second age' about earning and saving; the 'third age' about self-fulfilment and personal well-being; and the 'fourth age' about final dependency, decrepitude and death. This division does not follow chronological age, but pays attention to the diversity among the group of people we use to label 'old people' (the major discrepancy being between the third age as the top of the career and as a period of performance and self-fulfilment, and the fourth age as a period of decrepitude and dependency).

A persistent misconception today is to let the minority of old people living in institutions or being care receivers represent the whole group of older people. As Karisto (2002) has noticed, it is less relevant to study the third age from the typical problem and care-oriented perspectives, which de facto restricts the scope to the minority of elderly in the fourth age.

Karisto's main criticism of the third age/fourth age concept is based on the fact that the fourth age becomes a total contrast to and a negation of the third age (Karisto, 2002). The result is a growing cleavage between the healthy active leisure of the third age and the physical decrepitude and dependency of the fourth age, between 'go-go' and 'no-go' pensioners (Blaikie, 1999). The third age is generally much longer than the fourth, and a problem with using the third age concept is that it can hide the extensive heterogeneity in this prolonged stage of life (Karisto, 2002).

The Mannheim-inspired concept of 'generation' as groups of people who share a distinctive culture and/or a self-conscious identity by virtue of their having experienced the same historical events at the same time (Alwin and McCammon, 2003, p 43) is another collective concept contradicting diversity. An opposite of diversity is also immanent in the concept of 'institutionalisation of the lifecourse', introduced by Kohli (1986a, 1986b). Today this concept is used more frequently than Riley's (1972) concept of 'age stratification' (Conrad, 1992). The lifecourse can be defined as interdependent sequences of age-related social roles across life domains (for example, family, education, work, leisure). When these linkages are tightly coupled and universally salient in a population, their coherence and normative strength lead to a more highly institutionalised, age-graded lifecourse with little heterogeneity between the age-based social roles (O'Rand, 2003).

Following this exposition, we turn our focus in the contrasting direction: towards increased diversity and inter-individual heterogeneity in old age. First, from a lifecourse perspective, we will discuss this as a consequence of the de-institutionalisation of the lifecourse. Second, we will exemplify how increased diversity can be a consequence of data construction and presentation.

Towards increased diversity

When the linkages between the different life phases and social roles are loosely coupled, the diversity and variability in the lifecourse increases. Where the relationship of age to the transitions weakens and the synchronisation of roles across life domains becomes less standardised, we speak of a de-institutionalisation of the lifecourse. However, scholars do not agree on the extent of the de-institutionalisation of the lifecourse, and some argue that structural lags in the responses of social institutions to demographic shifts are slowing the process of de-institutionalisation (O'Rand, 2003). Irrespective of its extent, we argue that de-institutionalisation means increased age heterogeneity and diversity across the lifecourse with the resulting possibility that the body becomes less visible in the identity-formation process.

Ageing research concerning the concept of social clocks or normative timetables, referring to expectations of appropriate times and ages of important life transitions, was pioneered by Neugarten in the 1950s and helped to demonstrate the enormous diversity of people's lives and also how social norms give meaning, and even direct, individual trajectories. Discussions of an age-irrelevant society and of blurring of boundaries between life stages reflect the awareness of a growing flexibility in transitions during the lifecourse (Conrad, 1992; Elder et al, 2003).

According to George (2003), one focus in lifecourse research has been the examination of heterogeneity in the lifecourse and the social characteristics and conditions that generate such diversity (for example, gender, race and class). Lifecourse research would certainly be less complicated if there were an 'expectable' (or normative) lifecourse in which a majority, or even a significant minority, followed a modal pattern of transitions and trajectories. Such is clearly not the case. Evidence regarding the timing of significant lifecourse transitions demonstrates the absence of an empirical timetable that can be used as a template of the expectable lifecourse.

While men and women are generally treated as adults at age 18, there is much less agreement about the age at which a person enters or leaves middle age. As societies age, age grades may proliferate within the older population in response to increased diversity in perceived interests, orientations, health and service needs. As the proportion of an age group that diverges from the age norms for various roles and life transitions increases, the nature of age groupings becomes more ambiguous. For example, as retirement ages have continued to drop and a large proportion of people retire during an extended period of time, the link between retirement and an age grouping called older age becomes more and more tenuous (Atchley, 2001).

Weakening of age norms and beliefs about what is 'appropriate' for different stages of life means growing diversity. Many earlier lifecycle models have been criticised for neglecting the heterogeneity. For example, early models of social pathways generally centred on a single role sequence like that of a lifecycle. Children mature, marry, and have children who grow up and start a family as the cycle continues into another generation. Of course, this description is limited in that not everyone participates in familial reproduction (Elder, 2003).

Dannefer (2003) discusses the possibilities of lifecourse diversity in late modernity that is characterised by greater variability and inequality across individuals. According to Dannefer, as a part of postmodern deconstruction of modernity's 'grand narratives', the modern 'standard lifecourse' is now in a process of de-institutionalisation. The expression 'institutionalisation of the modern lifecourse' has often been equated with the 'three boxes' – education, work, retirement – and an age-graded sequence of social roles. This career imperative, however, has been criticised by arguments, for example, that in recent decades the events of cohabiting, childbearing and marriage have become 'disordered'. Dannefer (2003, p 651) takes other examples from subcultures or micro-cultures, such as urban street gang cultures in the US, where a 'normative lifecourse' may include an expectation of not surviving to age 30:

> Under such alternative configurations, thirtysomethings may be grandparents; elders are workers, parents mortgage their children, and children themselves are labourers and parents, prostitutes and soldiers, criminals and explorers. Some children become independent at a remarkably young age, while others lose their lives at an early age.

However, as Dannefer states, we currently have little knowledge about the extent to which effects of early lifecourse experiences and developments upon later life outcomes will hold in times of institutional or economic turbulence:

> To the extent that observed T1-T2 life course connections rely upon conditions of institutional predictability and certainty, these connections may weaken or disappear if the institutional matrix is eroded. (2003, p 654)

Lifecourse diversity can be illustrated by the study of a high-school class of 1972 (Rindfuss et al, 1987, cf George, 2003). The authors coded the participants' sequences of five roles – work, education, homemaking, military, and other – during eight years following high-school graduation. They report that 1,100 sequences were needed to describe the experiences of the 6,700 men in the sample; the corresponding number of sequences for the 7,000 women was 1,800. Consequently, a key challenge of lifecourse research is to simultaneously do justice to long-term patterns of change and stability and to the heterogeneity of those patterns.

One argument for a growing diversity stems from theories of modernisation. In the late modern societies, diversity more or less becomes an inherent part of everyday life. In late modernity, new definitions of ageing will emerge, where the ageing experience is transformed from a collective to a more individually and reflexively constructed experience. An increased individualisation of society is also affecting ageing in a more individualised direction. Self-identity is continuously revised through biographical narratives in the context of multiple choices. Lifestyle choices thus become increasingly important in the constitution of self-identity. As Giddens (1991, p 14) puts it:

> Modernity is a post-traditional order, in which the question, 'How shall I live?' has to be answered in day-to-day decisions about how to behave, what to wear and what to eat.

By emphasising actions and subjective and everyday experiences among older people, the agency perspective promotes diversity. Many earlier social gerontological theories, such as theories of disengagement, activity and age stratification, for example, have been criticised for neglecting agency, choice and the subjective aspects of ageing (Birren et al, 1996). Recent discussions of development and ageing have increasingly emphasised agency and choice. Individuals are seen as architects of their own lives (Hagestad and Dannefer, 2001), which increases the researcher's possibilities of identifying diversity and variation.

However, critique has been raised against an agency without structure perspective, an individualisation of the social where societal crises such as unemployment and poverty become cast as personal failures. Hagestad and Dannefer refer to paradoxical socialisation, where youth is socialised into an ideology of choice, a sense of choice that may have increased (with regard to leisure, for example) but where still fundamental patterns of social reproduction according to class remain.

From an agency perspective, it is obvious that people may experience their age differently. For example, in a study by Öberg and Tornstam (2001), 1,250 20- to 85-year-old Swedes were asked about their 'ideal age': "How old would you rather wish to be?" The responses showed that 72% would have preferred to be younger than their chronological age; 23% would prefer to be as old as they were, and 5% would have preferred to be older than they are.

From Figure 4.4, we can see the ideal age for the youngest age group (20-24) to be their own (chronological) age. For each successive age group, the discrepancy between chronological and ideal age is growing. In the age group 45-54, people in average would like to be about ten years younger; in the age group 75-85, almost 30 years younger than their chronological age.

There are certainly several reasons for the increasing discrepancy between chronological age and ideal age, for example, closeness to death or desire for an age associated with better health and functional capacity. In Figure 4.4, showing the mean age difference, the variance in the responses is concealed. This is also the traditional way of presenting quantitative gerontological research. The results in the scattergram in Figure 4.5 show a more differentiated picture.

Figure 4.5 shows how the diversity in ideal age is growing by age. This example of constructing and presenting data shows that individuals' unique experiences over the years produce increasing differences between them. One interpretation of these results is that the majority of the older respondents do not desire youthfulness as such; they may rather wish for an age when their health and functional capacity was better.

Epilogue

In this chapter we have showed, on the one hand, how diversity may increase or decrease by age (or remain unchanged). Furthermore, we have showed how diversity may decrease as a consequence of an institutionalisation, and increase as a consequence of a de-institutionalisation of the lifecourse. On the other hand, we have showed how gerontological research can contribute to the process of constructing increased or decreased diversity, depending on the study perspective and the way of presenting the results. For example, all collective identities conceal the heterogeneity in old age. We have also illustrated how qualitative research and studies with an inner perspective on ageing and everyday experiences can contribute to more diversified descriptions of old age.

Acknowledgement

We are grateful for valuable comments on the typescript from Marianne Winqvist and Lars Tornstam. This research is supported by the Swedish Council for Working life and Social Research.

Figure 4.4: The discrepancy between chronological age and ideal age for respondents in different age groups

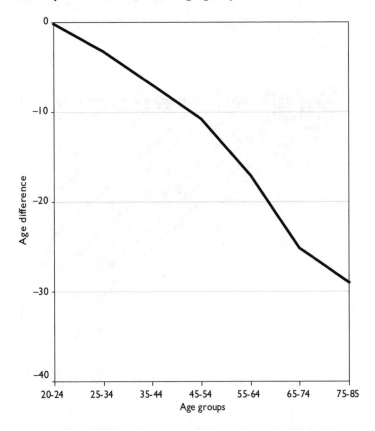

Figure 4.5: The distribution of the discrepancy between chronological age and ideal age for the same sample shown in Figure 4.4

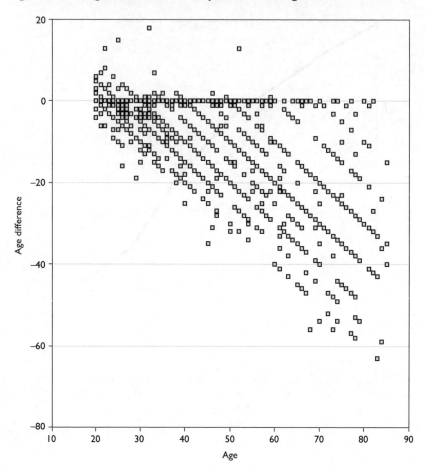

References

Alwin, D.F. and McCammon, R.J. (2003) 'Generations, cohorts, and social change', in J.T. Mortimer and M.J. Shanahan (eds) *Handbook of the lifecourse*, New York, NY: Kluwer Academic Publishers, pp 23-49.

Andersson, L. (2002) 'Ålderism – några infallsvinklar', in *Att åldras. Riv ålderstrappan! Livslopp i förändring*, (SOU 2002:29, Bilagedel A), Stockholm: Fritzes offentliga publikationer, pp 1-45.

Atchley, R.C. (2001) 'Age grading and grouping', in G.L. Maddox et al (eds) *The encyclopaedia of aging. Vol I*, New York, NY: Springer Publishing Co, pp 36-7.

Barrett, A.E. (2000) 'Marital trajectories and mental health', *Journal of Health and Social Behaviour*, vol 41, no 4, pp 451-64.

Binstock, R.H. (2002) 'In memoriam: Bernice L. Neugarten', *The Gerontologist*, vol 42, no 2, pp 149-51.

Birren, J.E., Kenyon, G.M., Ruth, J-E., Schroots, J.J.F. and Svensson, T. (eds) (1996) *Aging and biography. Explorations in adult development*, New York, NY: Springer.

Blaikie, A. (1999) 'Can there be a cultural sociology of ageing?', *Education and Ageing*, vol 14, no 2, pp 127-39.

Burgess, E.O. and Bengtson, V.L (2001) 'Theories in social gerontology', in G.L. Maddox et al (eds) *The encyclopaedia of aging. Vol II*, New York, NY: Springer, pp 1017-19.

Conrad, C. (1992) 'Old age in the modern and post-modern western world', in T.R. Cole, D.D. van Tassel and R. Kastenbaum (eds) *Handbook of the humanities and aging*, New York, NY: Springer, pp 62-95.

Dannefer, D. (2003) 'Toward a global geography of the life course. Challenges of late modernity for life course theory', in J.T. Mortimer and M.J. Shanahan (eds) *Handbook of the life course*, New York, NY: Kluwer Academic, pp 647-59.

Elder, G.H. Jr., Kirkpatrick Johnson, M. and Crosnoe, R. (2003) 'The emergence and development of life course theory', in J.T. Mortimer and M.L Shanahan (eds) *Handbook of the life course*, New York, NY: Kluwer Academic, pp 3-22.

Folkhälsorapport (2001) *Äldres hälsa och välbefinnande. En utmaning för folkhälsoarbetet*, Stockholm: Stiftelsen Stockholms läns Äldrecentrum.

George, L.K. (2003) 'Life course research: achievements and potential', in J.T. Mortimer and M.L Shanahan (eds) *Handbook of the life course*, New York, NY: Kluwer Academic, pp 671-80.

Giddens, A. (1991) *Modernity and self-identity*, Cambridge: Polity Press.

Hagestad, G.O. and Dannefer, D. (2001) 'Concepts of theories of aging. Beyond microfication in social science approaches', in R.H. Binstock and L.K. George (eds) *Handbook of aging and the social sciences*, San Diego, CA: Academic Press, pp 3-21.

Hertzman, C., Frank, J. and Evans, R.G. (1994) 'Heterogeneities in health status and the determinants of population health', in R.G. Evans, M.L. Barer and T.R. Marmor (eds) *Why are some people healthy and others not? The determinants of health of populations*, New York, NY: Aldine de Gruyter, pp 67-92.

Jylhä, M. (1994) 'Self-rated health revisited: exploring survey interview episodes with elderly respondents', *Social Science and Medicine*, vol 39, no 7, pp 983-90.

Karisto, A. (2002) 'Kolmannen iän käsitteestä ja sen käytöstä', *Gerontologia*, vol 16, no 3, pp 138-42.

Kohli, M. (1986a) 'The world we forgot: a historical review of the life course', in V.W. Marshall (ed) *Later life: The social psychology of aging*, Beverly Hills, CA: Sage Publications, pp 271-303.

Kohli, M. (1986b) 'Social organization and subjective construction of the life course', in A.B. Sørensen, F.E. Weinert and L.R. Sherrod (eds) *Human development and the life-course: Multidisciplinary perspectives*, Hillsdale, NJ: Lawrence Erlbaum Associates, pp 271-92.

Laslett, P (1989) *A fresh map of life: The emergence of the third age*, London: Weidenfeld and Nicholson.

Neugarten, B.L. (1974) 'Age groups in American society and the rise of the young-old', *Annals of the American Academy of Political and Social Science*, vol 415, pp 187-98.

Öberg, P. and Tornstam, L. (2001) 'Youthfulness and fitness – identity ideals for all ages?', *Journal of Aging and Identity*, vol 6, no 1, pp 15-29.

O'Rand, A.M. (2003) 'The future of the life course: late modernity and life course risks', in J.T. Mortimer and M.L Shanahan (eds) *Handbook of the life course*, New York, NY: Kluwer Academic, pp 693-702.

Riley, M.W, Johnson, M. and Foner, A. (1972) *Aging and society: A sociology of age stratification*, New York, NY: Russell Sage Foundation.

Romøren, T.I. and Blekeseaune, M. (2003) 'Trajectories of disability among the oldest old', *Journal of Aging and Health*, vol 15, no 3, pp 548-66.

Tornstam, L. (1982) 'Gerontology in a dynamic society', in T.K. Hareven and K.J. Adams (eds) *Aging and life course transitions: An interdisciplinary perspective*, New York, NY: Guilford Press, pp 183-220.

FIVE

Gender trajectories: how age and marital status influence patterns of gender inequality in later life

Sara Arber

Key points

- Older married men are advantaged on key aspects of quality of life, and nearly three quarters of older men are married.
- Widows are financially and materially disadvantaged, and widowhood is the norm for older women.
- Older divorced men and women face financial, material and health disadvantages, and are groups projected to grow rapidly.
- Older women are more likely to spend the final stage of their life in a residential setting, both because of higher levels of disability and widowhood.

Key readings

Arber, S., Davidson, K. and Ginn, J. (eds) (2003) *Gender and ageing: Changing roles and relationships*, Maidenhead: Open University Press.

Arber, S. and Ginn, J. (eds) (1995) *Connecting gender and ageing*, Buckingham: Open University Press.

Bernard, M. and Meade, K. (1993) *Women come of age*, London: Edward Arnold.

Calasanti, T. and Sleven, K. (2001) *Gender, social inequalities, and aging*, Walnut Creek, CA: AltaMira Press.

Thompson, E.H. (ed) (1994) *Older men's lives*, Thousand Oaks, CA: Sage Publications.

Introduction

Research on gender and later life has often taken a feminist political economy perspective, emphasising the disadvantaged position of older women in relation to pensions and access to health and social care (Arber and Ginn, 1991, 1995; Estes, 2001). This chapter extends this approach by examining diversity among older men and women according to marital status. It is important to see marital status in later life as reflecting an older woman's lifecourse, for example, in terms of how childrearing has constrained paid employment and therefore acquisition of pensions, while having children also influences an older person's potential available carers. There are many other bases of diversity in later life, such as class and ethnicity, which may crosscut and amplify gender inequalities (Calasanti and Sleven, 2001), but these are not considered here. Less attention has been paid to older men's lives (Thompson, 1994). This chapter aims to redress some of this imbalance by considering the extent to which the minority of non-partnered men in later life are disadvantaged in terms of financial and material well-being and access to carers.

Later life is a predominantly female world. In all developed societies, women live longer than men, resulting in increasingly more older women than men as age advances. The extent of this female numerical dominance varies between societies. In the countries of the former Soviet Union and central Europe, the life expectancy of women is over 10 years more than men (Mesle and Vallin, 2002), and the numerical gender differential is much greater than in the UK. In the UK, women in 2001 could expect to live 4.8 years longer than men – an expectation of life of 80.1 for women and 75.3 for men (ONS, 2003).

The numerical gender difference among older people varies between societies and over time within the same society. The UK has witnessed more rapid falls in male than female mortality over the past 30 years, evidenced by a reduction in the gender difference in life expectancy from 6.3 years in 1970. In 2001 in the UK, there were 138 women for every 100 men over age 65, which had fallen from 161 women to 100 men in 1971. The gender differential is now only 113 women for every man aged 65-74, but it rises rapidly with advancing age. In 1991 there were over three women for every man over age 85, but this fell to a sex ratio of 2.6 in 2001 (Arber and Ginn, 2004). These demographic changes mean that old age is becoming less feminised than it was in the later half of the 20th century.

The differential mortality rate of women and men also influences partnership status, which is intimately connected to other aspects of well-being in later life, but in gender-differentiated ways. This chapter examines gender differences across the age span from age 65, contrasting five-year age groups, from the late 60s to those over 85 years. Gender differences will be considered in a number of spheres that are central to quality of later life, namely income, material circumstances, health and disability, and living in a residential care setting, in each case examining to what extent these gender differences are due to variations between men and women in their marital status.

Gender, age and marital status

The chronological marker signifying the start of old age varies over time, between societies and across social groups within a particular society. Many chapters in this book consider variations in self-perceptions of whether individuals feel 'old' and the implications of this for their self-identity. Other markers relate to the age of eligibility for the state retirement pension, for free public transport, or age of retirement from paid employment. Across Europe, the age of leaving paid employment has decreased markedly over the past 30 years. The UK is fairly typical, with an average age of labour market exit of 61 for men and 57 for women. However, age of exit has increasingly diverged from the age of eligibility for a state pension, which in the UK has traditionally been 65 for men but for women is now being increased from 60 to 65.

This chapter considers women and men aged 65+, conforming to the state pension age in the UK – an age by which more than 90% are no longer in the paid labour force. Those entering this chronologically defined gateway can expect to live for a further 15-20 years. This period of later life is one of change and diversity, marked for many by the impact of the death of their partner and by increasing levels of disability. The gender-related implications of these two events are considered.

Gender differences linked to advancing chronological age may be the effect of various distinct processes:

- *physiological ageing*, that is, gender differences in changes in functional ability and disability that may occur with ageing;
- the longer-term effects of *gendered roles and relationships* across the lifecourse associated with marriage, childrearing and paid employment;
- *social changes* associated with advancing age that affect an individual, for example, the death of their partner (Arber and Ginn, 1995).

Age differences may also reflect *cohort* differences. People in their late sixties grew up after the Second World War, benefiting from the development of the welfare state and expansion of education, with women likely to return to employment following childrearing, whereas those in their eighties often experienced the war at first hand, after which women returned to the home and were only peripherally involved in the labour market during their adult lives. These cohort differences divide the current span of older people. There may be even greater cohort differences in future, as the 'baby boomers', who experienced their formative teenage years during the major societal changes of the 1960s, reach retirement age (Evandrou, 1997).

This chapter contrasts gender differences in income, material circumstances, health and disability, and living in a care home setting by comparing the 'youngest old' with the 'oldest old' based on data from the British General Household Survey (GHS). Using such cross-sectional survey data, it is not possible to distinguish between the effects of gendered roles across the lifecourse, age-related social changes, physiological ageing or cohort differences, although these four types of explanations need to be borne in mind throughout the chapter.

Marital status and living arrangements are pivotal to an older person's financial and material well-being, and their access to carers should they become frail or disabled. A significant transition for many older people begins when they are widowed. Widowhood often represents the loss of a partner of 40-50 years, who may have been the main source of companionship and support, especially for men (Askham, 1994; Davidson, 1999).

Most men over 65 years of age are married (71% in 2001 in the UK) and therefore have a partner for companionship, domestic service support and for care should they become physically disabled. Whereas half of older women are widowed, and only 40% were married in 2001 (Arber et al, 2003). Even among men aged 85+, 45% are married, compared with only 10% of women. Smaller proportions of older people are never married or divorced (about 6% were in each category in 2001), but the proportions divorced are projected to rise rapidly, reaching 13% of men aged 65+ and 14% of women by 2021 (Shaw, 1999; Arber and Ginn, 2004). Given the marked gender differences in marital status in later life, it is pertinent to consider to what extent marital status rather than gender per se may be responsible for some of the well-known gender inequalities among older people.

Gender inequalities in income in later life

Older women in the UK are much poorer than older men, and much of this difference relates to their lower level of private pension accumulation because of the interrupted and part-time paid employment careers of the current cohort of older women (Ginn, 2003). When assessing gender differences in poverty in later life, and how these vary by age and marital status, it is relevant to distinguish personal (or individual) income from household income. There are good reasons to measure individual incomes (Arber and Ginn, 2004). As discussed earlier, the majority of older women are not married and those who are married can expect to outlive their husbands. Sharing between spouses or cohabiting partners may not be equal, and having one's own income is qualitatively different from income that may be transferred by a partner.

The proportion of older women and men with an income of less than £100 per week is shown in Table 5.1a. Data are drawn from five years of the British GHS – a nationally representative survey of about 10,000 households per year, in which all persons aged 16+ in the household are interviewed, with a response rate of around 80% in the mid-1990s (Walker et al, 2001). Data from 1993 to 1996 and 1998 were combined, yielding a sample of more than 15,000 men and women aged 65+. Income in all years has been adjusted according to the Retail Price Index for 1998. Table 5.1a shows massive gender inequalities in personal income, with two thirds of older women having an income less than £100 per week, compared with only 30% of older men. Among men, the proportion with this low income level increases from 18% in their late 60s to almost half aged 85+. This is likely to primarily reflect cohort differences in the acquisition of private (occupational and personal) pensions, as well as the declining value of private pensions with advancing age. Among women, there is no age trend under 80, with over two thirds of women having this low personal income level, but above 80 there is a slight decrease in the proportion of low-income women, falling to 59% of women aged 85+. This diminution

Table 5.1: Income, material well-being and health by age and gender in Britain (age 65+)

	65-69 (%)	70-74 (%)	75-79 (%)	80-84 (%)	85+ (%)	All 65+ (%)	Odds ratios[c]
a) Personal income[a] below £100 per week							
Men	18	29	38	43	47	30	1.0
Women	68[e]	69[e]	68[e]	64[e]	59[e]	67[e]	4.7[e]
b) Household income [a,b] in lowest 25%, 65+							
Men	12	17	24	**26**	**30**	19	1.0
Women	20[e]	28[e]	34[e]	38[e]	40[e]	30[e]	1.8[e]
c) Does not own home – ie renter							
Men	26	31	33	**38**	**34**	31	1.0
Women	29[d]	37[e]	38[e]	43[d]	43[e]	36[e]	1.2[e]
d) No car in household							
Men	23	32	38	**54**	**66**	34	1.0[e]
Women	38[e]	51[e]	65[e]	73[e]	81[e]	56[e]	2.4[e]
e) Health perceived as 'not good'							
Men	20	20	21	**24**	**22**	21	1.0
Women	19	**22**	26[e]	**27**	30[e]	23[e]	1.1[e]
f) Severe disability – score of 6+							
Men	5.7	4.7	7.2	**16.7**	**20.6**	7.8	1.0
Women	7.6	9.7[e]	16.2[e]	20.5[e]	39.1[e]	14.8[e]	1.9[e]
Minimum number for a-e							
Men	2,212	1,929	1,283	735	383	6,542	6,542
Women	2,488	2,414	1,787	1,227	863	8,779	8,779
Number for f (disability)							
Men	918	844	517	318	165	2,762	2,762
Women	1,054	1,060	786	488	376	3,764	3,764

Notes:

Percentages above the average for all aged 65+ have been emboldened.

[a] Household income and personal income adjusted according to Retail Price Index 1998.

[b] Household income having adjusted for household composition using the McClements Scale.

[c] Odds ratios after controlling for five-year age groups (65-69, 70-74, 75-79, 80-84, 85+); reference category is men with odds defined as 1.0.

[d] Significance of gender difference = $p<0.05$.

[e] Significance of gender difference = $p<0.01$.

Source: General Household Survey, all variables 1993-96, 1998, except for f (disability) – 1994 and 1998

with age is likely to reflect changes in marital status, since widows receive a higher state pension than married women, and often inherit part of their husbands' private pension.

Poverty can also be considered in terms of household income, which assumes equal sharing in couples. Those living with others also benefit from economies of scale that may improve their standard of living. In this analysis, low household income is measured as those in the lowest quartile (25%) of the income distribution of those aged 65+ (after adjusting income levels to 1998 values using the Retail Price Index). The older person's household composition has been adjusted using the McClements income equivalising scales (DWP, 2002), so that the living standards of older people can be directly compared according to chronological age and marital status. With this measure of equivalised household income, 19% of older men and 30% of women are poor (Table 5.1b). There are highly significant gender differences in income within each age group across the age span of later life, but these differences are less stark than for personal income. In each age group, older women are 8-10% more likely to have a low household income. The chances of having a low household income double across the age span for both older women and men, from 12% of men in their late 60s to 30% over age 85, and the respective figures for women are from 20% to 40%. This age trend of increasing household poverty is likely to reflect cohort differences for men, and for women a mixture of cohort differences and changes in marital status associated with advancing age, which is considered in the next section.

Income and marital status in later life

Since women are much more likely to be widowed than men, this section examines to what extent the lower personal and household income of older women is linked to their marital status. It also brings into sharp relief the financial position of the smaller proportions of men who are non-partnered in later life, allowing a comparison between widowers who have lost their partner through death, divorced older men who have lost their partner usually somewhat earlier in their lifecourse (often in acrimonious circumstances), and men who have been lifelong bachelors, having never married.

The analysis uses logistic regression models to compare the differential effects of marital status on income for older women compared with men. Marital status is based on four categories: married/cohabiting, widowed, divorced/separated, and those who have never married. Thus, eight gender/marital status groups are identified, enabling comparison between each group with married men defined as the reference category. Age is controlled in five-year groups. Since widows are on average older than married and divorced women, controlling for five-year age groups provides a more accurate assessment of the relative financial position of each gender/marital status group.

Logistic regression is also used to provide a summary of the gender differences in income, while controlling for five-year age groups. Here men are defined as the reference category with an odds ratio of 1.0, and Table 5.1a (final column) shows that older women have 4.7 times greater odds of having a low *personal* income of less than £100 per week than men (having controlled for age). In contrast, women have 1.8 times greater odds of low *household* income than men.

The nature of the interaction between gender and marital status is examined in Table 5.2 using logistic regression; any gender/marital status category with an odds ratio higher than 1.0 is more likely to be disadvantaged than married men. In relation to personal income, married women are by far the most disadvantaged, with an odds of having an income less than £100 per week that is 15 times higher than that for married men. Divorced women also have a

Table 5.2: Odds ratios[c] of income, material circumstances and health by gender and marital status in Britain (age 65+)

	Men				Women			
	Married	Widowed	Divorced/ separated	Never married	Married	Widowed	Divorced/ separated	Never married
a) Personal income[a] below £100 per week	1.0	1.5[e]	2.2[e]	1.7[e]	*15.2[e]*	3.1[d]	*5.0[e]*	1.9[e]
b) Household income[a,b] in lowest 25% of those 65+	1.0	1.3[e]	2.2[e]	1.5[d]	1.2[d]	2.7[e]	*4.7[e]*	1.8[e]
c) Does not own home – ie renter	1.0	1.9[e]	*4.5[e]*	3.0[e]	1.1	2.1[e]	3.6[e]	2.0[e]
d) No car in household	1.0	2.0[e]	3.5[e]	4.2[e]	1.2[e]	*7.5[e]*	*7.0[e]*	*5.4[e]*
e) Health seen as 'not good'	1.0	1.1	1.8[d]	1.0	1.1[d]	1.3[e]	1.7[e]	1.1
f) Severe disability – score of 6+	1.0	1.0	1.5	1.1	1.8[e]	2.0[e]	2.1[e]	1.6[e]
Minimum number for a-e	4,673	1,196	284	389	3,651	4,160	372	596
Number for f (disability)	1,966	516	118	162	1,564	1,787	162	248

Note: Odds ratios above 4.0 are emboldened and above 2.0 are italicised.
[a] Household income and personal income adjusted according to Retail Price Index 1998.
[b] Household income having adjusted for household composition using the McClements Scale.
[c] Odds ratios after controlling for five-year age groups (65-69, 70-74, 75-79, 80-84, 85+); reference category is married men with odds defined as 1.0.
[d] Significance of gender difference = $p<0.05$.
[e] Significance of gender difference = $p<0.01$.
Source: General Household Survey, all variables 1993-96, 1998, except for f (disability) – 1994 and 1998

very high level of personal poverty – their odds ratio of low income is five times greater than for married men (odds ratio, OR=5.0), while the odds ratio of low personal income for widows is three times greater than for married men (OR=3.1).

The marital status differentials are less severe for household equivalised income, but apart from married women, the pattern is very similar. Divorced women are the group most likely to be in household poverty in later life with odds of poverty that are 4.7 times higher than for married men. The next most financially disadvantaged group are widows, with odds 2.7 times higher than for married men. This disadvantage is particularly salient, as almost half of older women are widows. The household income of widowers (OR=1.3) is not very different from that of married men, showing that among men there is little financial penalty attached to widowhood. Divorced men stand out as the most financially disadvantaged group of older men (OR=2.2). Among women living without a partner, never-married women are the least likely to be in household poverty

(OR=1.9). It is notable that widows have much higher odds of low household income (OR=2.7) compared with widowers (OR=1.3).

These findings suggest that one of the main effects of assuming equal sharing of income between partners through measuring equivalised household income is to obscure the financial position of older married women. Married women are by far the poorest on measures of personal income, but on household equivalised income have an income little different from that of married men. It is clear that following the breakdown of a marriage, whether through death of their partner or divorce, older women are financially disadvantaged. This is the case to an even greater extent for divorced older women than for widows, since the latter may 'inherit' part of their former husbands' private pension. Whether personal income or household income is used to compare income among older men, a similar pattern emerges, of divorced men being the poorest group, followed by never-married men. In each case, married men are the most advantaged, and as discussed earlier, they represent the majority of older men.

Material circumstances

Other aspects of material well-being in later life include owning a home and having a car available within the household. Home ownership in the UK represents an important capital asset, while social housing has become stigmatised over the past 20 years and often includes dwellings that are in undesirable residential areas, where there are greater concerns about safety and security. There are fairly small gender differences in whether older people rent their home, although older women are more likely to be renters than men in each age group (Table 5.1c). For both men and women, the probability of renting increases with advancing age, from 29% of women in their late 60s to 43% aged 85+. The comparable proportions for men show a smaller increase from 26% to 34%. This age-related trend may reflect both cohort differences in home ownership, and changes in residence associated with widowhood.

The relatively modest gender differences in home ownership shown in Table 5.1c hide much larger differences between gender/marital status groups. Table 5.2c shows that older widows and widowers have a comparable odds of renting, with about twice the odds of renting compared with married men and women. This suggests that during widowhood, some older people move into rented accommodation, because they cannot afford the upkeep of an owned home, to move nearer other family members, or to move into sheltered accommodation. These findings suggest that renting is associated with widowhood per se, since there are no clear differences by gender. The group least likely to own their home are divorced older men, with an OR of 4.5 of renting compared with married men, followed by divorced women (OR=3.6). The latter probably reflects the very disadvantaged financial circumstances of the divorced in later life. Never-married men have a higher OR of renting in later life (3.0) than never-married women (OR=2.0).

One aspect of quality of material life and well-being for older people is having a car, which depends on having a certain level of income. For both men and women, having a car in the household is a key factor in maintaining independence – their ability to shop, visit, enjoy leisure facilities, help with grandchildren, attend hospital appointments and so on. Yet among older cohorts of women the norm was to depend on their husband for transport for social purposes, shopping, or accessing healthcare facilities. It was less usual for these women to obtain a driving licence themselves. Thus, for older women, widowhood or divorce may represent more than the loss of a breadwinner and partner – it may include the loss of mobility.

Car ownership declines with increasing age, reflecting both age and cohort effects, and in each age group is lower for women than men (see Table 5.1d). Only 35% of women aged 75–79 and 19% aged 85+ have access to a car in the household, compared with 62% and 34% of men in these two age groups. Older women are much less likely than men to have a car in the household (OR=2.4). The major reason for these profound gender differences relates to marital status. Table 5.2d shows that the greatest difference is for widows, with odds of not having a car 7.5 times higher than for married men. The odds ratio for divorced women is 7.0 and for never-married women is 5.4. Thus, loss of a partner for women, whether by widowhood or divorce, has a profound impact by restricting their mobility through removing access to a car in the household. Never-married women are somewhat less disadvantaged, probably because they were more likely to have learnt to drive when younger, as well as being relatively better off financially and therefore more likely to be able to afford to run a car in later life.

There are also strong differences in car ownership among men by marital status. Married men are the most likely to have a car, followed by widowers (OR=2.0). Never-married men are least likely to have a car (OR=4.2), with divorced men also disadvantaged (OR=3.5). The lower level of car ownership for divorced and never-married men may partly reflect their low household income.

The pattern of car ownership varies fundamentally by gender – all groups of women without a partner are disadvantaged in their car access compared with men or married women. However, we can expect the gender division of car ownership to lessen for future cohorts in later life, since more younger women now learn to drive, although future cohorts of older women in the UK may still lack the financial resources to run a car (Ginn, 2003).

Health and disability

Health is fundamental to well-being and the ability to maintain independence and autonomy in later life, with previous research showing gender differences in health (Arber and Cooper, 1999; Annandale and Hunt, 2000). Research on marital status and health has focused primarily on working ages, finding that married men have better health than never-married or previously married men (Morgan, 1980; Wyke and Ford, 1992). The divorced and separated have been consistently found to have poorer health than the married, and single men but not single women report poorer health than their married counterparts (see, for example, Verbrugge, 1979; Morgan, 1980; Glaser and Grundy, 1997).

This section examines gender differences in subjective health and in disability, focusing on patterns with age and marital status in later life. Respondents in the GHS were asked whether their self-reported health over the past year had been 'good', 'fairly good' or 'not good'. Table 5.1e shows no variation in health with age among men, but the proportion of women who rate their health as 'not good' increases from 19% to 30% from the late 60s to late 80s. It seems likely that subjective perceptions of health are coloured by a person's expectations of health at more advanced ages, with their reference groups being other older people of the same age. There is little gender difference in self-assessed health, and in only two age groups (late 70s and aged 85+) are women significantly more likely than men of the same age to rate their health as 'not good'.

Self-reporting of 'not good' health is analysed according to gender/marital status groups while controlling for five-year age groups in Table 5.2e. The divorced report the poorest health, with an OR of 1.8 for divorced men and 1.7 for divorced women compared with married men (OR=1.0). There are only modest differences in self-reported health among the other marital status groups for both older men and women. It is notable that the differences between gender/marital status groups in subjective health are much smaller than those for income and material circumstances (Table 5.2a–d).

A more important indicator of health status in later life is whether people can independently perform Activities of Daily Living (ADL). A scale of functional limitations was constructed (using the 1994 and 1998 GHS) based on whether the older person could undertake six activities of daily living: cutting their own toenails, walking down the road, getting up and down stairs, getting around the house, washing or bathing, and getting in and out of bed. If the person could undertake the activity without difficulty, it was coded 0; if undertaken only with difficulty, the activity was coded 1; and if they could not perform the activity, it was coded 2. These six items were summed to form a scale in which a score of six represents a person with severe disability who is likely to require assistance on a daily basis to remain living in the community (Arber and Cooper, 1999).

The likelihood of severe disability increases markedly with age, but to a greater extent for women than men (Table 5.1f). In their late 60s, 7.6% of women compared with 5.7% of men have a severe disability. This gender differential increases to twice as many women as men having severe disability in their late 70s and aged 85+. Over age 85, two fifths of women living in the community compared with a fifth of men have this severe level of impairment, which would mean they need help on a regular basis to remain living in the community. The gender differential in severe disability can also be seen from the odds ratio of 1.9 for women having severe disability compared with men (OR=1).

Table 5.2f shows the odds ratios of severe disability according to gender/marital status groups after controlling for five-year age groups. There is little difference among men according to marital status in the proportion with severe functional limitations; only the divorced have a higher odds ratio than married men, but this difference does not reach statistical significance. In contrast, all older women irrespective of marital status have significantly higher levels of disability than married men, odds ratios of approximately 2.0 compared with married men. Thus, level of disability is primarily related to gender per se, and is largely unrelated to marital status. This contrasts with the analysis of income and material circumstances, which showed strong patterns of disadvantage according to marital status among both women and men.

Living in residential care settings

Entering a care home is usually considered a major threat to autonomy, and is something older people tend to resist until there is no alternative. Older women are more likely to spend the closing stages of their life living in a care-related communal setting. Analyses from the 2001 census for England and Wales show that over twice as many women as men aged 65+ (5.2% and 2.2% respectively) live in a nursing, residential or other health-related establishment (data supplied personally by ONS). Figure 5.1a shows there is a very rapid rise in such institutional living with advancing age. The increase is from 1% of women and men in their early 70s to 20% of women and 11% of men aged 85+. Above age 80, twice as many women as men are communal residents.

The main reason for the higher communal residence of older women than men relates to marital status, since the widowed and never-married are far more likely to live in care homes in later life than those who are married and these groups are disproportionately women (Arber and Ginn, 1991, 2004). In each age group, the never married are the most likely to live in a care-related setting (Figure 5.1b). They are five times more likely than the married to be communal residents in each age group below 85. The widowed are intermediate between these two extremes (as are the divorced, who are not shown in Figure 5.1b). Under age 80, the widowed have half the level of communal residence of the never married, illustrating the role of adult children in providing care. However, the widowed are three times more likely to live in a residential setting than their married counterparts, demonstrating the very major role of marital partners in providing intensive care and delaying residential admissions.

It is notable that within each marital status there is little gender difference in the proportions living in a residential setting under age 80 (Figure 5.1b). Only above this age are women more likely to be communal residents than men, reflecting the higher levels of disability experienced by older women, especially at advanced ages, as discussed earlier. Thus, whether older people can expect to spend the final stage of their life in a residential setting is influenced primarily

Figure 5.1: Percentage living in a communal establishment[a] by (a) age group and sex, and (b) marital status[b], age group and sex (age 65+)

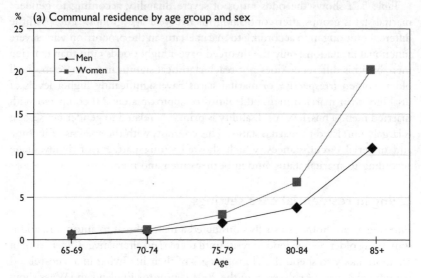

% (a) Communal residence by age group and sex

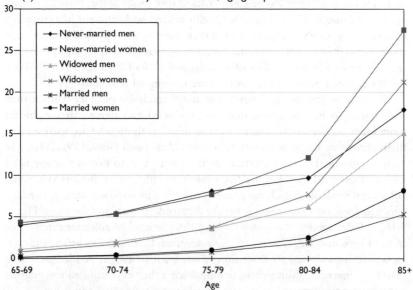

% (b) Communal residence by marital status, age group and sex

Notes: [a] Those living in nursing homes, residential homes, psychiatric hospitals/homes, general hospitals, other medical and care homes, and other establishments.

[b] The divorced and separated have been omitted, in order to show more clearly the differences between married, widowed and never-married older people.

Source: 2001 Census, England and Wales, from Arber and Ginn (2004, figure A6)

by their marital status, as well as by their degree of physical impairment, which in turn is associated with gender. Marital status can be interpreted as a proxy for the availability of family carers. The marital difference in care home residence demonstrates the very substantial role played by family carers in supporting older people to remain living in the community. The never married are least likely to have family carers, the widowed and divorced generally have children as potential carers, while married older people are likely to have their partner as their carer, unless they are too frail or disabled to perform this role.

Conclusions

The span of later life from age 65 upwards can be examined according to various bases of inequality (or diversity), including class, ethnicity and sexual orientation. This chapter has focused on three other sources of diversity: age, gender and marital status. Gender has divergent relationships with different aspects of quality of later life. Four key areas were examined: income, material circumstances, health and disability, and living in care homes. In each area, disadvantage increases with advancing age, but generally at a faster rate for women than men.

Older married people, irrespective of gender, are highly advantaged in terms of their household income, material circumstances and lower chance of living in residential or nursing care. However, this gender similarity must be tempered by the recognition that almost three quarters of older men are married, and most remain married until they die, whereas these advantages associated with marriage are the province of only a minority of older women. Widows, constituting about half of all older women, have about twice the odds of both living in poverty and of renting their home, seven times the odds of not having a car, and are three times more likely to live in a care home than married women. There are less striking differences in the material well-being of the numerically smaller group of widowed men compared with the majority group of married older men. Thus, gender influences the impact of marital status, with widowhood having a major adverse effect on the material well-being of older women, but less so for older men.

The proportion of divorced men and women among the older population is rapidly increasing. Many people who divorced earlier in their lifecourse are now entering later life, because of the high divorce rates in the UK over the past 30 years. Divorced older women are the most financially disadvantaged group in later life, mainly because they have no access to a partner's pension and their own paid working lives were severely hampered by childrearing. They are also less likely to own their home than other groups of older women. Divorced older men are also disadvantaged financially, and in terms of car and home ownership.

This chapter argues that analyses of financial and material well-being in later life should examine the *interaction* between gender and marital status, rather than treating them as separate (additive) variables. It is clear that being married is beneficial for both older men and women in terms of financial and material well-being, while both divorced women and men are disadvantaged. The never married show a divergent pattern by gender, with never-married women relatively advantaged compared with other non-partnered older women, whereas never married men show a broadly comparable level of disadvantage to the divorced. The position of the widowed diverges by gender, with widowers more similar to married men, compared with the larger material gap between widows and married women. These findings illustrate how gender relations across the lifecourse are implicated in the impact of marital status on material well-being in later life.

Although older women have a longer expectation of life than men, they also have a longer period in which they can expect to be disabled or living in a care home. The gender differential in disability means that older women are more likely to require both informal care and state health and welfare services. Older women's disadvantage due to higher levels of disability is compounded by their lower income in later life. Marital status has a critical impact on older people's need for care and support from relatives or others *outside* their household, and from state and private services.

Gender and marital status are associated with quality of later life, in varying ways according to different dimensions of quality of life. Disability is primarily influenced by gender per se, with older women experiencing higher levels of impairment in later life irrespective of their marital status. To understand the financial and material well-being of older people, it is necessary to consider the *interaction* of gender *and* marital status, since there are different gender-related processes impacting on women and men according to their marital status, which in turn reflect their lifecourse engagement in paid work and family building. In contrast, the likelihood of living in a care home in later life is primarily influenced by marital status, which provides a proxy for the availability of family carers. Gender has a broadly similar influence on the likelihood of living in a care home within each marital status under age 80. However, because of the higher disability levels of older women than men aged 80+ within each marital status, women are more likely to be communal residents than men. Thus, marital status and gender have an *additive* (rather than interacting) influence on whether older people spend the closing stage of their life in a care home.

References

Annandale, E. and Hunt, K. (eds) (2000) *Gender inequalities in health*, Buckingham: Open University Press.

Arber, S. and Cooper, H. (1999) 'Gender differences in health in later life: a new paradox?', *Social Science and Medicine*, vol 48, no 1, pp 61-76.

Arber, S. and Ginn, J. (1991) *Gender and later life: A sociological analysis of resources and constraints*, London: Sage Publications.

Arber, S. and Ginn, J. (eds) (1995) *Connecting gender and ageing*, Buckingham: Open University Press.

Arber, S. and Ginn, J. (2004) 'Ageing and gender: diversity and change', *Social Trends*, vol 34, London: The Stationary Office, pp 1-14.

Arber, S., Davidson, K. and Ginn, J. (eds) (2003) *Gender and ageing: Changing roles and relationships*, Maidenhead: Open University Press.

Askham, J. (1994) 'Marriage relationships of older people', *Reviews of Clinical Gerontology*, vol 4, pp 261-8.

Calasanti, T. and Sleven, K. (2001) *Gender, social inequalities, and aging*, Walnut Creek, CA: AltaMira Press.

Davidson, K. (1999) 'Marriage in retrospect: a study of older widows and widowers', in R. Miller and S. Browning (eds) *With this ring: Divorce, intimacy and cohabitation form a multicultural perspective*, Stamford, CT: JAI Press, pp 127-45.

DWP (Department for Work and Pensions) (2002) *Households Below Average Income*, London: DWP.

Estes, C. (2001) 'From gender to the political economy of ageing', *European Journal of Social Quality*, vol 2, no 1, pp 28-56.

Evandrou, M. (ed) (1997) *Baby boomers: Ageing in the 21st century*, London: Age Concern.

Ginn, J. (2003) *Gender, pensions and the lifecourse: How pensions need to adapt to changing family forms*, Bristol: The Policy Press.

Glaser, K. and Grundy, E. (1997) 'Marital status and long-term illness in Great Britain', *Journal of Marriage and the Family*, vol 59, pp 156-64.

Mesle, F. and Vallin, J. (2002) 'Mortality in Europe: the divergence between east and west', *Population*, vol 57, no 1, pp 157-96.

Morgan, M. (1980) 'Marital status, health, illness and service use', *Social Science and Medicine*, vol 14, pp 633-43.

ONS (Office for National Statistics) (2003) *Population Trends 112*, London: The Stationery Office.

Shaw, C. (1999) '1996-based population projections by legal marital status for England and Wales', *Population Trends*, vol 95, pp 23-32.

Thompson, E.H. (1994) 'Older men as invisible men in contemporary society', in E.H. Thompson (ed) *Older men's lives*, Thousand Oaks, CA: Sage Publications, pp 1-21.

Verbrugge, L. (1979) 'Marital status and health', *Journal of Marriage and the Family*, vol 41, pp 267-85.

Walker, A., Maher, J., Coulthard, M., Goddard, E. and Thomas, M. (2001) *Living in Britain: Results from the 2000/01 General Household Survey*, London: The Stationery Office.

Wyke, S. and Ford, G. (1992) 'Competing explanations for associations between marital status and health', *Social Science and Medicine*, vol 34, no 5, pp 525-32.

Section 11:
Social identifications

SIX

The search for ageing identities

Andrew Blaikie

Key points

- Socio-structural factors and modernist discourses determine lifecourse categories.
- By contrast, deconstructionist interpretations suggest that identities should be seen as developed 'from the self up'.
- A dialectical view posits negotiation between individuals, social structures and cultural representations. Reflexive selves identify with or reject definitions of ageing according to notions of difference – people understand who they are by knowing what they are not.
- Ethnographic approaches allow consciousness of age to be described, but selfhood is not straightforwardly amenable to communication since sociological analysis is limited by its reliance upon classification.

Key readings

- Cohen, A.P. (1993) *Self consciousness: An alternative anthropology of identity*, London: Routledge.
- Hockey, J. and James, A. (2003) *Social identities across the life course*, London: Palgrave Macmillan.
- Kohli, M. (1988) 'Ageing as a challenge for sociological theory', *Ageing and Society*, vol 8, pp 367-94.
- See generally *Journal of Aging and Identity*.

Introduction

Although personal and social identities are shaped as much by age as they are by gender, ethnicity or class, social theory has largely neglected the significance of ageing as a key ingredient. Logic dictates that this is a bad thing, for age represents "one of the key bases for the production of social identity, acting as a way to classify and order the passing of time in an individual's life" (Hockey and James, 2003, p 3). Equally, however, the imperative manner in which gender, 'race' and class frame each of us serves as a reminder that such articulation reduces mystique and uniqueness to categorical explanation. With a disciplinary historiography that has successively embraced activity theory, disengagement and structured dependency, gerontologists have been well advised to shift perspective towards approaches more sensitive to the range of individual experiences and behaviours, hence the acknowledgement of diversity in statements such as "there are different types of rurality, different racial and ethnic experiences, and different ways of growing old gay" (Marshall, 1987, p 83). Yet, can we conduct meaningful social-scientific analysis without recourse to classification and, by extension, generalisation about individuals? This chapter aims to clear some conceptual ground by exposing the distinctive apparatuses that have effectively imprisoned ageing identities.

Structural determination

Identity refers to a sense of self that develops through socialisation and social interaction. Rather than being an ascribed, immutable property of the individual, it is a condition that can only be understood as provisional: instead of simply being ourselves, we are forever in the process of becoming what we are (Jenkins, 1996). Nor are selves tangible and unitary; they are the slippery and often evanescent products of negotiations within and between individuals, ideologies and structures. However, these interactions have generally been perceived as one-sided, the massive and pervasive power of social structures being regarded as decisive in the production and reproduction of identities.

For every human being, the body is crucial to understanding ageing. Hockey and James (2003, p 126) note that "our perception of the world is always sited in a particular experience of embodiment". Since our bodies recognisably change and decay, ageing has been subjected to essentialist discourses where identities are perceived as inevitably defined and limited by biology. Equally, consciousness of one's own body significantly affects the psychological sense of identity while the appearance of the body conditions both everyday attitudes and institutional responses to it. Thus, in later life "an entire social history can be read off the old body" (Hallam et al, 1999, p 123), its vices and virtues evident in its very wrinkles and contortions (Hepworth, 1995). Ageing heralds constraints upon the body, and although these may feel personal enough they are to a degree the consequence of societal barriers imposed by medicalisation. In particular, the professionalisation of geriatric medicine has acted to classify older people's bodies as distinct from younger bodies, while simultaneously institutionalising a dichotomy between the positive stereotypes of 'normal' ageing and the negative, pathological ones associated with mental and physical decline. Ageing and illness have thereby become closely linked. Moreover, the development of social medicine has been such that geriatrics has effectively colonised the older population by according age-based attributes to members of the wider community *outside* the confines of the hospital and the nursing home (Armstrong, 1983). However, the continuing prominence of a problem-orientated medical model compared with the reality of ever-greater numbers of 'normal' ageing people is not simply the result of old age being ghettoised by means of scientific prescription.

The determinants of social status have clearly varied over time. While economic powerlessness, culture and religion were highly significant before the industrial revolution, several trends are specific to modernity (Minois, 1989). First, with dramatic rises in life expectancy, population ageing has necessitated a major rearrangement of the lifecourse. The experiences of becoming and being old, as we understand the term, are historically novel. Whereas in 1750, the median female age at death in Britain was 35, by the 1970s it had risen to 80 (Anderson, 1985). Most people in the developed world, once they reach 25, can expect to live beyond 70 (Laslett, 1987). This phenomenon is evident in the emergence of 'the third age', the unprecedented expansion of numbers of people no longer in paid work or raising their children but still fit and active. Second, however, despite this shift in the age balance of western populations toward the upper end of the chronological spectrum, the devaluing of older people through urbanisation, education and new technologies remains an insidious legacy of industrial progress (Fennell et al, 1988).

Third, this persists because of structured dependency. Paid work in modern societies has been widely regarded as a central feature underlying social identities, conferring independence and adult status. By contrast, those not engaged in paid work, primarily children and the retired, have been relegated to a condition of dependency that is structured both by labour market considerations and the machinations of the state. Not only are they marginalised through non-membership of the workforce, but also their exclusion is legally enforced through education policy, at the one end, and statutory retirement ages and pensions at the other. The commodification of labour has run in tandem with the granting of citizenship rights, while the welfare state, itself devised to alleviate the effects of capitalism upon those disqualified, has created dependency as much as it has addressed it (Twine, 1994).

The problem with categories

Arguably, biological essentialism, demographic determinism and structured dependency together reduce the scope for ageing identities, with older people simply pawns in a threefold process of medicalisation, marginalisation and modernisation. These determinations may conflict with one another. For example, during the earlier 20th century, retirement gradually developed as a rite of passage linked to a fixed chronological age precisely as the physiological and mental capacities associated with particular age bands became less amenable to rigid classification. Just when biological and sociological definitions of old age began to diverge, so policymakers sought to bind them together (Blaikie and Macnicol, 1989). Yet despite such inconsistencies, for the ageing individual pigeonholing is a constant threat.

While historians attempt to demonstrate that "the category of old age was constructed in moral ways to laud and censure forms of behaviour deemed appropriate and inappropriate" (Troyansky, 1998, p 97), Foucauldians have stressed the power of medico-social discourses about ageing to insinuate themselves into both institutional and popular understandings (Katz, 1996; Powell and Biggs, 2000). Meanwhile, modernisation theorists contend that traditional values became outmoded, as society became increasingly bureaucratic and differentiated. Older people were thus labelled as 'the elderly', a social and economic group delimited by chronological markers that disqualified them from the production process. Modernity generated a sharpened sense of stigma through pensions systems that increasingly classified older people as a sub-population, stereotyped via their implied decrepitude. Politically, this was a product of demographic calculation that cast a dark shadow over later life as a time of decline (Blaikie, 1999; Titmuss and Titmuss, 1942). Conceivably, an emergent postmodern period signals amelioration, as agelessness becomes a realisable possibility. However, for all its liberating rhetoric, postmodernity is not without its problems either, as we shall see.

Much has been said about the degree to which individual identities may be determined by generational shifts in experience, in particular the impact of historical conditions during childhood and early adulthood on attitudes in later life (Elder, 1974). Political behaviour, susceptibility to different consumer markets, and worldviews are among themes recruited to illustrate the underlying assumption that generation itself has a major bearing upon identity (Ostroff, 1989; Williams, 1990; Walker and Naegele, 1999). Intergenerational conflict has been similarly problematised (Turner, 1998; Johnson et al, 1989). Needless to say, such gross, macro-level assumptions by definition ignore the context-bound (but shifting) complexity of most people's lives. When market research primers lead by claiming that the sense of challenge of those born in the 1960s "will have a staggering effect on the growth of senior power", one is prone to be somewhat sceptical (Ostroff, 1989, p 38). People are not clones. Yet conflict of a gross sort is also evident in the differing conclusions drawn by successive generations of academic interpreters: the more scholars debunk the flimsy evidence of their predecessors, the more they create new orthodoxies. At the same time, ambivalent perceptions of ageing – at one time or place deeply discriminatory, at the next reassuringly enlightened – suggest that everyday attitudes are just as volatile. The interviewees in Thompson et al's (1990) book, *I don't feel old*, claimed that they were pleasantly surprised that their later lives turned out differently from the stereotypes they had expected to find (Thompson et al, 1990). Meanwhile, social policy histories are replete with tensions between the positive meanings offered through self-representation of individuals and the negative definitions developed through institutional regulation (Johnson and Thane, 1998). Who or what are we to believe?

Certainly the concern with social structure has limited the development of experiential approaches, and not only within sociology, where an anticipatory life stages model has emphasised "the social processes by which individuals are enabled to move into and out of ... categorical identities" (Hockey and James, 2003, pp 36-7). The social model of old age generated by historical determinism and articulated in both materialist and discourse-based perspectives finds further resonance in the social psychology of the lifecourse; for, while lifespan psychologists concentrate on sequences of events that may happen at different times and in different configurations, depending on the individual in question, they nonetheless suggest both predictable crises and predictable ways in which these may be resolved (Baltes and Baltes, 1990). Thus the notion of 'mid-life' is mooted, its characteristics examined and likely physical, cognitive and emotional changes related to critical transitions, such as menopause, empty nest, redundancy and bereavement (Sheehy, 1976, 1997). Personal transformation can then be managed through appropriate interventions based on generic developmental models (Sugarman, 1986). Whatever the plausibility of these nostrums, it is one thing to account for transitional phases within the lifecourse, but quite another to explain what having to negotiate these transitions feels like. And, unsurprisingly perhaps, the best approximations to a phenomenological perspective have grown out of literary evidence that, by its very fictional nature, presents considerable problems of interpretation (Hepworth, 2002).

Deconstructing the self

Whatever the motive force, the outcome has been the same: obligations and expectations have been yoked to membership of particular age groups, with the result that unwanted and ascribed identities have frequently been imposed upon individuals while desired identities (and the scope to achieve these) have been withheld. All classification has the effect of demeaning by homogenising, whether the reference group be 'the elderly', third and fourth ages, or simply lifecourse stage. Against the weight of structural determination, some theorists have suggested that identities may be better understood by working 'from the self upwards'. For example, Cohen (1993) argues that, paradoxically, we can only understand how society hangs together by looking at its opposite, the self and personal identity. This involves taking account of the individual's self-consciousness – an awareness of and capacity to reflect upon how we are each authors of our own experiences and behaviour. Thus, although sociologists tend to examine how 'society' determines individual behaviour, we might better understand both self and society if we begin by observing how individuals manage to maintain coherent identities. Whereas the traditional lifecycle, as a fixed set of stages occupied by people of particular age bands, was superseded by a modern lifecourse recognising the articulation between individuals and the production-based structures of the work society, the emphasis on plurality and flexibility within consumer culture heralds the deconstruction of age as a foundation for social classification (Featherstone and Hepworth, 1989). In this more individualised world, people have become increasingly detached from bonds of family, class and locality, and freed thereby to shape their own identities (Vincent, 1999). Significantly, the market provides a major locus for the nurture and maintenance of these fresh identities where personal fulfilment is the prime motive, not obligation to others. Lives become 'projects' that selectively plunder an awesome range of lifestyle choices. Meanwhile, the integrity of the coherent, modern self has been undermined by a constantly fracturing, 'saturated' self, which confuses what it presently is with all that it might become (Gergen, 1992). Although this signals a potential for choice that can be overbearing and carries considerable risk, identity clearly becomes an attribute that can and will change throughout the lifecourse.

Such thinking paves the way for consideration of the reflexive, free-floating self unleashed as an effect of the triumph of individualism. It is now understood as axiomatic not only that identities in western society have progressed from being production-based to being consumer-driven, but also that the individual is no longer the drone of high mass-consumption but the niche-defined specialist. People are no longer defined by their occupation, and the limits this imposes on what they might consume, so much as how, in a more affluent world, they exercise choice in constructing, even buying their own identities in the marketplace. But this, of course, is fundamentally attuned to creating demand by developing niches that allow both young and old to mould themselves anew; hence the segmentation of the grey market on the basis of pop-psychological evaluations based on cohort preferences. While this returns us to the imposition of external categories through acronyms like WOOPIES (well-off older persons), GLAMS (grey, leisured and moneyed), it is also stigmatising in that little interest is shown in wooing the mass of older people who do not possess the collateral to support the lifestyles being promoted (Blaikie, 1999).

Those who can afford to be persuaded may well reflect an emergent cultural trend towards third-age living, but their expanded embrace of a more youthful self reflects incorporation into a continuing capitalist mission as much as it marks resistance to the tyranny of growing old. Technologies that facilitate cyborg possibilities may poise a welcome counter to the fatalistic assumptions of biological essentialism, and the ageing body may no longer impose the constraints it once did (Gilleard and Higgs, 2000). Yet there remains an existential cost: flourishing third-age identities undoubtedly entwine cultural with bodily capital, but the creeping inevitability of deep old age and death ensures that these are strategies of denial.

This re-identification of age involves more than just "the paradoxical privileging of the tyranny of the flesh" (Hockey and James, 2003, p 109). In a media-dominated popular culture obsessed with visual presentation, outward bodily signs become mirrors of morality as well as reminders of mortality, the message being that a permanently youthful appearance can only be maintained through hard graft. Thus the work ethic of the old, production-based society survives in a highly personalised, but consumerist form, reinforced by Foucauldian self-surveillance. Clothing, diet, exercise, facelifts, liposuction, Botox, Viagra and HRT all testify to the current climate of high sensitivity towards masking the visible evidence of age. The inner-directed notion of self as moral character has arguably been replaced by the idea of 'personality' (Featherstone et al, 1991), a 'performing self' who, like a stage actor, learns a variety of scripts and acts out multiple roles depending on the requirements of the situation. This apparent social necessity has implications for identity, for, whereas the modern self was obsessed with building an identity and keeping it stable, in a climate of social uncertainty, the postmodern self is preoccupied with avoiding commitment and needs constantly to be able to mutate and move on. For Bauman, the old model individual pursued a single goal, measuring how far they had travelled by means of a biographical story and accumulating character through experience, but today's selves inhabit a continuous present where life is as fragmented, discontinuous and episodic. Rather than saving for the future, now we cannot afford to invest too strongly for fear of being bound to a single, potentially inescapable destiny (Bauman, 1992, 1996). However, whereas the problem might be one of preserving a coherent personal identity in a context where social identities are superficial, temporary and disposable, there is a danger of according too much agency to free-floating actors by creating a 'coat-rack' explanation: an identity is not simply "that which individuals pick up and discard as they age" (Hockey and James, 2003, p 121), not least because the market, far from being a liberating or empowering force, is yet another hegemonic and constraining structure (Nicholson, 1995). Equally, many observers highlight the notion of a continuity of self that underpins and directs the various other selves (effectively roles) that an individual presents. The 'performing self' follows Goffman's dramaturgical approach, which, drawing an analogy between social interaction and the theatre, characterises the self as both director and actor, managing back-stage the front-stage presentation that others see (Goffman, 1971). This has been developed in the idea of the 'mask of age', whereby, on the one hand, the visible ageing body disguises the ever-youthful self within, or, on the other, the external surface appearance is used as a template to present various personae, all of which with the aid of cosmetics and other props, can be used to reveal 'the self we would like to be' that is otherwise concealed by the bodily signs of age (Featherstone et al, 1991).

Dialectical pathways

Whether or not the desire for personal connectedness and continuity vies with social fragmentation, neither categorical identities nor philosophical problematics of the self address the processes whereby identities are forged. The nominal designation of 'older person' or 'uni-age self' has no meaning until we examine the response of that person to such classification. We can safely assume that older people do not blindly acquiesce to a rationale of dissolution and slowly fall apart. On the contrary, there is plentiful evidence that individuals attempt to maintain dignity and self-esteem even in the most extreme late-life circumstances (Blaikie, 1999). Indeed, it is precisely because we value the integral self that we struggle to maintain its ageless character (Kaufman, 1986). Nevertheless, if we accept the claim that identities are constructed through interaction with others, then we have to analyse the form and content of such negotiation. This requires that the scale of interrogation shift from structural representations to micro-sociology.

On one level, this involves conventionally observing the tension between structure and agency, or what C. Wright Mills (1959) called the distinction between 'the personal troubles of milieu' and 'the public issues of social structure'. Research should concentrate on the dialectical relationship between public and private worlds, noting the situationally specific antagonisms between older people's attempts to achieve a purposeful quality of life and the obstacles they encounter. In particular, incidents where individuals transgress age-appropriate boundaries – refusals to retire, insistence on playing sports, dressing in teenage clothes – are rich in data. So too are encounters between staff and inmates of institutions such as nursing homes, especially when residents refuse to accept the labels foisted upon them (Goffman, 1968).

It would be a mistake, however, to consider all identity formation as simply a set of responses to external impositions or irritations. Roles and relationships only acquire sociological significance when we know the meaning they hold for the persons concerned, for it is individuals who animate and embody social identities (Hockey and James, 2003, p 134). And they do this in dialogue with others. One of the more important insights of lifecourse analysis is that strategies for survival in later life draw on repertoires learned earlier in life. Thus, when ageing individuals meet challenges or encounter new roles, they rely not only on the resources immediately available within that context but also upon their insight and experience. The creative ability to use freedom from a life of paid work positively to gain fulfilment through activities as diverse as grandparenthood and gardening is considered crucial to sustaining or enhancing the quality of life in retirement, but it is not a competence that automatically comes with the territory. As agents, individuals will either reproduce, transform or fail to accommodate to new identities according to their historically achieved capabilities. These skills are not pre-given, for the ability to adapt in order to maintain and develop a coherent identity depends to a degree upon recollection.

The ongoing presentation of self requires that we can account for our present identities in terms of past biography. Consequently, ethnographers look to the remembered past to establish the socio-cultural foundations on which individuals have built their attitudes and understandings. The uncertainties of the present, particularly those aspects of globalisation that threaten the stability of place-bound existence, produce anxieties that might be salved by long-held convictions or religious faith. Similarly, ontological solace can be maintained by identification with the customs and conventions of lost partners or relatives, particularly though the evocation of 'better times' (Conway, 2003). Hints of such 'involuted' identities are evident from interviews and narrative accounts and in the popularity among older women of TV serials, magazines and literature that foreground nostalgic images of family, neighbourhood and community (Blaikie, 2004). Here a selective, romanticised vision of the past provides an ideological resource for sustaining continuity between the past-situated self and a perplexing present. Likewise, the value of household objects, photographs and souvenirs is enhanced for those whose lives become constricted as they age. An elderly widow moving to sheltered accommodation, and then to a nursing home, may cling to such possessions because they confer orientation by signalling the passage of time and, perhaps more importantly, because they have great personal meaning as markers reminding her who she is.

Memory is important, but so too is aspiration. Others, who are more favourably situated, are able to project their identities forward into their lifestyle projects. By such are the glossy mythologies of retirement magazines, real estate agents and holiday companies inspired. But whether an individual conforms more closely to the backward-looking, involuted type or to the forward-seeking, aspirational model, dealing with ageing in the present requires attempts to harmonise both past and future senses of self. Imagination is thus a major resource.

Alterity and difference

Thus far little has been said of the significant impact of popular cultural representations upon ageing identities. Writers, painters, photographers, advertisers, magazine editors, television scriptwriters and a host of other cultural entrepreneurs construct and reproduce ideals of later life that vary from the tawdry stereotypes of dirty old men and little old ladies to the celebrities whose looks and lifestyles make them icons of 'positive ageing'. However, in what ways do older people themselves interpret such diverse images? How might we discern self-referential vocabularies that question, oppose or play with such an imaginary?

In deploying the concept of alterity, or 'otherness', cultural theorists posit the idea that identities are constituted less by what people are than by what they are not. That is to say, it is in knowing the difference between ourselves and others that we understand what makes us distinctive. In placing ourselves, we find common ground with some individuals as well as points of departure, or complete unconnectedness from others. Doing this is an active process of *identification* that requires an awareness of the contingency of our lives (Hall, 1996). Such thinking is relational, since identities only emerge once the 'other' has been established. Yet, rather than working at an empirical or phenomenological level, Hall (1996, p 5) argues that alterity and difference are best comprehended when applied to textual analysis where cultural representations may be interpreted as the "discourses and practices which attempt to 'interpellate', speak to us or hail us into place as the subjects of particular discourses". Thus 'age' is understood as a discourse, positing over-arching notions of how we should live; 'adulthood' exists because of the aged 'other', of later life as what adulthood is not (and also because it is not 'childhood'). Similarly, 'normal ageing' or 'positive ageing' each arise because they are not in keeping with the pathological stereotype of old age as constructed through the medical model.

If this yet again implies codification, there is a link here to the sociology of knowledge that renders individuals themselves important agents in the social construction of later life. Discourses of ageing, be they framed by political economy, lifespan psychology or postmodern sociology, try to represent identities in many ways; but this does not mean we know what is going on in the minds of the figures who dot their imagined landscapes. In accessing such personalised data, we can work with the heuristic dictum that accounts should be sufficient unto the complexity they purport to describe. Yet biographies, like maps, invoke symbolic abstractions that are "comprehensible to consciousness" rather than co-extensive with the areas they aim to represent (Thompson, 2000, p 106). To better understand ourselves we must simplify, and in so doing we will inevitably convey abbreviated, even caricatured impressions when we talk to others. This is the essence of language, of communication through 'intersubjectivity' in the service of socially constructing reality (Berger and Luckmann, 1991). Intriguingly, Jenkins (1996) makes a distinction between individual or personal identity (the coherent sense of self that underlies whatever else we might be) and social identity (the identities inhabited through the roles we play in social life). He contends that social identities are more robust because they are not vulnerable to change in the biographical way that individual identities are. They are also reified and made to appear as given and somehow 'natural' attributes. Individuals take objectified images, categories and stereotypes and relate to them subjectively such that they feel themselves to become those categories or to have those attributes. Thus the only language in which one can convey the experience of being old is that through which a person establishes themselves in relation to the popularly held meaning of the term. If I say 'I feel old', I am indicating that I appear to be acting out the destined ageing script; when I say 'I don't feel old', I am suggesting that the script needs changing because, for me, it no longer feels right. This perspective assumes that identities emerge through a reflexive process that requires each of us to envision ourselves as others see us, or, to use Mead's (1934) term, by relating to the 'generalised other'.

Since we regard 'ageing' (as an internalised social norm, but not, of course, the only way of interpreting it) as 'natural', it becomes our paramount reality: it is obdurate, it will not go away. Yet its very persistence ensures that people will devise ways to side-step or delay its inevitability. These 'escape attempts' range from routine distractions, such as watching television, to planned excursions such as cruise holidays, to wholesale body modification (Cohen and Taylor, 1992). However, they have two differentiating characteristics: first, they are necessarily temporary and liable to collapse (ultimately one's ageing will reassert its dominance); second, they are not evenly distributed – the ability to select desired routes of escape will depend upon mental and physical health, income and personal domestic circumstances, including obligations towards partners and kin.

Conclusions

Otherness and difference assume that identities have boundaries. Age distinctions may be straightforwardly spatialised, as in, for example, the education of children in schools or the containment of geriatric patients within separate hospitals. The disciplines and discourses that legitimise these zones of separation may have been questioned by postmodernist elaboration, but any elasticity of arrangements remains under-girded by strategies of surveillance, be these at the level of institutional survey or via the self-policing of reflexive selves. It is, indeed, modernity that forces us to see ageing as we do. Although the symbolism of ageing is suffused with representations that constrain, these are framed by a modernist discourse that vaunts at the same time the cult of individualism and the attendant cultivation of individuality. Thus ageing involves constant comparison between one's mental and bodily capabilities and received conceptions of behaviour appropriate to different lifecourse stages.

The discussion of structural determinants indicates that the hegemony of medicalised and socially exclusionary generalisations is considerable, while a particular interpretation of the lifecourse, coterminous with modernity, has exerted itself as the paramount reality. As Kohli (Kohli, 1986, pp 286-7) has argued, modern bureaucracies have created a number of structural problems to which the institutionalisation of a 'moral economy of the lifecourse' has been a solution:

> Chronological age is apparently a very good criterion for the rational organisation of public services and transfers. It renders the lifecourse – and by that, the passage of individuals through social systems – orderly and calculable.

Of course, old age does not reflect a single, shared experience, any more than female-ness, black-ness or working-class-ness. Nevertheless, standards of living are determined by socio-structural factors, as are many prejudices that constrain the expression of full individuality: for older women, sexism colludes with ageism, while for ethnic elders racism supplies the partner. One of the formative elements in the diversity of later life is inequality. Thus, rather than bemoaning the failure of social scientists to interpret ageing as an organising principle like class, ethnicity, gender or cohort, we ought perhaps to welcome the reticence further to categorise our elders. In particular, we should note the insights of social theorists who indicate that the unitary notion of the self as constructed by family, work and other primary structures of socialisation and identification no longer suits conditions of late modernity or postmodernity (Featherstone et al, 1991; Giddens, 1991; Cohen, 1993; Bauman, 1996).

In their study of identities through the lifecourse, Hockey and James (2003, pp 209, 210) conclude that "in the last analysis, the *experience* of ageing – like that of time passing – is essentially imperceptible". We can only register its effects on the mind and body and apprehend the social consequences. Thus, they argue, the ageing process is "an absent presence, unacknowledged yet fundamental and inescapable". Certainly, any shared understanding will always be limited by its social context. Thus, the individual accessible to those who care to 'read' her is one we perceive via a filter of pre-coded meanings. Although we acknowledge different ways to grow old or various types of older person, the way we organise knowledge determines our interpretation – and in the wish to celebrate diversity we will impose fresh categories through our own typification. Such ultimately reductive framing not only reflects the limits of social science methodologies in handling the evidence of ageing, but also indicates that selfhood itself may be essentially incommunicable. Motives may be gleaned by asking why people identify with particular characterisations of age (Blaikie, 2002). However, while these cannot always be articulated or expressed, conditions such as dementia undermine the very basis of coherent identity (Grant, 1998). Or we run up against a deficit of empathy since we cannot possibly know what old age or dying is like until we get there, and we cannot reflect upon it afterwards since we will no longer exist (Elias, 1985). These are merely extreme instances of the more general predicament of consciousness. Ultimately, despite the best efforts both of ethnographers and their ageing subjects, raw identities – rather than descriptions of those identities – remain intractable.

References

Anderson, M. (1985) 'The emergence of the modern life-cycle in Britain', *Social History*, vol 10, pp 69-88.

Armstrong, D. (1983) *Political anatomy of the body: Medical knowledge in Britain in the Twentieth Century*, Cambridge: Cambridge University Press.

Baltes, P.B. and Baltes, M.M. (1990) 'Psychological perspectives on successful aging: the model of selective optimisation with compensation', in P.B. Baltes and M.M. Baltes (eds) *Successful aging: Perspectives from the behavioural sciences*, New York, NY: Cambridge University Press, pp 1-34.

Bauman, Z. (1992) *Mortality, immortality and other life strategies*, Cambridge: Polity Press.

Bauman, Z. (1996) 'From pilgrim to tourist – or a short history of identity', in S. Hall and P. du Gay (eds) *Questions of cultural identity*, London: Sage Publications, pp 18-36.

Berger, P. and Luckmann, T. (1991) *The social construction of reality: A treatise in the sociology of knowledge*, Harmondsworth: Penguin.

Blaikie, A. (1999) *Ageing and popular culture*, Cambridge: Cambridge University Press.

Blaikie, A. (2002) 'The secret world of subcultural aging: what unites and what divides?', in L. Andersson (ed) *Cultural gerontology*, Westport, CT: Greenwood Press, pp 95-110.

Blaikie, A. (2004: forthcoming) 'Imagined landscapes of age and identity', in G.J. Andrews and D.R. Phillips (eds) *Ageing and place*, London: Routledge.

Blaikie, A. and Macnicol, J. (1989) 'Ageing and social policy: a twentieth century dilemma', in A.M. Warnes (ed) *Human ageing and later life*, London: Edward Arnold, pp 69-82.

Cohen, A.P. (1993) *Self consciousness: An alternative anthropology of identity*, London: Routledge.

Cohen, S. and Taylor, L. (1992) *Escape attempts: The theory and practice of resistance to everyday life*, London: Routledge.

Conway, S. (2003) 'Ageing and imagined community: some cultural constructions and reconstructions', *Sociological Research Online*, vol 8, no 2 (www.socresonline.org.uk).

Elias, N. (1985) *The loneliness of the dying*, Oxford: Blackwell.

Elder, G.H. (1974) *Children of the great depression*, Chicago, IL: University of Chicago Press.

Featherstone, M. (1991) 'The body in consumer culture', in M. Featherstone, M. Hepworth and B.S. Turner (eds) *The body: Social process and cultural theory*, London: Sage Publications, pp 170-96.

Featherstone, M. and Hepworth, M. (1989) 'Ageing and old age: reflections on the postmodern life course', in B. Bytheway, T. Keil, P. Allatt and A. Bryman (eds) *Becoming and being old: Sociological approaches to later life*, London: Sage Publications, pp 143-57.

Featherstone, M. and Hepworth, M. (1991) 'The mask of ageing and the postmodern life course', in M. Featherstone, M. Hepworth and B.S. Turner (eds) *The body: Social process and cultural theory*, London: Sage Publications, pp 371-89.

Featherstone, M., Hepworth, M. and Turner, B.S. (eds) (1991) *The body: Social process and cultural theory*, London: Sage Publications.

Fennell, G., Phillipson, C. and Evers, H. (eds) (1988) *The sociology of old age*, Milton Keynes: Open University Press.

Gergen, K. (1992) *The saturated self: Dilemmas of identity in contemporary life*, New York, NY: Basic Books.

Giddens, A. (1991) *Modernity and self-identity*, Cambridge: Polity Press.

Gilleard, C. and Higgs, P. (2000) *Cultures of ageing: Self, citizen and the body*, London: Prentice Hall.

Goffman, E. (1968) *Stigma: Notes on the management of spoiled identity*, Harmondsworth: Pelican.

Goffman, E. (1971) *The presentation of self in everyday life*, Harmondsworth: Pelican.

Grant, L. (1998) *Remind me who I am, again*, Cambridge: Granta Books.

Hall, S. (1996) 'Introduction: who needs identity?', in S. Hall and P. du Gay (eds) *Questions of cultural identity*, London: Sage Publications, pp 1-17.

Hallam, E., Hockey, J. and Howarth, G. (1999) *Beyond the body: Death and social identity*, London: Routledge.

Hepworth, M. (1995) 'Wrinkles of vice and wrinkles of virtue: the moral interpretation of the ageing body', in C. Hummel and J. Lalive D'Epinay (eds) *Images of ageing in western societies*, Geneva: University of Geneva, pp 39-68.

Hepworth, M. (2002), 'Using cultural products in researching images of ageing', in A. Jamieson and C. Victor (eds) *Researching ageing and later life: The practice of social gerontology*, Buckingham: Open University Press, pp 80-95.

Hockey, J. and James, A. (2003) *Social identities across the life course*, London: Palgrave Macmillan.

Jenkins, R. (1996) *Social identity*, London: Routledge.

Johnson, P., Conrad, C. and Thomson, D. (eds) (1989) *Workers versus pensioners: Intergenerational justice in an ageing world*, Manchester: Manchester University Press.

Johnson, P. and Thane, P. (eds) (1998) *Old age from antiquity to post-modernity*, London: Routledge.

Katz, S. (1996) *Disciplining old age: The formation of gerontological knowledge*, Charlottesville, VA: University Press of Virginia.

Kaufman, S. (1986) *The ageless self: Sources of meaning in later life*, Madison, WI: University of Wisconsin Press.

Kohli, M. (1986) 'The world we forgot: a historical review of the life course', in V.W. Marshall (ed) *Later life: The social psychology of aging*, London: Sage Publications, pp 271-303.

Laslett, P. (1987) 'The emergence of the third age', *Ageing and Society*, vol 7, pp 113-60.

Marshall, V.W. (ed) (1987) *Aging in Canada: Social perspectives*, Markham, Ontario: Fitzhenry and Whiteside.

Mead, G.H. (1934) *Mind, self and society*, Chicago, IL: Chicago University Press.

Mills, C.W. (1959) *The sociological imagination*, Oxford: Oxford University Press.

Minois, G. (1989) *History of old age: From antiquity to the renaissance*, Cambridge: Polity Press.

Nicholson, L. (1995) 'Interpreting gender', in L. Nicholson and S. Seidman (eds) *Social postmodernism: Beyond identity politics*, Cambridge: Cambridge University Press, pp 39-67.

Ostroff, J. (1989) *Successful marketing to the 50+ consumer: How to capture one of the biggest and fastest growing markets in America*, Englewood Cliffs, NJ: Prentice Hall.

Powell, J. L. and Biggs, S. (2000) 'Managing old age: the disciplinary web of power, surveillance and normalisation', *Journal of Aging and Identity*, vol 5, no 1, pp 3-13.

Sheehy, G. (1976) *Passages: Predictable crises of adult life*, New York, NY: Dutton.

Sheehy, G. (1997) *New passages: Mapping your life across time*, New York, NY: HarperCollins.

Sugarman, L. (1986) *Life-span development: Concepts, theories and interventions*, London: Methuen.

Thompson, P., Itzin, C. and Abendstern, M. (1990) *I don't feel old: The experience of later life*, Oxford: Oxford University Press.

Thompson, W. (2000) *What happened to history?*, London: Pluto.

Titmuss, R.M. and Titmuss, K. (1942) *Parents revolt: A study of the declining birth-rate in acquisitive societies*, London: Secker and Warburg.

Troyansky, D. (1998) 'Balancing social and cultural approaches to the history of old age and ageing in Europe', in P. Johnson and P. Thane (eds) *Old age from antiquity to post-modernity*, London: Routledge, pp 96-109.

Turner, B.S. (1998) 'Ageing and generational conflicts: A reply to Sarah Irwin', *British Journal of Sociology*, vol 49, no 2, pp 299-304.

Twine, F. (1994) *Citizenship and social rights: The interdependence of self and society*, London: Sage Publications.

Vincent, J. (1999) 'Consumers, identity and old age', *Education and Ageing*, vol 14, no 2, pp 141-58.

Walker, A. and Naegele, G. (eds) (1999) *The politics of old age in Europe*, Buckingham: Open University Press.

Williams, R. (1990) *A protestant legacy: Attitudes to illness and death among older Aberdonians*, Oxford: Clarendon Press.

SEVEN

New ageism: age imperialism, personal experience and ageing policy

Simon Biggs

Key points

- Policy on ageing has moved from responding to particular problems to defining what it is to 'age well'.
- Diversity in ageing is restricted by trends toward positive or productive ageing.
- Distinctions between hidden parts of the self and outward appearance marks the management of age identity.
- Age imperialism from one age phase to another requires a re-evaluation of ageism, plus a concentration on the processes as well as the content of ageism.

Key readings

- Estes, C., Biggs, S. and Phillipson, C. (2004) *Social theory, social policy and ageing*, Buckingham: Open University Press.
- Morrow-Howell, N., Hinterlong, J. and Sherraden, M. (eds) (2001) *Productive aging: Concepts and challenges*, Baltimore, MD: Johns Hopkins.
- European Community (2002) 'Europe's response to world ageing: promoting economic and social progress in an ageing world: a contribution to the 2nd World Assembly on Ageing', www.europa.eu.int/comm/employment_social/news/2002/apr/ageing_en

Introduction

With an increasing awareness of demographic change, contemporary experiences of adult ageing have become issues of public policy, so much so that social policy appears to be moving from its traditional concern with isolated problems to the question of how adult ageing is socially perceived and personally encountered. The implications of this change are considerable and have a direct effect on the possibilities for diversity in the pathways of ageing that are capable of official recognition. In particular, the question arises of how far definitions of 'ageing well' become an attempt to fix the possibilities of ageing and channel them into predictable patterns. In this context, it is very difficult to consider the psychic life of ageing as a source and expression of multiplicity, without addressing the policy context within which certain narratives of ageing are given life.

This chapter critically assesses two aspects of age identity in the light of the above.

First, most people like to be thought of as successful. It is part of the seduction of current trends in policy that many gerontological aims have been taken on board. Active, successful and productive ageing has taken on a moral significance that mediates our everyday understanding of what it is to age well. However, these notions of success appear limiting and socially conforming when compared with psychological and psycho-dynamic understanding of ageing and the existential priorities of the second half of life.

Second, few people like to be thought of as lacking depth. It is suggested here that one of the ways that individuals negotiate the contradictions of contemporary ageing is through the development of masquerade. Social connection and conformity are separated psychologically from an imaginative world of self. It is within this inner realm that personal development and integration may take place.

The tension between an external logic largely mediated through public policy and an inner logic of ageing forms a key aspect the relationship between age and personal identity. The expression of diversity, and on occasion even the possibility of thinking about alternative states of being, is at stake in such an encounter, as is the degree of harmony allowed to exist between these inner and outer realities.

Age, identity and policy

In examining the relationship between personal experience and ageing policy, this chapter constitutes an attempt to shed some light on the way that policy shapes the way we see old age, its potential and the spaces that might be created in which to live a good old age. Ageing, like many other aspects of identity, is a site upon which power is distributed and power games are played out. And we need to take this into account when examining the assumptions that lie behind policy. When examining such questions through the lens of adult ageing along with other dimensions of power, policy needs to be seen as the product of one age group as applied to another and as such is inherently intergenerational in its patterning and implications.

Two lines of debate within gerontology are striking here. One focuses on the social-psychological and psychodynamic nature of adult ageing and intergenerational relationships. Another arises from the social construction of later life. One perspective is driven from within and privileges the expression of personal experience, from inner to outer worlds. The other is much more concerned with the power of external structures that shape, or at least impinge upon, one's sense of who one is. This second often poses the problem from the perspective of an observer looking in, while the former takes the stance of the individual looking out.

This relationship, between internal and external worlds, requires negotiation, even though in much writing on the subject they often appear as if they are the same thing. One elides the other, makes it opaque, colonises it and in so doing reduces its inherent diversity. It is but a small step from thinking about ageing and identity in this way to assuming that social policy reflects what ageing is actually like, or, from the perspective of personal experience, subtly assuming that policy is saying something that it is not but is in some way more personally palatable.

Highlighting the tension between the inner and the outer opens up a space, then, where these competing perspectives require conscious negotiation. The negotiation is also inter-personal; it takes psycho-sociological form between younger and older adults, between professionals and laypersons, between the well and the ill and between different cultural groups. Age identity, then, is something that is negotiated: it has a fluidity, but exists between relatively fixed points.

The current standard view of identity is neatly summed up by this statement, from the work of Dan McAdams (1993, p 35):

> Defining the self through myth may be seen as an ongoing act of psychological
> and social responsibility. Because our world can no longer tell us who we
> are and how we should live, we must figure it out on out own.

In gerontology, a similar view has been expressed about the 'blurring' of the adult lifecourse (Featherstone and Hepworth, 1991). Pre-existing structures that could be relied upon to shape life experience, such as the life stages identified by Erik Erikson in the 1950s and 60s, are said to become more fluid and less fixed. In the absence of these structures, originally conceived of as descriptions of a core reality and now more likely to be thought of as historically contingent narratives (Lynott and Lynott, 1996), we must, as McAdams tells us, "figure it out on our own".

Adult ageing has stretched this perspective, often identified as post-modern, almost to breaking point. The flexibility opportuned by social phenomena spanning a landscape as broad as consumer lifestyles, retirement communities, plastic surgery, plus virtual and internet opportunities for identity building, occasions a confrontation between the promise of an almost inexhaustible array of identity alternatives and the increasing inflexibility of the ageing body itself (Tulle, 2003). Such observations have provoked Featherstone and Hepworth (1991) to propose that the defining axis of contemporary ageing identity lies between an aged body and a youthful self attempting to get out, a contradiction they label 'the mask of ageing'. Personal expression thus becomes a self-consuming battle between oneself and one's body.

This view, while conceptually both satisfying and challenging, has important policy implications. It both feeds and draws upon attempts to overcome the ageing body and in the final analysis death itself. We enter then the territory of longevity, its commercial potential and accompanying inequalities of access to extended life. In terms of identity, we are talking about the possibilities of re-invention and a denial of limits. In many ways this approach also reflects the 'outside-looking-in' perspective in so far as personal experience is bounded by the possibilities that the external world makes available for action and feedback.

Another way of thinking about negotiated identity is, however, to think of adult ageing as a journey that occasions expanded personal potential, and, in psycho-dynamic terms, increased ownership of previously repressed or projected parts of the self (Jung, 1932). This mature imagination, however, still exists within an essentially ageist, and thus hostile, social environment (Biggs, 1999). In order to subsist, this inner world of maturity needs to form a bridge to the wider social world, but also requires protection from it. So, if the 'mask of ageing' entails masking as a negative ossification of the body that has to be overcome, here the emphasis is upon a form of masquerade, a performed identity that protects and connects.

An additional difference between the two models is that the first assumes that, in the 'young' self trying to find expression, there is a continuity of identity across the lifecourse. The goals of later life, in other words, are more or less the same as those of youth. The second model assumes the opposite, that there are markedly different existential priorities in the first and second halves of life. As such it is founded on discontinuity and difference between parts of the adult lifecourse. This is explained partly by a new freedom to express parts of the self that had to be curtailed during earlier phases of adult life that entailed the demands of work or child rearing, and partly by an increased awareness of finitude, the limits to life and to the time left in which to live.

The policy implications of this second model would be to seek out and enhance opportunities for the expression of the mature self and reduce the barriers to that expression. It sees the struggle for adult identity in similar ways to the disability movement: to change the social and material world, rather than to manipulate a potentially 'ageless' body.

Clearly there is truth in both of these perspectives and in the assertion that the psycho-social processes of identity in later life involve an amalgam of social ageism, increased personal integration and bodily challenges.

The mechanics of identity management in mature adulthood identify the contradictory nature of ageing. On the one hand, a situation arises of increased personal integration and expansion of self-identity, different existential priorities to earlier phases of the adult lifecourse and undeniable bodily challenges. On the other, there are restricted opportunities for self-expression, a focus on a continuity of goals across the lifecourse and an emphasis on maintaining an ageless psycho-social and bodily identity.

The asymmetry of this contradictory state of affairs bears a strong resemblance to the different priorities of younger and later adulthood. The 'mask of ageing' viewpoint closely follows a pathway of continuation, of the themes and processes of the first half of life for as long as possible, whereas the 'mature imagination' does not.

Positive, active and productive ageing in social policy

If policy shapes our everyday understanding of ageing, it is important to discover which pathway it promotes. A brief excursion into historical change and social policy indicates that the legitimacy of particular forms of ageing is a highly contingent state of affairs. What becomes visible, though the searchlight of policy, and what is obscured varies as a social phenomenon regardless of the biological bases of ageing bodies, and this affects the ground upon which one can build a legitimate identity. Other potential identities are suppressed, sometimes institutionally and sometimes through personal psychology. While this observation is often used to indicate that there is no one 'natural' state or process of adult ageing, it is also true that the visible, residual, age identity is legitimised by particular dynamics of power.

An example of changing policies and identities can be seen in 20th-century Britain. Here, older people moved from being survivors subject to decline and dependency, to 'ageless' consumers in a privatised and medicalised market, marked by both age awareness and age avoidance, to active and productive ageing resources to others and to each other (see Estes et al, 2004). The first position, of the noble if sometimes wretched survivor, was certainly around following the Second World War and the birth of the modern welfare state. Care for older people was not, however, a priority during this period, and the assumption that old age was a time of withdrawal from society was rarely questioned. The second period saw the erosion of traditional welfare supports and a social dynamic that commodified old age as a potential new market for pharmaceutical products, with the most vulnerable older adults themselves becoming commodities within private systems of nursing care. At the same time, elders, as with all newly discovered customers of welfare, were characterised as ageless consumers exerting market choice. In a third period, while the economic dynamic of the second has been left largely unchallenged, a model has emerged positioning elders as potentially productive participants and therefore included in broader social agendas. It is this last incarnation that is now turned to as a case example of the reinvention of age identity through policy and the new risks that accompany it.

Positive ageing policies have been particularly attractive to gerontologists and to age activists because they appear to draw inspiration from radical streams of gerontology and the age movement itself. Attempts to identify active, successful or productive ageing are well intended in their recognition that growing numbers of affluent older adults plus medical advances make many decrements previously associated with old age modifiable and in some cases reversible (Rowe and Kahn, 1987). It suggests a means of countering negative stereotyping of older people and increasing their social inclusion. When looking at ageing, it promises the possibility of being critical of stereotypes of decline, yet still conforming to wider values in society. Posing the question of social ageing in terms of success and productivity draws attention to the ways that structural and personal components of identity interact. It also supplies techniques for the invention of ageing selves and the role of public policy in creating an atmosphere that fosters one view of ageing rather than another.

Positive ageing policies are becoming increasingly popular in Europe (Walker, 2000) and are largely replacing assumptions that old age is a time of dependency and decline. They emphasise the value of work and work-like activities (Biggs, 2001) and of leisure (Katz, 2000). A variety of descriptors have been used almost interchangably to name this 'new' approach to ageing. For example, a statement submitted to the UN World Assembly on Ageing, reads:

> A new vision of ageing was proposed that accepts the realities of a fundamental genetically driven bio-molecular process leading to death, but with the prospect of achieving healthy, active, productive, successful and positive ageing to the very end through lifestyle modification and interventions that work. (Andrews, 2002, p 1)

Active and productive forms have become the most common means of elaborating what 'positive' ageing is all about. Each implies a moral as well as an objective basis on which to grow old, the questions of later life and suggested remedies that can be deployed.

A debate between activity and disengagement as alternative routes through later life marked the beginnings of modern theorising in gerontology (Lynott and Lynott, 1996), with activity theory providing the better fit with a moral 'problem-solving' approach adopted by the new discipline. Further, a clear series of objectives made it attractive to social workers, nurses and physicians alike. According to this perspective, older people needed to maintain their existing activities for as long as possible and replace ones that they had lost with new ones. Activity theories are a response to the problematisation of older people as non-productive, by allowing the active body to colonise one's sense of self-worth. This is then rendered quantifiable and can be turned into measures and regimes; the world then becomes divided into active elders and those described as 'potentially active'.

Productive ageing meets the problem of social conformity head on. It examines the question of ageing through the lens of economic usefulness, so that Hinterlong et al (2001, p 4) argue that "society simply cannot afford to continue to overlook the potential of the older population to serve as a resource for social change and economic growth".

Policy assumptions that older people have become a burden are stood on their head as the productive ageing approach maintains that productivity does not decrease with age. It appears radical because it takes as its object the negative stereotyping of older people and is a reaction to intergenerational equity debates in US public policy (Minkler and Robertson, 1991). Indeed, much of the discussion around productive ageing has centred on definition. Caro et al (1993, p 6) describe productive ageing as:

> Any activity by an older individual that contributes to producing goods and services or develops the capacity to produce them.

Butler and Schechter (1995, p 211) have proposed:

> The capacity of an individual or population to serve in the paid workforce, to serve in volunteer activities, to assist in the family, and to maintain himself or herself as independently as possible.

Bass and Caro (2001) extend their original economic definition to include activity that would otherwise "need to be done by someone else", but not those done simply for personal gain or self-enhancement – such as meditation, excursions, carrying on correspondence, worship, or visiting with family and friends. Indeed, it has been observed that including activities that occur outside the formal market raises problems of measurement and valuation (Morrow-Howell et al, 2001).

Thus productive ageing is unashamedly economic in its foundation and uses efficiency as its core argument. The solution to the problem of ageing becomes finding a way for older people to be economically useful, either directly, or as some revisionist definitions imply, indirectly. As such, productive ageing answers any liberal avoidance of purpose, with older adults finding personal value through becoming a pool of surplus labour, although an economic rather than an ideological justification for the claims of actual productivity has been hard to find (Schultz, 2001).

Productive ageing, however, is a powerful means of reducing ambiguity around the role and place of older people in society. The 'problem' of ageing is solved by capitulation to the dominant values that have contributed to the problem in the first place. As Katz (2000) points out, an original emphasis on activity as a means to well-being has now become a mechanism for the management of everyday life and a neoliberal narrative of self.

The move toward a 'productive' understanding of positive ageing is not simply a North American phenomenon. It can be seen in European policy towards old age and in national interpretation of the same trends such as in the UK. *Europe's response to World Ageing: Promoting economic and social progress in an ageing world* (European Community, 2002) recognises a "profound transformation in the experience and meaning of old age" based on "changes in age structure, health and patterns of employment". A narrative emerges of flexible retirement, increased longevity with people being healthier for longer and needing to play a valued role in society if intergenerational solidarity is not to be threatened. Ageing is seen as a site for potential conflict, remedied by increased efforts at social inclusion.

The ideas of productive ageing and a lifecourse approach will inform policy responses to ageing in Europe "for the foreseeable future". The key challenges identified include:

- maintaining growth and sound public finances;
- responding to the challenge of an ageing and shrinking workforce;
- ensuring adequate, sustainable and adaptable pensions;
- and securing access to high-quality health and long-term care while ensuring the financial stability of services.

The UK New Labour government (1997-present) has been particularly enthusiastic in its redefinition of adult ageing, with innovation occurring in parallel with developments in EU policy. A consolidating document, entitled *Winning the generation game* (Cabinet Office, 2000, p 1), states that:

> Unless we encourage older people to remain actively engaged in socially valued activity, whether paid or unpaid, everybody in Britain will miss out on the benefits of their experience and social commitment.

Four key areas are identified as the engine for change:

- to raise the expectations of older people and stop making judgements based on their age rather than their 'true value';
- to encourage persons aged 50+ to stay in work;
- reverse 'perverse incentives' to retire early; and
- increase volunteering among persons already retired.

An attempt is made to turn the so-called burden of old age into an opportunity. From a situation of a falling workforce and increasing pension payments, policies are aimed at creating an increasing workforce resulting in falling pension payments. This is social inclusion of a sort. The axis of the statement, however, turns on the notion of being paid or unpaid; and one is paid or unpaid for work. As policy becomes refined, the role created for older people becomes one of work, or work-like activities, with an accompanying postponement or erosion of pension rights and an expectation of engagement in the voluntary sector.

This is a highly communitarian view of social inclusion with a strong family resemblance to the debate on productive ageing. Thus even within the rhetoric of inclusion, which itself restricts the potential for self-development in later life, we encounter further restriction in the interpretation of legitimised identity. The vacuum left by the erosion of traditional definitions of ageing identity has been filled with work or, failing that, work-like activities. As such, new ageing policy equally constitutes an attempt to regulate identity in later life.

Positive ageing, ageism and age imperialism

When viewed from a discontinuous approach to the lifecourse, the 'productive' solution to age policy begins to look seriously one-sided. It resembles a form of age imperialism, if one agrees that first and second halves of life have markedly different priorities.

By age imperialism here is meant the imposition of the goals, aims, priorities and agendas of one age group onto and into the lives of other age groups. This may be consciously done, for reasons of political or economic expediency, or done unknowingly as if these priorities are simply commonsense, especially when one happens to be in the dominant age position. It involves an unwillingness to consider diversity based on adult age and an assumptive world in which the most powerful perspective acquires a moral dimension. If one ends up on the wrong side of this equation, one lives ones life according to principles that are out of kilter with emerging life priorities.

The narrative being created through contemporary policy shows clear elements of age imperialism in the sense that the values of work and care for others had, until very recently, been identified with earlier stages of the lifecourse. Under such circumstances, it is worth asking who the decision takers are in terms of age and who they are taking decisions about and on the basis of which assumptive realities. This interpretation of ageing owes much to imperatives independent of the priorities of later life itself and is linked to other forms of power, particularly economic ones.

Social inclusion on the terms of work and work-like activities appears limited when compared with alternative possibilities for an ageing identity, as have been identified through gero-transcendence (Tornstam, 1996) and the mature imagination (Biggs, 1999). As Moody (2001) has argued, a defining feature of the 'productive' narrative is 'lets make 'em like us'. This statement has two interpretations, both of which shed light on the limitations of 'new' ageing. First, it implies that the objective of policy is to make older adults acceptable to dominant power relations in wider society. Second, it indicates a way to do that, namely, by becoming the same as the dominant group in terms of values and attitudes toward age and identity. Further, work is not a neutral context: it implies hierarchy, discipline and power inequalities. As Schultz (2001) has indicated, there is no guarantee that older workers will be valued for the skills that emerge with maturity and they may simply find themselves competing on ground favouring competencies and attitudes arising in the first half of life.

Viewed like this, new ageing looks suspiciously like the intrusion of one age group into the life space of another. It is a more sophisticated ageism than a simple dislike of old age because the remedy is defined as access back into the life world of a different age phase. The possibility of self-integration and the recovery of suppressed material, of existential differences based on age, of spirit and reflection, dissent and resistance are left out. Similarly, bodily changes associated with age are not addressed, as productivity takes no notice of them other than in terms of output. We are treated as if we are all the same, and that sameness assumes a baseline that is not drawn from later life itself.

Personal experience and ageing policy revisited

In terms of process and personal strategies, a number of features arise for identity management with respect to age that reflect the inequities of this age-imperialist situation.

First is a core distinction between surface appearance and depth, with a hidden inner self that needs protecting and is difficult to express directly. Second is a tension between connection and separateness in spanning these internal and external worlds. We all need contact with other people, even if that contact is sometimes disconfirming and causes us to withdraw. Age dominance would form one important constituent of that context. Third, attention is drawn to the likelihood that the internal world can be expressed in any one external space. If there is a high degree of harmony between the external, social world that impinges here on the surfaces of identity, then a more authentic form of self-expression might take place. It allows us to ask whether particular policies facilitate or inhibit the expression of this inner logic in the social world. Where the likelihood of expression is greater, so would the possibilities of more genuine self-development and a more liberating context identifiable. Fourth, these observations free us from recourse to particular content in identifying ageist practice. The issue is no longer that ageism is expressed in terms of disengagement, decline and dependency. New forms of 'ageing well' explicitly reject this formulation, yet spawn new forms of ageism based on unending productivity. If attention is paid to process, then it matters less whether dependency, activity or productivity-based policies describe the legitimating expression of particular aspects of ageing. Each may be a liberating or constraining force depending on the social-historical circumstances. Likelihood provides a conceptual tool for interrogating the spaces that policy might create for the performance of age and identity. In different policy contexts, different things might be hidden and expressed, but processes of likelihood and harmony remain.

This in itself would suggest that we think less in terms of whether, say disengagement or activity, or gero-transcendence or productivity, are the right answers to the question of age and identity. We might think more in terms of the processes engendered by particular policy spaces and how the contents encourage or exclude specific forms of identity performance and negotiation between generations.

As narratives of ageing change, the contents of identities that are perceived to be legitimate also change. However, this says little in itself about the appropriateness of these narratives for ageing.

To address this problem, there must be a return to the question of depth. An analysis taking depth of experience into account would ask whether it is enough for notions of success simply to refer to surface appearances providing admission into a world marked by social conformity. Beyond this external logic lies an interior space, where aspects of the self that are not allowed legitimate expression can exist. Being mindful of these hidden aspects of an ageing identity recognises the protective function of the masquerade. It raises questions about what happens to parts of the self that are beyond the limitations set by legitimising social narratives. In any novel policy context, it should be asked what will be made explicit and what hidden in the new narrative that emerges, and thus what will become conforming and what subversive.

When the factors identified above are taken into account, initially seductive and seemingly pro-gerontological policies leave very limited room for the expression of diversity in ageing.

Conclusions

An attempt has been made critically to assess the personal strategies through which age and identity are managed under contemporary conditions, and draw out some implications of the rapid changes to which the rhetoric of late life policy has been subject. It has been argued that the processes involved in negotiating identity, particularly with respect to the inner and outer logic of personal and social identity, may be relatively stable. However, the contents and the inversions of content that context can provoke create significant sources of risk and uncertainty for social-psychological development in later life. The possibilities for harmony, identified as an ability to express deeper aspects of identity in particular social spaces, and the likelihood that inner and outer logic coincide, would provide a means of identifying positive future development in the relationship between policy rhetoric, personal experience and the imaginative spaces that arise between them.

References

Andrews, G. (2002) 'Valencia Forum: a meeting of gerontological researchers, educators and providers in support of the international plan of action on ageing 2002', Introduction: 1-6, www.valencia-forum.org

Bass, S.A. and Caro, F.G. (2001) 'Productive aging, a conceptual framework', in N. Morrow-Howell, J. Hinterlong and M. Sherraden (eds) *Productive aging: Concepts and challenges*, Baltimore, MD: Johns Hopkins.

Biggs, S. (1999) *The mature imagination: Dynamics of identity in midlife and beyond*, Buckingham: Open University Press.

Biggs, S. (2001) 'Toward critical narrativity: stories of aging in contemporary social policy', *Journal of Aging Studies*, vol 15, no 4, pp 303-16.

Butler, R. and Schechter, M. (1995) 'Productive aging', in G. Maddox (ed) *The encyclopaedia of aging*, New York, NY: Springer.

Cabinet Office (2000) *Winning the generation game*, London: Cabinet Office.

Caro, F., Bass, S. and Chen, Y. (1993) *Achieving a productive aging society*, Westport, CT: Auburn House.

Estes, C., Biggs, S. and Phillipson, C. (2004) *Social theory, social policy and ageing*, Buckingham: Open University Press.

European Community (2002) 'Europe's response to world ageing: promoting economic and social progress in an ageing world: a contribution to the 2nd World Assembly on Ageing', www.europe.eu.int/comm/employment_social/news/2002/apr/ageing_en

Featherstone, M. and Hepworth, M. (1991) 'Ageing and old age: reflections on the post-modern life-course', in B. Bytheway (ed) *Becoming and being old: Sociological approaches to later life*, London: Sage Publications, pp 143-57.

Hinterlong, J., Morrow-Howell, N. and Sherraden, M. (2001) 'Productive aging: principles and perspectives', in N. Morrow-Howell, J. Hinterlong and M. Sherraden (eds) *Productive aging: Concepts and challenges*, Baltimore, MD: Johns Hopkins.

Jung, C.G. (1932) *Collected works. Vol 7*, London: Routledge.

Katz, S. (2000) 'Busy bodies: activity, aging and the management of everyday life', *Journal of Aging Studies*, vol 14, no 2, pp 135-52.

Lynott, R.L. and Lynott, P.P. (1996) 'Tracing the course of theoretical development in the sociology of ageing', *The Gerontologist*, vol 36, no 6, pp 749-60.

Minkler, M. and Robertson, A. (1991) 'The ideology of age-race wars', *Ageing and Society*, vol 11, no 1, pp 1-22.

Moody, H. (2001) 'Productive aging and the ideology of old age', in N. Morrow-Howell, J. Hinterlong and M. Sherraden (eds) *Productive aging: Concepts and challenges*, Baltimore, MD: Johns Hopkins, pp 175-96.

McAdams, D. (1993) *The stories we live by*, New York, NY: Morrow.

Morrow-Howell, N., Hinterlong, J. and Sherraden, M. (eds) (2001) *Productive aging: Concepts and challenges*, Baltimore, MD: Johns Hopkins.

Rowe, J.W. and Kahn, R.L. (1987) 'Human aging: usual and successful', *Science*, vol 237, no 4811, pp 143-9.

Schultz, H.J. (2001) 'Public policy ambiguity', in N. Morrow-Howell, J. Hinterlong and M. Sherraden (eds) *Productive aging: Concepts and challenges*, Baltimore, MD: Johns Hopkins, pp 145-74.

Tornstam, L. (1996) 'Gerotranscendence: a theory about maturing into old age', *Journal of Aging and Identity*, vol 1, no 1, pp 37-50.

Tulle, E. (2003). 'Sense and structure: toward a sociology of old bodies', in S. Biggs, A. Lowenstein and J. Hendricks (eds) *The need for theory: Critical approaches to social gerontology*, Amityville, NJ: Baywood, pp 91-104.

Walker, A. (2000) 'Aging in Europe', *Hallym International Journal of Aging*, vol 2, no 1, pp 27-39.

EIGHT

Sexuality in gerontology: a heteronormative presence, a queer absence

Ann Cronin

Key points

- The presence of heteronormative thinking and practice in the social scientific study of later life has contributed to the marginalisation of the experiences of older lesbian and gay adults.
- Sexuality in later life has either been ignored in later-life studies or underpinned by a biomedical of sexuality, which does not pay sufficient attention to the social construction of sexuality.
- The inclusion of sexual diversity in late life studies helps us understand the experiences of older lesbian and gay adults and demonstrates the way in which the institution of heterosexuality structures the lives of all older adults.

Key readings

- Cruz, M. (2003) *Sociological analysis of ageing: The gay male perspective*, New York, NY: Haworth Press.
- Fullmer, E., Shenk, D. and Eastland, L. (1999) 'Negating identity: a feminist analysis of the social invisibility of older lesbians', *Journal of Women and Aging*, vol 11, no 2/3, pp 131-48.
- Rosenfeld, D. (2003) *The changing of the guard: Lesbian and gay elders, identity, and social change*, Philadelphia, PA: Temple University Press.

Introduction

Traditional gerontological models of 'normal ageing' have in recent years been challenged by a growing awareness that individual and social diversity across the lifespan leads to multiple different realities in later life (Dannefer, 1996). The majority of the research on social diversity or heterogeneity among older people has focused on gender, class, race/ethnicity and cultural diversity (for example, Arber and Ginn, 1991; Conway-Turner, 1999; Griffin and Aitkin,

1999; Evandrou, 2000; McFadden, 2001). Alongside the move to understand social diversity, there has also been a move to explore sexuality in later life. While not dismissing the problems associated with defining and measuring the non-heterosexual population, Age Concern in the UK (Age Concern, 2002) claims that one in 15 users of its services is lesbian or gay. The small but growing body of research examining the experiences of older lesbian, gay and bisexual adults (for example, Almvig 1982; Berger and Kelley, 1986; Friend, 1990; Dorfman et al, 1995; Herdt et al, 1997; Fullmer et al, 1999; Rosenfeld, 2002) documents both the structural disadvantages faced by this older group of adults, while simultaneously helping to dispel the myth that older lesbians and gay men will automatically face a lonely old age due to familial and societal rejection. Yet, the experiences of this small but significant minority are relegated to the margins of mainstream gerontology.

Therefore, the purpose of this chapter is, first, to offer an explanation for gerontology's failure to take sufficient account of sexual diversity; second, to explore the experiences of this group of older adults. This chapter is divided into three sections. The first begins with an overview of the current debate about social diversity, before the second moves on to explore why sexual diversity has yet to be fully incorporated into this debate. This is centred on the argument that gerontology, in common with many other academic disciplines, is underpinned by heteronormative assumptions and practices. This theoretical framework is developed in the following section, which compares the current findings of research on sexuality in later life with data from my own research with older self-identified lesbians. In the third and final section, I return to the theme of social diversity to explore the diversity of experiences among older lesbian and gay adults.

The data for this chapter comes from qualitative research with 22 self-identified lesbian women aged 45-68, with a mean age of 54, living in either the UK or the US. The women were recruited through a variety of different sources: word of mouth, national organisations and websites and bulletin boards on the Internet. Twelve face-to-face interviews and two email interviews were conducted with women living in the UK. The remaining 10 interviews with US women were conducted via email. Four couples participated in the research: three through face-to-face joint interviews and one couple through separate email interviews. All the participants were white and, on the basis of educational background and occupational profession could be classified as middle class. However, women who had married prior to embracing a lesbian lifestyle were more likely to be in a worse economic situation than never-married women. The interview schedule used open-ended questions to explore both past and present experiences, focusing on the relationship between individual biography and socio-historical context, participation in lesbian and gay social networks and attitude towards and experience of ageing. Qualitative methods, akin to grounded theory, were used to code and analyse the data, with particular attention paid to the subjects' own categories rather than imposing my own external categories.

The heteronormativity of gerontology

Yee (2002) suggests that the inclusion of social diversity in research will both reward and challenge gerontologists. Developing this theme, Yee (2002, p 1) argues that:

> Diversity is about the recognition and celebration of the differences that exist
> in our society.... Diversity is about recognising barriers that prevent access to
> our social systems and building a broader community infrastructure.

This dual understanding of social diversity – celebration and constraint – should form the basis of any empirical investigation of this subject. Calasanti (1996) cautions against using a 'normal' model of ageing as a reference point through which to compare and measure patterns of difference as this methodology fails to consider existing hierarchies of power thus reinforcing power differentials. For example, women and men experience later life differently, yet, despite being in the majority, the experiences of older women are often compared with the experiences of older men. This reinforces the normality of the reference group's experiences while minimising the differing social reality of groups who stand outside the socially constructed norm. This reductivist approach assumes we can only understand the experiences of a particular social group by the mere fact that they do not belong to the dominant reference group; yet being female is different from not being male.

Addressing these problems, Calasanti (1996) suggests that empirical investigations into social diversity should begin with the assumption that reality will differ according to social location and group membership, thus permitting us a rich insight to what Dannefer (1996) terms the many different realities of ageing. As Yee (2002) suggests, this must begin with a commitment by gerontologists to reflect critically on both individual and collective constructions of normalcy. While an analysis of sexuality is currently missing from the study of social diversity, the theoretical framing underpinning social diversity is suitable for an analysis of lesbian and gay experience of later life. Although older lesbians and gay men will in part share a common reality with all older people, the structural organisation of sexuality privileges heterosexuality over other forms of sexuality; therefore it can be assumed that older lesbians and gay men will experience later life differently from their heterosexual counterparts. Mary, a 68-year-old self-identified lesbian living in the US, writing about the experience of ageing as a lesbian states:

> Issues facing me? Hmm, discrimination as a woman first, as a senior citizen
> on top of that and in addition a lesbian makes it a triple whammy.

So why have the experiences of older lesbian and gay adults been ignored by gerontology for so long? Queer theorists and feminists have used the concept of heteronormativity to explore the social construction and institutionalisation of heterosexuality. Heteronormativity refers to the way in which the structural organisation of western societies is predicated on the belief that heterosexuality is biologically, psychologically and sociologically superior to other forms of sexuality. Thus, heterosexuality does not simply refer to opposite-sex relationships but represents an axis of power and the dominant mode for conducting intimate relationships, which in turn is linked to ideas concerning gender-appropriate sexual behaviour. For example, the culturally dominant belief that men are sexually active and women are sexually passive maintains a double standard of sexual behaviour, while limiting both the understanding and practice of heterosex and reinforcing gender power relations.

Furthermore, heterosexuality as ideology and normative principle dominates both the legal system (Weiss, 2001) and the cultural system, thus legitimating differential treatment of those who stand outside the heterosexual regime. While not dismissing the gains made from 30 years of political activism by the lesbian and gay movement, the dominant institutional and cultural framework remains heteronormative. For example, it was only as recent as December 2002 that the present Labour Government announced its intentions to allow lesbian and gay couples to register their partnerships, thus permitting them access to a range of legal and financial benefits that are the right of married heterosexuals. While this government initiative is to be welcomed, marriage as both institution and practice remains a heterosexual privilege. As VanEvery (1996) notes, while heterosexuality is the hegemonic form of sexuality in western societies, marriage is the hegemonic form of heterosexuality.

The concept of heteronormativity increases our understanding of both the structural disadvantages faced by those who stand outside the heterosexual regime and the way in which institutionalised heterosexuality limits and constrains those who identify as heterosexual. Therefore, extending the current analyses of the performance of institutionalised heterosexuality to the domain of later life and the ageing process can only be of benefit to all. However, broadening our understanding of the triple whammy of gender, age and sexuality must begin by deconstructing the paradigm of heteronormativity that informs gerontological theory and practice.

Sexuality in later life

Calasanti and Slevin (2001) argue that older people have been culturally constructed as:

- first, no longer sexual desirable;
- second, no longer sexually desirous;
- third, sexually incapable or dysfunctional.

Hall et al (1982) argue that older people are regarded as being physically unattractive, while Deacon et al (1995) highlight the link between sex and youth, lending credence to Hodson and Skeen's (1994) claim that the sexualised body is the young body, while the older body is stripped of its sexuality. Spence (1992) argues that existing cultural myths persuade people (including health professionals and older people) that older people should not/cannot be sexual and if by some miracle they are able to be sexual they should keep quiet about it.

These cultural myths and stereotypes are reinforced in the practices of everyday life, for example, popular jokes and media depictions of sex in later life (Vasil and Wass, 1993; Hooyman and Kiyak, 1999). While not disagreeing with this analysis, the image of the dirty old man or the aggressive marketing of Viagra to older men accompanied by jokes about older women hiding a husband's Viagra not only reflect ageist assumptions concerning sexuality but also gendered ones. In a similar manner, while older women having children late in life are subject to ridicule and moral condemnation, older men are congratulated for their continued virility. Cultural understandings of sexuality in later life are filtered through a gendered lens that reinforces the existing gendered active/passive dichotomy, while limiting definitions of 'real sex' to penile penetration. Furthermore, while the older (gendered) body is denied the right or ability to be sexual, it nevertheless remains a heterosexual body – homosexuality is ignored.

Although gerontology has not actively promoted such crude stereotypes, its traditional silence on sexuality has contributed to the 'cultural illiteracy' that Calasanti and Slevin (2001) suggest surrounds sexuality in later life. The lack of an alternative discourse has enabled misinformed myths and stereotypes to flourish, thus reinforcing the hegemonic belief that 'sex belongs to the young'. Fortunately, there is evidence to suggest that this omission is beginning to be addressed in gerontology (Quam, 1993), with recent research focusing on managing and overcoming the physiological impact of the ageing process on sexual ability and function. While not negating the importance of biomedical research, Sanders (1999) declares that research addressing the psychological and sociological factors that structure the meaning and practice of sexuality in later life is either rare or underpinned by limited understandings of what constitutes sexuality. For example, Peate (1999, p 175) acknowledges the psychosocial dimension of sexuality, yet draws on the language of essentialism to construct sex as a primary drive and limits sexual acts to "behaviours that involve the genitalia, e.g. stimulation of the erogenous". This privileges a phallocentric understanding of sex, which discounts other ways of expressing sexual desire and pleasure, which is detrimental to heterosex and renders lesbian sexuality invisible.

Therefore, while the move to understand sexuality in later life is to be welcomed, much of the research is theoretically flawed due to its failure to address the role sexuality plays in the social organisation and regulation of society. Gerontology's failure to reflect critically on the gendered and heteronormative framework in which it operates accounts for both the biomedicalisation of sexuality and an unproblematic acceptance of the heterosexual/homosexual divide, which help to explain the continued social exclusion of older lesbian and gay adults. Gerontology needs to move beyond its current simplistic and reductive focus on sexual behaviour, to incorporate an analysis of the socio-historical construction of sexuality that focuses on the relationship between socio-historical contexts and individual constructions of sexual meaning, identity and practice.

Situating the construction of sexual identity

This last point can be illustrated through comparing my own research with older lesbians with existing research on the sexuality of older people. Brecher's (1993) large-scale survey of sexual attitudes and behaviours among the over-50s is based on a sample he describes as "overwhelmingly heterosexual". Among other things, he notes that 97% of the sample had been married at least once and three quarters were married at the point of participation in the study. Thus, Brecher makes the assumption that marriage (past or present) is evidence of a heterosexual identity. Although on the surface this might seem a reasonable assertion, it is underpinned by a patriarchal and heteronormative understanding of gender and sexuality. Any endorsement of the western ideological view of marriage as an institution freely entered into for reasons of romantic love ignores both socioeconomic context and cultural diversity. It also reinforces a fixed and essentialist understanding of sexuality, which pays little attention to the socially constructed nature of sexuality and sexual identity.

Eleven of the 22 women in my study were either divorced or separated. The age at which women married ranged between 20 and 25 years, while age at the point of divorce ranged between 40 and 50 years. Ten of the 11 women had children, with the majority having waited until their children left home before divorcing and adopting a lesbian lifestyle. Two women had adolescent children still in their care. None of the remaining 11 never-married women had children. While individual variation existed, the majority of the 'never-married' women had embraced a lesbian lifestyle in early adulthood. Nevertheless, only three of the 11 women had lived an exclusively lesbian lifestyle, the remaining eight referring to occasional attempts to have sexual and intimate relationships with men. These findings, whether they relate to the incidence of marriage among lesbians or sexual experiences with men, cast doubt over the assumption that marriage is an automatic indication of a heterosexual identity. In the case of Brecher's study, this is further exacerbated by patriarchal and heteronormative interpretation of accounts regarding same-sex experiences. Addressing the implications of the statistically proven gender imbalance in later life on women's ability to be sexually active, Brecher (1993, p 109) writes:

> Some unmarried women discuss entering into a sexual relationship with another woman as a solution to the dearth-of-unmarried-men problem; but only a few have taken that course.

The implication here is that same-sex relationships would not be a first choice for women, but would only be considered if there were a lack of men.

'Situational' explanations for homosexuality in which the individual involved is classified as a 'pseudo' homosexual have a long history in both biological and psychological discourses on homosexuality. Working within an individualist framework devoid of social context, the assumption is that the majority of individuals are innately heterosexual and will only engage in homosexual activity when a preferred heterosexual alternative is not available. This has long been a favoured explanation for the occurrence of homosexual behaviour in same-sex institutions such as prisons, or single-sex schools, and now, according to Brecher, in later life. Elaborating on this Brecher (1993, p 109) writes:

> The overwhelming majority of our respondents are primarily heterosexual. Quite a few however, report pre-adolescent sexual encounters with others of their gender (with little or no harm reported); and quite a few essentially heterosexual women and men report one or more homosexual partners or encounters after 50. These respondents seem to view such homosexual contacts as an additional, rather than an alternative, form of sexual activity.

Leaving to one side Brecher's assumption that same-sex experiences might be harmful (one has to ask how such harm would be defined and measured?), both my own data and existing research offer an alternative understanding of married women who have had same-sex experiences and feelings in both adolescence and later life. Jensen (1999) argues that it is only possible to understand the apparent contradiction between identity and behaviour if we locate women's individual biographies in their socio-historical context. Elaborating on this, Rosenfeld (2002) distinguishes between two 'identity cohorts' of older lesbians and gay men. The first 'identity cohort', primarily consisting of the 'old old', are adults who became aware of their sexuality prior to the Gay Liberation Movement. Lacking an alternative discourse, they drew on the discursive construction of homosexuality as a stigmatised and potentially discreditable identity to construct their own self-image. Given that this discourse was supported by extreme "moral, social and legal injunctions against homosexuality" (Quam, 1993, p 10), lesbians and gay men often felt they had no option but to adopt lifelong survival strategies such as secrecy and passing. Furthermore, despite a change in social attitudes towards homosexuality, thus increasing the possibility for lesbians and gay men to be more open about their sexuality, it is likely that this cohort of old-old lesbians and gay men will continue to be secretive about their sexuality (Rosenfeld, 2002), thus impeding access to this group.

Rosenfeld's second 'identity cohort' consists primarily of the 'young old', women and men who embraced a lesbian or gay identity and lifestyle either during the Gay Liberation Movement, or in the period directly following it. Unlike the first 'identity cohort', this cohort had access to a self-affirmative and celebratory discourse, thus affecting personal conceptualisations of their sexual identity. Furthermore, the formation of a sexual identity that stood outside or in opposition to the heterosexual norm was more likely to be undertaken with others than in isolation. This group is more likely to be visible, belong to social networks and communities and lobby for services.

The identification of these two 'identity cohorts' provides a valuable insight into the social diversity of the older lesbian and gay population. However, other identity cohorts exist, which may or may not be age-related, for example older lesbians and gay men, who for a variety of reasons did not adopt a lesbian or gay identity until later in life, often following marriage and children. Confining the discussion just to women, it can be argued that this cohort of women, growing up in a period of intense homophobia and heterosexism, combined with a post-war enforcement of strict gender norms, found it difficult to challenge what was expected of them. Rich (1980), focusing primarily on the sexual domination of women by men, argues that the compulsory nature of heterosexuality ensures that men retain their physical, economical and emotional control over women. For Rich, the institution of heterosexuality is dependent upon ensuring that the experiences of lesbians either remain invisible or are associated with disease and illness. The cultural validation of heterosexuality over the denigration of homosexuality contributed to the difficulty that the women in my research faced concerning their sexuality. For example, Lesley, a 54-year-old, writes:

> I was brought up in a middle-class Jewish family in New York City. Although the typical concepts of wife, children, and white picket fence were never mentioned in so many words, I think it was more understood than actually discussed. The concept of *not* getting married (as my two older sisters had done) was never an issue. ... I was trying to 'do what was right' by society's standards, even if they weren't right for me.

Such accounts juxtaposed with Brecher's dismissal of same-sex experience in both adolescence and later life offer an alternative socially situated account of sexual identity that highlights the slippage between identity and practice. These 'once-married' women do not have relationships with women in later life because of a dearth of available men. Instead it is a conscious desire for authenticity between identity and practice, a desire that could only be acted upon in later life partly because of changes in the status of homosexuality and changing gender norms. The women talked at length of their adolescent and young adulthood feelings for women. For these women, such feelings were indicative of their sexual identity, which they considered to be 'primarily lesbian', not 'primarily heterosexual'.

> As a child, once I realised I was attracted to other girls/women, I didn't actually 'think' about it. I just knew that I was and knew that, deep down inside, it was totally natural. It felt like the 'real me'. I was comfortable with it until I got old enough to realise (about the age of 12) that this was not, seemingly, the natural order of things. That's when I knew I had to hide my light under a bushel, so to speak. It was at this point that I felt like a misfit.

I didn't quite fit in with the other girls. We didn't have the same interests. While they were worrying about boys, I wanted to ride my bike, roller skate, climb trees – have fun! To me, flirting with boys wasn't fun; it wasn't natural; it was a waste of time. I felt out of kilter from then on. (Chris, 56 years old, UK)

In this section, I have deconstructed some of the heteronormative assumptions underpinning gerontology's understanding of sex and sexuality. This has centred on unpicking the implications of using a biomedical understanding of sexuality, which pays little attention to the social and historical context in which sexuality and sexual identity is constructed and performed. Two key issues have emerged from this discussion: one concerns sexual identity; the other addresses the theme of social diversity. While separated for ease of discussion, they are in practice connected.

The sexual identity of an individual may not be what it at first appears. While this might seem an obvious statement, it is something that has too often been overlooked on the basis that the overwhelming majority of people can be defined as heterosexual. The dismissal of same-sex experience is only possible through conflating heterosexual behaviour with heterosexual identity; that is, through theorising an unproblematic relationship between 'doing' and 'being' that fails to consider how the social may constrain and limit behaviour. This results in the construction of heterosexuality as an authentic identity, supported by a biological discourse, while non-heterosexual experiences, which might be an indication of an alternative identity, remain unacknowledged.

This in turn relates to my second point concerning the social diversity that exists among lesbian and gay adults, as evidenced by the stories told by the women in my study. Use of categories such as lesbian and gay will always exclude adults who live a non-heterosexual lifestyle but, for a variety of reasons, choose not to incorporate such experiences into a discrete sexual identity. This illustrates the paucity of the language of sexuality, and as the analysis of Brecher's study indicates, is equally applicable to those designated heterosexual. Leaving to one side the thorny issue of sexual categories, the last section of this chapter, drawing on the concept of social support, explores how the diversity that exists among self-identified lesbian and gay adults affects later-life experience.

Queering social support

Cooper et al (1999, p 9) define social support as:

The companionship and practical information and esteem support which the individual derives from interactions with members of his or her 'social network', including friends, colleagues, acquaintances and family members.

Elaborating on this, House and Kahn (1985) distinguish between structural and functional aspects of social support. Structural aspects of social support focus on the nature and frequency of social relationships and social activities, and also include a consideration of living status, for example living alone or with a partner. Functional aspects of social support focus on the psychosocial benefits to be gained from positive involvement in social activities. Aside from helping the individual to integrate into wider society and providing access to help and information, involvement in social relationships and networks provides an individual with a place to express feelings and develop self-esteem.

The operationalisation of this multidimensional concept in research on older people has focused on measuring access to and levels of social support based on different social variables, for example, gender or marital status. Ross and Mirowsky (1989) state that married people report higher levels of familial-based social support than single people do, while Cooper et al (1999) show that marriage may act as a deterrent against the development of friendship networks. Belle (1987) points to the structural factors that favour women over men regarding both the quality and quantity of social support networks both through out the lifecourse and particularly in later life. Bearing in mind women's greater life expectancy, O'Connor (1992, p 119) argues that female friendship in later life is likely to be "one of the few available sources of social integration, status and companionship" available to older women. Utilising Rich's (1980) concept of 'compulsory heterosexuality', O'Connor argues that heterosexual women have been prevented from developing strong friendships with women, thus placing them at a disadvantage in later life. Unfortunately, O'Connor falls short of assessing the implications of this thesis for non-heterosexual women, who free from marriage and the micro-politics of gender may have invested more energy in female friendships, with all the implications this may contain for later life. Rose (2000) argues that the study of women's romantic and friendship relationships has been dominated by a heterosexual ethic through which all relationships are understood, rendering lesbians invisible or misrepresented, while denying agency to heterosexual women. Just as older lesbian and gay adults have been ignored or marginalised in the recent debate on sexuality in later life, they have also been excluded from the examination of social support in later life. The unacknowledged emphasis on heterosexual-based forms of social support in later life partially explains the traditional image of the lonely older lesbian or gay man who has been rejected by both society and family (Kehoe, 1991; Walters and Simon, 1993). This stereotype is only able to exist because heterosexual-based social networks have been used as a reference point to understand the experiences of older non-heterosexual adults. To paraphrase Calasanti, heterosexuality is presented as the 'normal model' and everything else is judged against this – and found wanting.

Counteracting this image, Dorfman et al (1995) demonstrate that, while older lesbian and gay adults, unlike older heterosexual adults, are less likely to receive support from family members, they do receive high levels of social support from friends, leading to the term 'friendship families'. Similarly, lesbians throughout the lifecourse are more likely to depend on friends and partners than relatives for support (Aura, 1985). Meanwhile, Friend (1990) argues that the achievement of an 'affirmative' lesbian or gay identity encourages the development of psychological strength that can be drawn upon in later life. Kimmel (1978) asserts that successful negotiation of the 'coming-out' process and subsequently, learning to manage the challenges posed by living in a homophobic society leaves an individual with increased 'ego strength'. Berger and Kelly (1986, p 209) use the term 'mastery of stigma' to refer to the successful management of the threat posed to an individual's identity from 'coming out', leading to the conclusion that "being gay or lesbian actually facilitates adaptation to ageing". This would suggest that, far from being depressed and socially isolated, older lesbian and gay adults have the potential to be part of identity-affirming and supportive networks. My own research with older self-identified lesbians offers qualified support to this claim; yet, as the discussion below indicates, greater attention must be paid to social diversity among older lesbian and gay adults themselves.

Analysis of the women's accounts suggests three major sources of social support. The first source of social support is via membership and active involvement in lesbian social networks. Social networks can be divided into three types: locally situated networks, geographically dispersed networks and Internet-based networks. Often, these networks overlap with each other. Three out of the 22 women talked about their involvement in mixed-sex social networks, the majority claiming a preference for women-only networks. The second source of social support is based on nuclear and extended family networks, while the third is via involvement with friendship networks not based on sexuality, for example work-based groups or community-based friendships.

Although involvement in one type of network did not prevent involvement in another, there did appear to be a relationship between the first and third forms of support. High levels of involvement in lesbian social networks, particularly local ones, were paralleled by low levels of involvement in work-based or other friendship networks; a low level of involvement in lesbian communities led to a higher reliance on other sources of social support, be they the immediate neighbourhood or work-based friendships. The level of involvement in family networks was mediated by two factors: first, whether a woman had disclosed her sexuality to her family, and second, how this information was received by family members. While the response of individual family members differed, women who had either not disclosed their sexuality or had been rejected by their family on disclosure had very limited contact and did not expect them to be a source of support in later life. Moreover, while not dismissing the importance of ties beyond the lesbian community, the majority of the women prioritised the unique form of social support to be found from a community based on shared experiences and identity:

> I have many straight acquaintances, people that I work with, people in my apartment complex, but I choose to reserve any meaningful/emotional feelings to lesbian friends. (Cathy, 54 years old, UK)

> All of my friends in Georgia are lesbians, so my social life is directly related to my sexual identity! I do have friends back in New Jersey who are straight and who accept me totally. They will always be my friends and even will come to visit me in Georgia. But they don't understand, down deep inside, that there is a difference between us. They don't understand how I can not get excited about the same things they do (all 'het' things). Only one friend understands, since her brother-in-law and daughter are both homosexuals. (Donna, 58 years old, US)

While these findings are broadly consistent with the research findings discussed earlier, a deeper analysis of the data suggests the presence of three interrelated factors influencing access and participation in lesbian communities: relationship status, the length of time a woman had lived a lesbian lifestyle and geographical location. The longer a women had lived a lesbian lifestyle, the higher the probability of first being in a relationship and, second, being in a long-term relationship. A high proportion of single women had identified as a lesbian in the last five years. Women in long-term relationships had relatively low levels of involvement in lesbian networks than those either in relationships of a shorter duration or currently single. For these women, the end of a relationship, either through separation or death could result in social isolation, although there was some evidence to suggest that this could be counteracted by life-long friendships, which may provide access to wider social networks. Women who have always lived a lesbian lifestyle and were currently in short-term relationships or single were most likely to be actively involved in social networks, be they locally situated, geographically dispersed, electronic or a combination of all three. These women expressed high levels of satisfaction with their lives and, and felt confident that the social networks to which they belonged would continue to be the main source of support in old age.

Women who had embraced a lesbian lifestyle later in life, often following marriage and children, expressed a similar sentiment, yet were able to access and participate in lesbian communities. The major barrier to participation was lack of a locally based lesbian network and an inability to move to one due to either a lack of financial resources or existing family ties. This situation was particularly acute for women with children still living at home and/or were not in paid employment. Women who were unable to move to an established lesbian and gay enclave found it extremely difficult, if not impossible, to either initiate an intimate relationship or become involved in lesbian and gay networks. For these women, use of the Internet was considered an important access point to lesbian networks. While much has been written about lesbian, gay or queer uses of the Internet (see Wakeford, 2000, for an overview), none of this has directly examined the experiences of older women or men and therefore this needs further investigation.

This brief discussion of both the different sources of social support available to older self-identified lesbians and the issues affecting access and participation is based on an understanding of the complexity of lesbian identity, made possible by prioritising the relationship between individual biography and social context. Just as gerontology has often assumed an unproblematic relationship between 'doing' and 'being' – practice and identity – it is possible that existing research on older lesbian and gay adults has adopted a similar approach, thereby paying insufficient attention to social diversity within this cohort of older adults. Again, this understanding should inform future research in this area, just as future research on social support in later life should seek to understand the role that sexuality may play in access and participation in supportive social networks. While not dismissing the detrimental impact of discriminatory attitudes and practices on later life, research in this area, my own included, indicates that older lesbian and gay adults who are able to access and participate in sexual identity-based networks may in some respects be better off in later life than their heterosexual counterparts. This in itself lends weight to the argument that the inclusion of sexual diversity in mainstream gerontology first improves our understanding of the experiences of older lesbian and gay adults and, second, illustrates the way in which the institution of heterosexuality structures the lives of all older adults. This perspective should to be reflected in future gerontological research and analysis. Until this happens, sexuality in gerontology will remain a heteronormative presence and a queer absence.

References

Age Concern (2002) 'Older lesbian and gay people – forgotten no more' (www.ageconcern.org.uk/sitesearch/news).

Almvig, C. (1982) *The invisible minority: Aging and lesbianism*, New York, NY: Utica College of Syracuse University.

Arber, S. and Ginn, J. (1991) *Gender and later life: A sociological analysis of resources and constraints*, London: Sage Publications.

Aura, J. (1985) 'Women's social support: a comparison of lesbians and heterosexual', unpublished dissertation, University of California, Los Angeles.

Belle, D. (1987) 'Gender differences in the social moderators of stress', in R.C. Barnett, L. Biener and G.K. Baruch (eds) *Gender and stress*, New York, NY: Free Press.

Berger, R.M. and Kelly, J. (1986) 'Working with homosexuals of the older population', *Social Casework*, April, pp 203-10.

Brecher, E. (1993) 'Love, sex and ageing', in J. Johnston and R. Slater (eds) *Ageing and later life*, London: Sage Publications and Open University Press.

Calasanti, T.M. (1996) 'Incorporating diversity: meaning, levels of research and implications for theory', *The Gerontologist*, vol 36, pp 147-56.

Calasanti, T.M. and Slevin, K.F. (2001) *Gender, social inequalities, and aging*, Walnut Creek, CA: Alta Mira Press.

Conway-Turner, K. (1999) 'Older women of color: a feminist exploration of the intersections of personal, familial and community life', *Journal of Women and Aging*, vol 11, no 2/3, pp 115-30.

Cooper, H., Arber, S., Fee, L. and Ginn, J. (1999) *The influence of social support and social capital on health: A review and analysis of British data*, London: Health Education Authority.

Dannfer, D. (1996) 'The social organization of diversity, and the normative organization of age', *The Gerontologist*, vol 36, pp 174-7.

Dorfman, R., Walters, K., Burke, P., Hardin, L., Karanik, T., Raphael, J. and Silverstein, E. (1995) 'Old sad and alone: the myth of the aging homosexual', *Journal of Gerontological Social Work*, vol 24, no 1/2, pp 29-44.

Deacon, S., Minichello, V. and Plummer, D. (1995) 'Sexuality and older people: revisiting the assumptions', *Educational Gerontology*, vol 21, pp 497-513.

Evandrou, M. (2000) 'Social inequalities in later life: the socio-economic position of older people from ethnic minority groups in Britain', *Population Trends*, vol 101, Autumn, pp 32-9.

Friend, R.A. (1990) 'Older lesbian and gay people: a theory of successful aging', *Journal of Homosexuality,* vol 20, pp 99-118.

Fullmer, E., Shenk, D. and Eastland, L. (1999) 'Negating identity: a feminist analysis of the social invisibility of older lesbians', *Journal of Women and Aging*, vol 11, no 2/3, pp 131-48.

Griffin, G. and Aitkin, L. (1999) 'Visibility blues: gender issues in elder abuse in institutional settings', *Journal of Elder Abuse and Neglect*, vol 10, no 12, pp 29-42.

Hall, A., Selby, J. and Vanclay, F.M. (1982) 'Sexual ageism', *Australian Journal on Aging*, vol 1, pp 29-34.

Herdt, G.I., Hostetler, A.J. and Cohler, B.J. (1997) 'Coming of age: gays, lesbians, and bisexuals in the second half of life', *Journal of Gay, Lesbian, and Bisexual Identity*, vol 2, pp 87-308.

Hodson, D. and Skeen, P. (1994) 'Sexuality and aging: the hammerlock of myths', *Journal of Applied Gerontology*, vol 13, pp 219-35.

Hooyman, N. and Kiyak, H.A. (1999) *Social gerontology*, Boston, MA: Allyn and Bacon.

House, J. S. and Kahn, R. (1985) 'Measures and concepts of social support', in S. Cohen and L. Syme (eds) *Social support and health*, New York, NY: Academic Press.

Jensen, K.L. (1999) *Lesbian epiphanies: Women coming out in later life*, London: Harrington Park Press.

Kehoe, M. (1991) 'Loneliness and the aging homosexual: is pet therapy the answer?', *Journal of Homosexuality*, vol 20, no 3/4, pp 137-41.

Kimmel, D.C. (1978) 'Adult development and aging: a gay perspective', *Journal of Social Issues*, vol 34, pp 113-30.

McFadden, S. (2001) 'Feminist scholarship as a meeting ground for age and disability studies', *The Gerontologist*, vol 42, no 1, pp 133-7.

O'Connor, P. (1992) *Friendships between women: A critical review*, London: Harvester Wheatsheaf.

Peate, I. (1999) 'The need to address sexuality in older people', *British Journal of Community Nursing*, vol 4, issue 4, pp 174-80.

Quam, J.K. (1993) 'Gay and lesbian aging', *SIECUS Report*, vol 21, no 5, pp 10-12.

Rich, A. (1980) 'Compulsory heterosexuality and lesbian existence', *Signs*, vol 5, no 4, pp 631-60.

Rose, S. (2000) 'Heterosexism and the study of women's romantic and friendship relationships', *Journal of Social Issues*, vol 56, no 2, pp 315-28.

Rosenfeld, D. (2002) 'Identity careers of older gay men and lesbians', in J.F. Gubrium and J. Holstein (eds) *Ways of aging*, Oxford: Blackwell Publishers, pp 161-81.

Ross, C.E. and Mirowsky, J. (1989) 'Explaining the social patterns of depression: control and problem-solving – or support and talking', *Journal of Health and Social Behavior*, vol 30, no 2, pp 206-19.

Sanders, A. (1999) *Mid-life sexuality: The need to integrate biological, psychological, and social perspectives*, SIECUS Report, vol 27, no 3, pp 3-7.

Spence, S.H. (1992) 'Psychosexual dysfunction in the elderly', *Behaviour Change*, vol 9, pp 55-64.

VanEvery, J. (1996) 'Heterosexuality and domestic life', in D. Richardson (ed) *Theorising heterosexuality*, Buckingham: Open University Press, pp 39-54.

Vasil, L. and Wass, H. (1993) 'Portrayal of the elderly in the media: a literature review and implications for educational gerontologists', *Educational Gerontology*, vol 19, pp 71-85.

Wakeford, N. (2000) 'Cyberqueer', in D. Bell and B.M. Kennedy (eds) *The cybercultures reader*, New York, NY: Routledge, pp 403-15.

Walters, K.L. and Simon, J.M. (1993) 'Lesbian and gay male group identity attitudes and self-esteem: implications for counselling', *Journal of Counselling Psychology*, vol 40, no 91, pp 94-9.

Weiss, J. (2001) 'The gender caste system: identity, privacy and heteronormativity', *Law & Sexuality*, vol 10, pp 123-86.

Yee, D. (2002) 'The most urgent issues for practitioners and policy makers', *Generations*, vol 26, no 3, pp 1-3.

Section III:
Migration and otherness

NINE

Making sense of the construct of successful ageing: the migrant experience

Sandra Torres

Key points

- Research on international migrants' understandings of successful ageing shows that ideas about what it means to age well are just as processual as the strategies that elders use to guarantee a good old age.
- The process of international migration could challenge the understandings of successful ageing that people uphold.
- The state of being in-between cultures that this process presupposes offers a fruitful point of departure for theory formulation and development in social gerontology.
- Social gerontological research on international migrants is relevant beyond the scope of ethno-gerontology and the planning and provision of elderly care services that cater to these elders' needs.

Key readings

Castles, S. and Miller, M.J. (1998) *The age of migration: International population movements in the modern world*, London: Macmillan Press.

Keith, J., Fry, C.L., Glascock, A.P., Ikels, C., Dickerson-Putman, J., Harpending, H.C. and Draper, P. (1994) *The ageing experience: Diversity and commonality across cultures*, Thousand Oaks, CA: Sage Publications.

Sokolovsky, J. (ed) (1997) *The cultural context of ageing: Worldwide perspectives*, Westport, CT: Bergin and Garvey.

'Transnationalism', *Ethnic and Racial Studies*, vol 22, no 2 (Special Issue).

Introduction

This chapter addresses the state of theoretical affairs of research concerned with one of gerontology's most debated constructs; that is, successful ageing. Hereby, it is argued that much could be learned if we were to treat international migrants as sources of theoretically fruitful information about the way in which understandings of successful ageing are shaped and reformulated through the lifecourse. This argument, however, is not a new one since I have been trying to raise social gerontology's awareness of the unexplored potential embedded in studying international migrant populations ever since it dawned to me that theory development in social gerontology was often a native (not to mention western-only) endeavour. The sections that follow will be, to a certain extent, a reiteration of what has been briefly argued elsewhere (Torres, 1998, 2001a, 2003c), namely that the migrant experience and the destabilisation of lifecourse continuity inherent to it offer interesting angles for theory building in social gerontology.

The argument that will be put forth is not exclusively theoretical, however. Empirical illustrations on the challenges that the process of migration poses to the way in which understandings of successful ageing are shaped will be used to show that the international migrant experience offers a relatively unexplored yet fruitful point of departure for social gerontological research. However, before these areas can be explored it seems necessary to highlight what makes the migrant experience unique and how I came to regard elders with such backgrounds as potential sources of information about how notions of successful ageing are constructed through the lifecourse.

International migration and the hybridity of the migrant experience

International migrants constitute, by virtue of their sheer numbers, a population to be reckoned with in the globalised era in which we are living. This is the case because over the past half a century we have witnessed the intensification and globalisation of international migration movements (Castles, 1998) and the various implications these have had for both societies and individuals across the world. Castles and Miller (1998, p 5) have asserted, for example, that "there can be few people in either industrial countries or less developed countries today who do not have personal experience of migration and its effects". This is the case because:

> International migration is hardly ever a simple individual action in which a person decides to move in search of better life-chances, pulls up his or her roots in the place of origin and quickly becomes assimilated in the new country. Much more often migration and settlement is a long-drawn-out process, which will be played out for the rest of the migrant's life, and affect subsequent generations too. (Castles and Miller, 1998, p 19)

Most of us associate, therefore, the act of migrating to a foreign country with the leaving behind of the social, cultural and environmental contexts that have given meaning to one's life. International migrants are therefore often assumed to encounter new social, cultural and environmental contexts that must be understood. This combination of uprooting and new challenges has been primarily thought to be concomitant with various losses and difficulties (Weeks and Cuellar, 1983; Gelfand, 1989; Angel and Angel, 1992; Torres, 2002), even though there is also ample research that has attested to the numerous possibilities that the process of international migration can bring (for example, Moghaddam et al, 1987; Brady 1989; Ahmadi and Tornstam, 1996).

The extent to which the impact of the migratory process is characterised by losses and difficulties is thought to be partially contingent upon the age factor. In comparison to those who migrate early in life, late-in-life migrants are believed to be unable smoothly to incorporate new ways, norms and values in their behavioural repertoire (Gelfand, 1989). Hence "the adjustment to a new culture is more difficult for older immigrants than it is for younger ones" (Gelfand, 1994, p 39). Angel and Angel (1992) have also studied the difficulties that older migrants experience. Their conclusion is that migration in later life can potentially sever a person's social networks of affiliations indefinitely. On a similar note, Weeks and Cuellar (1983) have found that recent older immigrants are more isolated than elders with other migrant backgrounds, followers of children being among the most isolated in spite of their strong kinship ties. Similar findings have been reported by Moon and Pearl (1991) among elderly Korean immigrants to the US, by Die and Seelbach (1988) among elderly Vietnamese immigrants to the US, and by Tran (1991), who found that older Indochinese refugees to the US have a poorer sense of adjustment than their younger counterparts. Against the backdrop that such research results offer, it is interesting to note that "gerontological research has tended to play down the significance of migration and large-scale population movements for the ageing process" (Blakemore, 1999, p 763). The fact that the migratory process is mostly characterised by inevitable confrontation with various demands for different kinds of change is an issue that is also often underplayed by the social gerontological research that focuses on migrant elders.

The demands posed by the process of international migration concern most spheres of life; from the easily tangible and behaviour-related (such as an immigrant's networks of affiliations, preferred lifestyle, ways, customary norms and everyday routines) to the not so equally discernible (such as the culture and values that shape the way in which these migrants make sense of their surroundings). The process of migration is therefore a trying one, not only because of the various challenges it poses to migrants' behavioural repertoires, but also because it questions the very essence that gives their preferred behavioural patterns their meaning. In light of this, I have elsewhere argued (Torres, 1998, 2001b) that international migrants are bound to question not only the ways in which they approach life, but also the ways in which they understand all of life's spheres. This is the case because of the state of being in-between cultures that the migratory process presupposes and the hybridity of cultural values, perspectives and ways of thinking to which international migrants are unavoidably exposed.

With regard to this hybridity, it must be mentioned that our understanding of what it means to be a migrant elder is being challenged in the globalised era in which we live (Torres, 2004b: forthcoming). This is the case not only because the volume of international migration movements has increased through globalisation, but also because improvements in communication and transportation systems have allowed resourceful international migrants to maintain transnational social ties and to stay in contact with their countries of origin in ways that were not at all possible before (Kivisto, 2001). The transnationality of the contemporary migrant experience means that some migrants are being constantly influenced by an array of cultural values, attitudes and understandings that might not always be compatible with one another. Most international migration and ethnic relations researchers agree, therefore, with the assertion that:

> transnational social ties may work against melting into the majority core – predicted by classical assimilation theories – thus leading to more cultural autonomy and even cultural hybrid identities. (Faist, 2000, p 190)

It is this hybridity that makes the lifecourses of international migrants interesting. With regard to this, Nederveen-Pieterse (1994, p 180) has argued that "hybridisation is a contribution to a sociology of the in-between, a sociology from the interstices". My contention is that the same could be said for social gerontology. The theoretical and empirical potential that is inherently embedded in the international migrant experience is a fruitful source of information about the way in which the ageing process is experienced and understood. One reason for this is that a migrant's lifecourse is not characterised by the kind of continuity and stability through time that most social gerontological theory takes for granted (Blakemore, 1999). As Phillipson (2002, p 8) has asserted:

> The experience of migrants is invariably one of discontinuity rather than continuity over the life course. This will inevitably have implications for adjustment in middle and late life and may require some re-thinking and re-assessment of theoretical models in gerontology which often assume a measure of linear development through the life course.

On the basis of this assertion, it seems appropriate to exemplify how the continuity and stability paradigm operates through an abridged presentation of the state of affairs in research on successful ageing, since it is on the basis of that debate that the decision to explore the international migrant experience was made.

Successful ageing: a construct and its various meanings

The construct of successful ageing is a highly debated one within social gerontology (Thomas and Chambers, 1989; Scheidt et al, 1999; Torres, 2001a). This is the case because the adjective successful implies "a contest in which there are winners and losers" and this makes most social gerontologists ill at ease (Strawbridge et al, 2002, p 728). The fact that there can never be, as Pahl (1995) has asserted, a universalistic approach to success criteria complicates matters further, as does the acknowledgement that it is inherently problematic to depart from a construct that is such a blatant "imposition of the Western template" (Thomas and Chambers, 1989, p 199). In spite of this, ideas of what it means to age well permeate most gerontological practice and have relevance to most social gerontological research and work. They can also, at times, be used as guidelines in the formulation of social policy for the elderly population.

Conceptualisations of what it means to age well are, in other words, at the very core of our discipline. This might be the reason why most gerontologists seem to find it difficult to disregard the ongoing debate on understandings and strategies for a good old age, even though we have yet to agree on how to refer to understandings of and/or strategies for successful ageing. Some talk, for example, of managing the process of ageing successfully (Baltes and Carstensen, 1996; Rowe and Khan, 1997), while others prefer to speak of ageing well (Herzog and House, 1991); productively (Riley and Riley, 1994); healthily (La Croix et al, 1997); and/or to speak of a good old age, as Fry et al do (1997).

With reference to the study of ageing and the advancements that have been made within the gerontological realm to which successful ageing studies belong, it must be brought to mind that old age was once believed to be a precarious stage characterised by various physiological, psychological and social challenges. The underlying assumption at that time was that for successful ageing to be ensured, we needed to cope with these challenges. Numerous gerontological understandings of the state of successful ageing were thought to be concordant with this stage-like understanding of the process of growing into old age. Among these were understandings of successful ageing that stressed activity (Havighurst et al, 1968); autonomy (Rowe and Kahn, 1987): tolerance, optimism and courage (Keith et al, 1990); capacity for self-care (Days, 1991); coping strategies aimed at the maintenance of a positive outlook (Fisher, 1992); the reaching of one's potential (Gibson, 1995); generativity (Fisher, 1995); the avoidance of disease, the maintenance of high physical and cognitive functioning and an active social life (Rowe and Kahn, 1997); and being happy, remaining hopeful, and developing our sense of self and our connections with others (Fisher and Specht, 1999). According to Baltes and Carstensen (1996), this first phase of the gerontological debate regarding successful ageing was, in other words, characterised by the belief that ageing was one of life's final stages, and by the state-oriented approach that seems to have been concomitant with that belief.

It was in the 1990s that lifespan gerontologists started to question social gerontology's state-like understanding of successful ageing. Through the process-oriented approach that is often characteristic of their work, they managed to shift the focus of gerontology from the 'outcome or the what' of successful ageing (the state-oriented approach) to the 'strategies or the how' of a successful old age (the process-oriented approach) (Baltes and Baltes, 1990; Featherman,

1992; Baltes, 1993; Abraham and Hansson, 1995; Steverink et al, 1998). Examples of the latter can be found in the work of Brandtstädter and Renner (1990), who advocate an understanding of successful ageing characterised by a gradual shift in coping strategies. This shift guarantees elders their well-being and the experience of life satisfaction in the midst of the various challenges that ageing poses. The process-like approach has also been associated with the development of a planning orientation to problem solving (Featherman, 1992); with the concept of adaptive competence (Featherman, 1992; Featherman et al, 1990); and with the continuous attainment of goals (Steverink et al, 1998). Finally, there is the selection, optimisation and compensation (SOC) model for the process of successful ageing first proposed by Baltes and Baltes in 1990, which is the process-oriented approach to successful ageing that has received the most attention over the past decade (see, for example, Baltes, 1993; Baltes and Carstensen, 1996).

With regard to the SOC model, it can be mentioned that among the arguments utilised by the Baltes and Baltes and their associates in the launching of the process-oriented approach to successful ageing that their SOC model implies was the fact that the gerontological conception of successful ageing had been normative and that ageing had usually been regarded in an either/or fashion (either as decline or as growth). It was because of this that Baltes and Carstensen (1996) argued that the primary focus on outcomes and the persistent disregard for fluidity in old age was a hinder to gerontologists' understanding of successful ageing. According to them, the shift in focus that was taking place – from having been exclusively concentrated on the 'what' (or, *the outcome*) to becoming interested in the 'how' (or, *the process*) as well – was necessary for the furthering of gerontologists' understanding of the construct in question and for the tackling of the lack of fluidity that was characteristic of understandings of successful ageing at that time.

Making sense of what it means to age well in the context of migration

It was on the basis of the anticipated fruitfulness of studying understandings and strategies for ageing in a context that had the potential to bring the crystallisation of lifecourse fluidity to the fore that I set out to make a preliminary test of a culturally relevant theoretical framework for the study of successful ageing (Torres, 1999, 2001a, 2003b) through vignette-based interviews (Torres, 2003a) with 30 Iranian immigrants to Sweden. These were conducted in order to tap into the manner in which international migrants make sense of the construct of successful ageing by addressing four different areas: nature, activity, time and relationships. Another of the project objectives was to explore how the migratory process challenges the way in which notions of successful ageing are shaped through the lifecourse.

Summarily speaking, the results gathered in this study attest to an enormous variety when it comes to the way in which the respondents' notions of ageing well were shaped and the manner in which these seem to have changed through the lifecourse. Different understandings of successful ageing besides those that are often taken for granted in the gerontological literature were also brought to the fore in this project. With regard to the being in-between that the migratory process presupposes, it became clear that international migration does seem to challenge people's understandings of successful ageing. Of interest in this respect is that it was mostly those that upheld an understanding that they deemed to be different from what they regarded as typical of their host culture's understandings that reported having felt compelled to reformulate the approach they deemed to be conducive to ageing well after migration (Torres, 2001a, 2001b, 2002).

In regard to the manner in which one relates to physiological decline, some of the respondents claimed, for example, to have abandoned their surrendering perspective on ageing for a more master-oriented approach to ageing well once they settled in Sweden. According to those that claimed to have done so, surrendering to nature is the norm in their country of origin, which is why they used to think that in order to age well one needs to give up once physiological decline becomes a fact. After having lived in a society that does not necessarily equate successful ageing with resignation to the inevitability of physiological decline, these respondents claimed to have abandoned their surrendering approach to successful ageing in favour of the mastering approach, which they deemed to be more characteristic of their new surroundings. Of interest in this regard is that, when explaining why this change had occurred, some alluded to the fact that scientific advancements are more readily available in Sweden than in Iran. According to them, this means that one is constantly surrounded by a master-nature mentality, which takes for granted that scientific knowledge gives mankind some power over Mother Nature. That mentality seems to have made some respondents reconsider the kind of resignation that they claim to be typical of Iranian ways of thinking when it comes to mankind's power over Mother Nature, natural catastrophes and/or the various debilitating changes that ageing bodies are assumed to undergo. After a few years in a society that does not seem to equate ageing well with surrendering, these respondents claim to have started to understand not only that the ageing body can be 'handled', but also that resignation to physiological decline is not good for one's psychological well-being.

Similar changes were also reported when it came to ideas regarding activity and time. Some of the respondents claimed that the Iranian culture was filled with numerous unspoken rules of propriety in old age. According to most of the respondents interviewed in this project, the Iranian approach to ageing well equates the process of growing older with becoming dignified. This, in turn, was assumed to equate with following all the conventions for how old people ought to behave. A busy schedule and a future-oriented outlook in old age are apparently not really appropriate ways to tackle the later stages of life. To age successfully in Iran is therefore the same as slowing down and living a much quieter, disengaged and passive life than that lived as a younger adult.

The way in which the ageing process seems to be tackled by most elderly Swedes, therefore, appeared quite strange to some of the respondents when they first settled in the host society they now regard as home. According to the respondents, Swedish elders did not seem to follow a specific dress code, nor did they seem to have a passive lifestyle. In fact, some of the respondents reported being in awe when they realised that Swedish elders' lifestyles resembled the busy lifestyles that were deemed to be exclusively reserved for younger generations in Iran. After a few years, some of the respondents indicated having abandoned their being and past-orientated understandings of successful ageing for the doing and either the present or the future orientation that they deemed more typical of Swedes' notions of ageing well. In regard to this, it must be mentioned that some talked about Sweden's restriction-free approach to ageing well as liberating and as something that had led them to look forward to old age. Some mentioned also that old age is synonymous with the 'waiting for death' period in their country of origin, which is why they found it alluring to see that elderly Swedes continued to look forward and to plan for the future.

Even the importance accorded to having autonomy in old age changed in the context of migration. The vast majority of the respondents claimed to have taken for granted that ageing well was synonymous with dependence upon the younger generation prior to migration. To age successfully was, for most of them, a question of having their own adult children take care of them. The idea that successful ageing is synonymous with the kind of autonomy that is often taken for granted in the social gerontological literature was foreign to most of the respondents before they settled in Sweden. However, most of them indicated that they had started to change the manner in which they thought about the relationship between familial obligations and successful ageing once they had become established in their host society. Some of them did so because they had ideologically changed the way they conceived of a successful old age (meaning that some claimed to have started to equate autonomy – instead of dependency – with successful ageing after having seen how elderly Swedes lived), while others reported having changed their understandings of successful ageing for more pragmatic reasons (as with those that mentioned that their children were being socialised in Sweden and they could not really expect to be cared for by them in their old age). Regardless of which kind of change the respondents alluded to, it was clear that the migratory process and the exposure to different cultural values that this presupposes had challenged what they thought constitutes a successful old age.

It is perhaps necessary to finish this section by briefly addressing some of the general trends that were found in this project. First, it seems necessary to mention that intra-cultural variation was found not only in regard to the understandings of successful ageing that the respondents claimed to have upheld prior to migration, but also in terms of the notions of ageing well that they said they held at present. The ways in which they made sense of their host culture showed considerable variation as well. Thus, although there was much more consensus regarding what they assumed to be typical of their culture of origin, they did not seem to agree about what they regarded as typical of their host culture. Despite of this, all the respondents who claimed to have abandoned the understandings of successful ageing they upheld prior to migration in favour of a more context-appropriate understanding did so on the basis of what they deemed to be typical Iranian and Swedish notions of what it means to age well. One can claim, therefore, that the hybridity discussed earlier seems to have been experienced by these respondents. In one way or another, they all seem to have felt compelled to handle the being in-between cultures that the migratory process presupposes. Of interest is also that some of the international migrants interviewed lived not only in-between cultures but also in-between different generations' notions of what it means to age well. This meant that although they had abandoned certain understandings of successful ageing in the context of migration, they still had to act in accordance with them when they took care of their elderly parents. Thus, although this study has only tackled how the process of international migration challenges understandings of successful ageing, it seems theoretically feasible that the context in question could also challenge the strategies for successful ageing that are used by international migrants.

The immigrant experience as a theoretically fruitful source of information

Most researchers working on successful ageing would probably agree that focusing on elders' actual strategies for successful ageing has indeed brought to the fore the heterogeneity of older people, the acceptance of multiple outcomes and the diversification of success standards that was lacking during the first phase of successful ageing studies. However, my own research on Iranian immigrants' understandings of successful ageing shows that the shift that was adamantly advocated (from studying understandings to focusing on strategies) is not the only way we could have tackled the lack of fluidity that was characteristic of the first phase of successful ageing studies alluded to earlier in this chapter. This is because there is at least one other context that has the theoretical potential of being conducive to the crystallisation of lifespan changes in the way in which successful ageing is understood. This is the context of international migration and the being in-between cultures that is characteristic of it. The results heretofore presented show that the dichotomy that successful ageing researchers seem to have been assuming (that is, that understandings of this construct are stable while strategies for successful ageing are fluid/processual) might not really be as applicable when it comes to international migrants.

Notions of what it means to age well are contextually determined, which is why a transition from one context to another has the potential to bring about the re-formulation of people's understandings of successful ageing. However, not all understandings are challenged in the migratory process. The data suggest that it is mostly those notions of successful ageing deemed to be ill fitting for the new context that are revised. Age upon migration also seems to play a role, since those who maintained understandings of successful ageing deemed to be incompatible with what was regarded as most typical of the new surroundings were those who had migrated late in life. While the sample was small for any conclusions to be drawn, the data show that the context of migration is theoretically profuse. The variation that was brought to the fore in this project points therefore to the fruitfulness of launching more successful ageing studies with migrant populations.

At the beginning of this chapter, I alluded to the fact that this is not the first time I have tried to raise awareness of the fact that gerontological research on migrant and minority populations is interesting at various levels, and not only the empirical. In this regard, it could anecdotally be mentioned that, although most of my work has tried to contribute to theory development, not a single one of the many conference papers I have presented over the years has been accepted for presentation in a 'mainstream' session in successful ageing. It may seem unnecessary to point this out, but the truth of the matter is that it is quite symptomatic of the way in which most social gerontologists relate to research that focuses on migrant and minority ageing. The impression one gets from this and other similar observations is that gerontological research on these populations is regarded as empirically interesting for those who cater to these elders' needs but not necessarily theoretically profuse in terms of mainstream gerontology. The results alluded to in the previous section about what the migrant experience has to offer points hopefully to the inadequateness of such an assumption. The intensification and globalisation of international migration movements and the transnational communities that these are creating mean also that the international migrant experience can no longer be relegated to the periphery of social gerontological knowledge (Torres, 2003c, 2004b: forthcoming).

In this respect, it must be acknowledged that others have also tried to bring international migrant research to the forefront of social gerontology. Blakemore (1999), for example, has tried to do so through his discussion regarding British social gerontology's lack of interest in exploring the relationship between migration and later life and its failure to acknowledge the various challenges that international migration poses to social care and elderly policy. Most recently, Phillipson (2002, p 8) has tried to draw our attention to transnational migration as a potentially interesting field for social gerontologists by stating that:

> through intensification of migration flows, the notion of what it means to grow old, when age begins, and normative behaviours for old age, will all show much wider variation in one society than has historically been the case.

The results presented in the previous section indicate that this might in fact be the case, since not only did the respondents in this study differ in the ways they thought about what successful ageing means, but they also had different ways of handling the notions of ageing well with which they were faced in their new surroundings. International migrants, however, remain relatively peripheral to theory development within social gerontology at this point in time. This is probably the case for a variety of reasons – from the fact that they constitute the 'other' (Torres, 2004a and b: forthcoming) in social gerontology to the fact that theory development in our field presupposes a linear development that does not really accommodate their reality. On the basis of the data briefly alluded to heretofore, it seems counterproductive to continue to attempt to advance theory exclusively on the basis of the linear lifecourse of natives. The discontinuity that characterises the lifecourse of international migrants is a theoretically profuse angle from which social gerontological research could be launched, since numerous unexpected trends are brought to the fore when we concentrate on the challenges that international migrants face on a daily basis as they revise their points of departure and adapt to their new surroundings. In globalised times such as ours, it therefore seems wasteful to continue to regard the migrant experience as an ethno-gerontological only affair. The key to the expansion of our gerontological imagination may lay in our ability to explore the hybridity that is characteristic of the international migrant experience. My contention, therefore, is that much could be learned if we were to regard these elders as potential protagonists in research that aims for theory formulation and development; a role that seems so far to have been reserved for native elders. In the words of Nederveen-Pieterse (1994), time has come for us to venture into a social gerontology of the in-between.

References

Abraham, J.D. and Hansson, R.O. (1995) 'Successful aging at work: an applied study of selection, optimization, and compensation through impression management', *Journal of Gerontology: Psychological Sciences*, vol 50B, no 2, pp 94-103.

Ahmadi, F. and Tornstam, L. (1996) 'The old flying Dutchmen: shuttling immigrants with double assets', *Journal of Aging and Identity*, vol 1, no 3, pp 191-210.

Angel, J.L. and Angel R.J. (1992) 'Age at migration, social connections, and well being among elderly Hispanics', *Journal of Aging and Health*, vol 4, no 4, pp 480-99.

Baltes, M.M. and Carstensen, L.L. (1996) 'The process of successful aging', *Ageing and Society*, vol 16, pp 397-422.

Baltes, P.B. (1993) 'The aging mind: potential and limits', *The Gerontologist*, vol 33, no 5, pp 580-94.

Baltes, P.B. and Baltes, M.M. (1990) 'Psychological perspectives on successful aging: the model of selective optimization with compensation', in P.B. Baltes and M.M. Baltes (eds) *Successful aging: Perspectives from the behavioral sciences*, New York, NY: Cambridge University Press, pp 1-34.

Blakemore, K. (1999) 'International migration in later life: social care and policy implications', *Ageing and Society*, vol 19, no 6, pp 761-74.

Brady, P. (1989) *Americans in Sweden: An assimilation study*, Uppsala: Department of Sociology, Uppsala University.

Brandtstädter, J. and Renner, G. (1990) 'Tenacious goal pursuit and flexible goal adjustment: explication and age-related analysis of assimilative and accommodative strategies for coping', *Psychology and Aging*, vol 5, no 1, pp 58-67.

Castles, S. (1998) 'Globalization and migration: some pressing contradictions', *International Social Science Journal*, vol 156, pp 179-86.

Castles, S. and Miller, M.J. (1998) *The age of migration: International population movements in the modern world*, London: Macmillan Press.

Days, A.T. (1991) *Remarkable survivors: Insights into successful aging among women*, Washington, DC: Urban Institute Press.

Die, A.H. and Seelbach, W.C. (1988) 'Problems, sources of assistance and knowledge of services among elderly Vietnamese immigrants', *The Gerontologist*, vol 28, no 4, pp 448-51.

Faist, T. (2000) 'Transnationalization in international migration: implications for the study of citizenship and culture', *Ethnic and Racial Studies*, vol 23, no 2, pp 189-222.

Featherman, D.L. (1992) 'Development of reserves for adaptation in old age: personal and societal agendas', in N.E. Cutler, D.W. Gregg and M.P. Lawton (eds) *Aging, money and life satisfaction: Aspects of financial social gerontology*, New York, NY: Springer, pp 135-68.

Featherman, D.L., Smith, J. and Peterson, J.G. (1990) 'Successful aging in a post-retired society', in P.B. Baltes and M.M. Baltes (eds) *Successful aging: Perspectives from the behavioral sciences*, New York, NY: Cambridge University Press, pp 50-93.

Fisher, B.J. (1992) 'Successful aging and life satisfaction: a pilot study for conceptual clarification', *Journal of Aging Studies*, vol 6, no 2, pp 191-202.

Fisher, B.J. (1995) 'Successful aging, life satisfaction and generativity in later life', *International Journal of Aging and Human Development*, vol 41, 3, pp 239-50.

Fisher, B.J. and Specht, D.K. (1999) 'Successful aging and creativity in later life', *Journal of Aging Studies*, vol 13, no 4, pp 457-72.

Fry, C.L., Dickerson-Putman, J., Draper, P., Ikels, C., Keith, J., Glascock, A. and Harpending, H.C. (1997) 'Culture and the meaning of a good old age', in J. Sokolovsky (ed) *The cultural context of ageing: Worldwide perspectives* (2nd edn), Westport, CT: Bergin and Garvey, pp 99-123.

Gelfand, D.E. (1989) 'Immigration, aging, and international relationships', *The Gerontologist*, vol 29, no 3, pp 366-71.

Gelfand, D.E. (1994) *Aging and ethnicity*, New York, NY: Springer.

Gibson, R.C. (1995) 'Promoting successful and productive aging in minority populations', in L.A. Bond, S.J. Cutler and A. Grams (eds) *Promoting successful and productive aging*, Thousand Oaks, CA: Sage Publications, pp 279-88.

Havighurst, R.J., Neugarten, B.L. and Tobin, S.S. (1968) 'Disengagement and patterns of aging', in B.L. Neugarten (ed) *Middle age and aging: A reader in social psychology*, Chicago, IL: University of Chicago Press, pp 161-72.

Herzog, A.R. and House, J.S. (1991) 'Productive activities and aging well', *Generations*, Winter, pp 49-54.

Keith, J., Fry, C.L. and Ikels, C. (1990) 'Community as context for successful aging', in J. Sokolovsky (ed) *The cultural context of aging: Worldwide perspectives*, Westport, CT: Bergin and Garvey Publishers, pp 245-61.

Kivisto, P. (2001) 'Theorizing transnational immigration: a critical review of current efforts', *Ethnic and Racial Studies*, vol 24, no 4, pp 549-77.

La Croix, A.Z., Newton, K.M., Leveille, S.G. and Wallace, J. (1997) 'Healthy aging: a women's issue', *Western Journal of Medicine*, vol 67, pp 220-32.

Moghaddam, F.M., Taylor, D. and Lalonde, R.N. (1987) 'Individualistic and collective integration strategies among Iranians in Canada', *International Journal of Psychology*, vol 22, pp 301-13.

Moon, J.H. and Pearl, J. (1991) 'Alienation of elderly Korean American immigrants as related to place of residence, gender, age, years of education, time in the US, living with or without children and living with or without spouse', *International Journal of Aging and Human Development*, vol 32, no 2, pp 115-24.

Nederveen-Pieterse, J. (1994) 'Globalization as hybridization', *International Sociology*, vol 9, no 2, pp 161-84.

Pahl, R. (1995) *After success: Fin-de-siècle anxiety and identity*, Cambridge: Polity Press.

Phillipson, C. (2002) *Transnational communities, migration and changing identities in later life*, Paper presented at the 34th EBSSRS Symposium on Ageing and Diversity, Bergen, 29-31 August.

Riley, J.W. and Riley, M.W. (1994) 'Beyond productive aging: changing lives and social structure', *Ageing International*, June, pp 15-19.

Rowe, J.W. and Kahn, R.L. (1987) 'Human aging: usual and successful', *Science*, vol 237, pp 143-9.

Rowe, J.W. and Kahn, R.L. (1997) 'Successful aging', *The Gerontologist*, vol 37, no 4, pp 433-40.

Scheidt, R.J., Humphreys, D.R. and Yorgason, J.B. (1999) 'Successful aging: what is not to like', *The Journal of Applied Social Gerontology*, vol 18, no 3, pp 277-82.

Steverink, N., Lindenberg, S. and Ormel, J. (1998) 'Toward understanding successful ageing: pattterned change in resources and goals', *Ageing and Society*, vol 18, no 4, pp 441-67.

Strawbridge, W.J., Wallhagen, M.I. and Cohen, R.D. (2002) 'Successful aging and well-being: self rated compared to Rowe and Khan', *The Gerontologist*, vol 42, no 6, pp 727-33.

Thomas, L.E. and Chambers, K.O. (1989) 'Successful aging among elderly men in England and India: a phenomenological comparison', in L.E. Thomas (ed) *Research on adulthood and ageing: The human science approach*, New York, NY: SUNY Press, pp 183-203.

Torres, S. (1998) *Broadening social gerontology's understanding of successful aging by focusing on the context of migration*, Paper presented at the 14th Nordic Congress on Social Gerontology, Trondheim, 24-27 May.

Torres, S. (1999) 'A culturally-relevant theoretical framework for the study of successful ageing', *Ageing and Society*, vol 19, no 1, pp 33-51.

Torres, S. (2001a) *Understanding successful aging: Cultural and migratory perspectives*, Uppsala: Department of Sociology, Uppsala University.

Torres, S. (2001b) 'Understandings of successful ageing in the context of migration: the case of Iranian immigrants to Sweden', *Ageing and Society*, vol 21, no 3, pp 333-55.

Torres, S. (2002) 'Relational values and ideas regarding successful aging', *Journal of Comparative Family Studies*, vol 33, no 3, pp 417-31.

Torres, S. (2003a) 'Exploring cross-cultural issues through vignettes: the pros and cons of this data collection method', in K. Lumme-Sandt, J. Outi and N. Mäkinen (eds) *The cultural in gerontology: Challenges, approaches and methods*, Programme and proceedings for the 4th International Symposium on Cultural Gerontology, Tampere, 24-27 May, pp 19-29.

Torres, S. (2003b) 'A preliminary empirical test of the culturally-relevant theoretical framework for the study of successful aging', *Journal of Cross-Cultural Gerontology*, vol 18, pp 73-91.

Torres, S. (2003c) 'Ageing in the midst of globalization: the implications of cultural values for understandings of ageing well', Paper presented at the European Study of Adult Well-Being (ESAW), 'Ageing Well in Europe' Seminar, Lund University.

Torres, S. (2004a: forthcoming) 'Elderly immigrants in Sweden: otherness under construction (Scheduled to appear in an upcoming special issue on migration and aging', *Journal of Ethnic and Migration Studies.*

Torres, S. (2004b: forthcoming) 'Culture, migration and inequality in globalized times: challenges to ethno- and anthropogerontology', in J. Baars, D. Dannefer, C. Phillipson and A. Walker (eds) *Ageing, globalization and inequality: The new critical gerontology*, New York, NY: Baywood.

Tran, T.V. (1991) 'Family living arrangements and social adjustment among three ethnic groups of elderly Indochinese refugees', *International Journal of Aging and Human Development*, vol 32, no 2, pp 91-102.

Weeks, J. and Cuellar, L. (1983) 'Isolation of older persons: the influence of immigration and length of residence', *Research on Aging*, vol 5, no 3, pp 369-88.

TEN

Older foreign migrants in Europe: multiple pathways and welfare positions

Tony Warnes

Key points

- Two groups of older migrants are increasing in number throughout western Europe: labour migrants who moved from the 1950s from southern Europe and other continents to the north, and affluent northern Europeans who move in the 'third age' for retirement to the south.
- There are other substantial groups of older migrants, such as the labour migrants who return to their native countries, as in Ireland, southern Europe and rural areas throughout, and those who move for 'family-joining' reasons in complex interchanges between all countries.
- 'Older migrants' are immensely diverse, but among them are some of the most deprived and socially excluded older people in Europe, as well as many who are pursuing innovative, positive approaches to their own old age. Few of the migrant populations have been studied by social gerontologists.
- A high level of international migration is an inevitable consequence of recent technological changes in communications and transport technologies and of the importance that European governments place on continued economic growth and the consequent labour recruitment policies. There should be more recognition of the valuable economic roles that migrants play, and more sympathetic and supportive policies for those who become sick or frail.

Key readings

Ackers, L. and Dwyer, P. (2002) *Senior citizenship? Retirement, migration and welfare in the European Union*, Bristol: The Policy Press.

King, R., Warnes, A.M. and Williams, A.M. (2000) *Sunset lives: British retirement migration to the Mediterranean*, Oxford: Berg.

O'Reilly, K. (2000) *The British on the Costa del Sol: Trans-national identities and local communities*, London: Routledge.

Warnes, A., Friedrich, K., Kellaher, L. and Torres, S. (eds) (2004) Older migrants in Europe, *Ageing and Society*, vol 24, no 3 (Special Issue), pp 307-476.

Introduction

During the past few years, researchers, clinicians and welfare professionals throughout Europe have become increasingly aware that the older population is becoming ethnically and culturally more diverse, and that among the minority ethnic and recent immigrant groups there are many with exceptional health and social problems. Both 'ageing' and 'international migration' have been studied intensively, but rarely have the interactions between the two socio-demographic processes been examined. Most gerontologists are familiar with analyses of population ageing, but few are well read in the vast international migration literature. There are innumerable theoretical formulations: for a valuable overview, see Petersen (1975, pp 279-334), and for recent work, see Castles and Miller (2003) and Joppke and Morawaska (2003). There is of course nothing new about large and sustained flows of international migration. From early in the 19th century, Europe's experience was mainly to send people to other continents, not to receive migrants. Only in the past half century has the net movement reversed, and since the 1980s another radical change has occurred: Greece, southern Italy, Spain and Portugal, which through most of the 20th century were regions of rural depopulation and emigration to northern European countries, the Americas and Australia, have become regions of immigration from Eastern Europe and other continents (King, 2002; Fonseca et al, 2002).

At the same time, among 'older migrants' are an increasing number of affluent northern Europeans pursuing positive approaches to old age through innovative residential strategies, including moving their permanent homes to southern Europe, or making seasonal moves between two or more homes. Whether deprived or privileged, by moving to a country in which they are not citizens or long-term residents, all migrants compromise their eligibility to state-funded, subsidised or managed services and have difficulties in accessing services – they inevitably have less knowledge of services in a foreign than in their home country and, for most, language differences are a barrier. This chapter synthesises the scarce evidence on the growth and characteristics of 'older migrants' across western Europe, explains why their number is likely to increase substantially in the coming decades, and argues that both policy makers and researchers should give more attention both to their diverse circumstances and to their disentitlement from many benefits and services that are offered to nationals and to those with continuous employment and residence records in the country.

The political and economic background

Europeans increasingly take the continent's contemporary political economy for granted. More and more assume that democratic governments must prevail, and that their executives are pursuing collective or communitarian goals while 'checked and balanced' by multi-party legislatures, national and international courts, and (if haphazardly) public opinion through regular elections and the media. These conditions are not yet fully realised in eastern Europe, but gross departures from the ideals are deemed not only tragic but also aberrant, as in the Balkans during the 1990s. In northern Europe, even minor deviations are internationally disparaged, as with Italian Prime Minister Berlusconi's self-serving decrees that have restricted magistrates' powers to seek financial information (about his business transactions) from foreign banks (Willan, 2001; Carlin, 2004). Compared with the 1930s, or even the early 1960s, Europe's contemporary governance is remarkably faithful to liberal democratic principles.

Two ambitions underlie the apparently secure establishment of progressive democracies: the determination to end destructive conflicts among Europe's states, and the strong desire for economic growth and more wealth. As neither ambition is new, other factors must have enabled their realisation during the second half of the 20th century. A full explanation is the concern of historians, but evident factors include the vision of the founders of the EC and its success, America's policing of European governance and macroeconomic management, the 'Cold War', the race for economic growth between Europe and the US and Japan, and European electorates' decreased enthusiasm for utopian ideologies and increased support for the political parties they believe are most likely to raise prosperity and welfare.

Sustained economic growth has partly been responsible for, and has certainly interacted with, two major developments in Europe's population: 'demographic ageing' and increased immigration and cultural diversity. Both processes are symptoms of more fundamental socioeconomic trends. 'Population ageing' to date has primarily come about through lowered fertility, itself the outcome of the mass adoption of new contraceptives by young adults seeking improved life chances and a better 'quality of life'. The aspiration to 'improve oneself in material respects' and for an improved quality of life have also stimulated international migration, but its causes are multiple and complex. Improved standards of living in much of Europe have led to rising levels of educational and work skills, and these in turn to shortages of menial, low-wage labour. To sustain national competitiveness and to restrain rising labour costs, the pragmatic policy response throughout the EU (and in North America and Australia, but not Japan) has been to encourage immigration (if not always overtly). At the beginning, in the 1950s, some policy makers assumed that the incoming unskilled labourers would stay for limited terms and eventually return to their countries of origin. While the *gastarbeiter* approach prevailed for several decades in Germany and with less rigour in Switzerland, Austria and Belgium, elsewhere it soon evaporated as the permanence of the labour shortages became apparent. Gradually, it came to be accepted that workers have families, their children require schools, and a civilised country should promote the integration of the migrant workers into the national society and its local communities.

The migration of young adults has implications for old age, because there are strong connections between people's lifetime 'activity space' – that is, where they have lived and visited often for education, training, work, their personal lives and recreation – and the places that they stay in or move to when they stop work (Warnes, 1992). Another important foundation of the growing number of older migrants, therefore, has been the internationalisation of leisure trips, work and education, yet another outcome of rising incomes, new aspirations, and advances in transport and communications technology. The growth of foreign holidays has been the main driver of increased 'amenity-seeking' migration from north to south in Europe, most particularly to the Spanish coasts and islands. It is apparent, then, that older international migrants in western Europe today include some of the most deprived and socially excluded, but also some of the most advantaged, resourceful and innovative among those exploring positive approaches to old age.

When the deep economic and social roots of increased international population mobility are recognised, two implications become clear. First, as the Secretary General of the UN recently reminded the European Parliament, increased immigration and cultural diversity is an inevitable consequence of the priority now given to economic growth (Annan, 2004). Second, the number of older people who have been international migrants and who are culturally different from the host population will undoubtedly increase during the coming decades. Given the valued economic role played by immigrants from other countries, there is a good case for more sympathetic and proactive attention to the problems and structured disadvantages that older migrants face.

Foreign migrants in Europe

Statistics on the foreign population and migrants are problematic for several reasons: 'entries' and 'exits' to and from a country are imperfectly recorded, there is considerable illegal migration, and the labelling of people from different countries and of different parentage is inconsistent. For example, France does not regard residents born in its overseas *départements* and resident in metropolitan France as foreigners, and some nations regard people born in the country of one or two foreign parents as themselves foreigners.

The total population of Europe in 1998 was around 810 million, and of these the recorded foreign population was 21 million, 2.6% of the total. Most of the foreign residents were in western European countries, with the highest concentrations in Luxembourg (35% of the population) and Switzerland (19%). Other countries with relatively high shares (around 9%) were Austria, Belgium and Germany (Haug et al, 2002). In the EU and European Free Trade Association (EFTA) countries in 1998, there were 19.8 million foreigners, of whom 12.9 million (65%) were Europeans. The largest foreign national groups continue to be from the southern European countries (Italy, Portugal, Spain and Greece) and Turkey, but there were also 3.1 million Africans and 2.2 million Asians. Germany has been the predominant destination for non-EU member state foreign nationals (Table 10.1). It is notable that, in recent decades, it is the southern European countries that have had the highest rates of growth of the foreign population.

Table 10.1: Foreign citizens in selected European countries (1980-2001)

	Thousands of foreign citizens				Annual change (%)	
	1980	1990	1998	2001	1980-90	1990-2001
Austria	283	456	737	754	4.9	4.7
Belgium	886	905	892	853	0.2	−0.5
France	3,714	3,608	3,260	a	−0.3	−1.1
Germany	4,453	5,242	7,320	7,297	1.6	3.1
Italy	299	781	1,250	1,465	10.1	5.9
Netherlands	521	692	662	668	2.9	−0.3
Spain	182	408	720	924	8.4	7.7
Sweden	422	484	500	477	1.4	−0.1
Switzerland	893	1,100	1,348	1,424	2.1	2.4
United Kingdom	1,601	1,875	2,207	2,460	1.6	2.5

Note: [a] No data: the growth rate in the far right column is for 1990-98. Available online at http://europa.eu.int/comm/eurostat/
Source: Eurostat, *Estadísticas Euro-CAN 2003*, Office des Publications Officielles des Communautés Européennes, Luxembourg 2003, Table 2.3

Age structure of the foreign populations

The are few figures on the age structure of migrant and foreign populations except in the north-western countries with 'continuous population registration'. A recent survey for the Council of Europe found that there are no data for Austria, France and Greece, and few for Iceland, Italy, Norway and Portugal, and that statements on long-term trends are possible only for Switzerland, Germany, Denmark, Greece, the Netherlands, Sweden and the UK. There are, however, sufficient national and comparative studies to enable broad generalisations (Warnes, 1996; Bolzman et al, 2001; Lie, 2002; Poulain and Perrin, 2002; Pérez, 2003).

The majority of labour migrants are young adults, and in the early decades of a mass migration the population has few older people and the average age is low. The pioneer 1950s and 1960s labour migrants are now entering old age and some of the flows have slowed. The result in many countries, as Belgian data show, is that the average age of the foreign population is increasing towards the national average (Figure 10.1). In most of western Europe, foreign immigrants are dominated by southern Europeans, north Africans and Turks, but the 'pioneer waves' of inter-continental migrants are also entering old age, such as Afro-Caribbeans and Indians in London and Latin Americans in Iberia. For the next two decades, it will be the younger elderly population (aged 60-74 years) that grows most quickly, as regional and city studies have shown (Simpson, 1997; Warnes, 1997, 2002; Spence, 2003). By the 2020s, there will be a rapid growth of the older population among migrants from more distant origins, particularly south and south-east Asia. Given the scarcity of Europe-wide data on older foreign migrants, for detailed information we turn to the unusually detailed Norwegian data.

Figure 10.1: The average age of nationals and foreigners in Belgium (1930-2000)

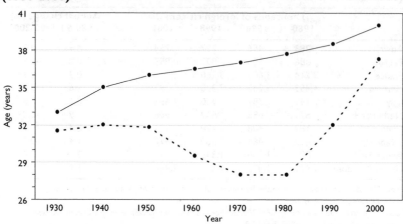

Source: Poulain and Perrin (2002, Figure 4.1)

Norway's foreign and immigrant residents

Norway's continuous population register provides an unusually detailed profile of migrants and the foreign population. On 1 January 2001, there were about 180,000 foreign citizens in the country and another 300,000 residents who had been born abroad – more than 30,000 of these had been adopted or born abroad of two Norwegian-born parents, and 23,000 had one Norwegian-born parent (Lie, 2002). At present, *Statistics Norway* defines the immigrant population as 'people with two foreign-born parents': in 2001, one sixth had been born in Norway. It has published valuable data on the post-1970 immigrants' origin countries and continents. Two features are apparent (and probably characteristic of other north-west European countries). The greatest change has been the very large increase in migrants from other continents besides North America and Australasia: the share of the total increased massively from 6% in 1970 to 51.5% in 2001. The other clear trend has been the substantial rise since 1989 in the number originating from eastern Europe: the share of the total increased from 9.8% in 1970 to 16.2% in 2001. The numbers of immigrants from other regions did not greatly decrease over the three decades, but because those from Asia and Africa (particularly) grew so strongly, the shares fell substantially; for example, from the Nordic countries from 45% in 1970 to 18% in 2001; from the rest of western Europe from 26% to 11%; and from North America and Australasia from 14% to 3% over the same period.

On average, the immigrants were younger than the general population of Norway in 2001, and most of those born in Norway of two foreign-born parents were still very young. The age structure of the foreign population had a different profile to that of the total Norwegian population (Figure 10.2). Only 10.5% (31,000 people) of the foreigners were aged 60+, compared with approximately 21.5% of the total population. The value of the population pyramid is its visual indication of the timing and relative scale of the increases in the near future of different age groups, although it should be remembered that population projections of migrant groups based entirely on 'cohort survival' (that is, the application of age–specific mortality rates to the current stock of people) are less reliable than for the general population. For one thing, the mortality of minority and migrant groups is sometimes significantly different from that of the general population. Another consideration is that both 'in' and 'out' migration can have substantial effects on a foreign population, through respectively 'family joining' and 'return' moves. Taking the immigrant population as a whole, however, it is apparent that by the 2020s there is likely to be a rapid increase of those entering old age (or passing 60 years of age). By extension, only from the late 2030s will the population of advanced old age (75+ years) show very high rates of growth.

The diversity of older migrants

The data from Norway show patterns that are corroborated in other countries not only by national sources but also by local censuses and surveys. Two older migrant populations are increasing rapidly in number in Europe. The most numerous are the millions of labour migrants who, from the 1950s onwards, moved either from south to north within Europe or into Europe, and subsequently have 'aged in place'. Many in the first waves were from the areas

Figure 10.2: The age structure of the immigrant and total populations of Norway (2001)

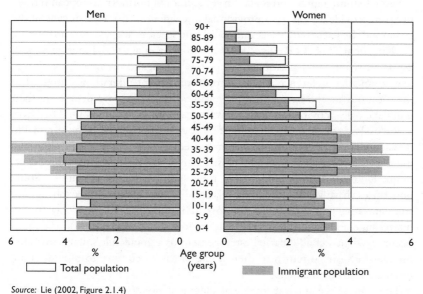

Source: Lie (2002, Figure 2.1.4)

of severe agricultural decline in southern Europe, while others came from regions of similarly constricted opportunities in north Africa and east Asia (in Germany's case, especially Turkey). By the 1960s, there were substantial flows from other continents, especially the Caribbean, the Indian subcontinent and south-east Asia. Many of the migrants had little education, and the majority entered low-skilled and low-paid manual work. In short, in comparison with the host populations, they have had a lifetime of disadvantage and deprivation, including poor healthcare and housing conditions, few opportunities to learn the local language, and very often the insults of cultural and racial discrimination.

The other rapidly expanding group are northern Europeans who, when aged in the 50s or 60s, permanently or seasonally migrate to southern Europe for retirement. Most are property owners, have occupational pensions, and worked and lived in the larger cities of north-west Europe. They finance their moves or 'residential circulation' by the sale of their high-value metropolitan homes, and move to improve the quality of their lives. A warmer climate that enables a more active, outdoor lifestyle is a strong draw. The rapid growth since the 1960s (at about 7% a year) of these 'amenity-seeking' southerly retirement migrations has been enabled by several technological, political and economic changes (Warnes, 2001). The improved accessibility to Mediterranean regions brought about by the jet plane and frequent, charter and low-cost scheduled services has been a prerequisite. It has enabled mass tourism, which both prompted investment in modern services and infrastructure, and enabled hundreds of thousands of northern Europeans to gain experience of visits and stays in southern European countries. Other technological changes, as in telecommunications, satellite and cable television, high-speed roads and retail banking, have also been important factors.

Several ethnographic and social survey studies of northern European retirees in Spain provide a basis for a provisional assessment of the kin contacts of the group and their access to health and social care services (for reviews and sources, see King et al, 2000; O'Reilly, 2000; Casado-Díaz et al, 2004; Rodríguez et al, 2004). Broadly, it is partnered couples who engage in 'amenity-seeking', 'environmental preference' or 'heliotropic' retirement migrations unrelated to the locations of children and other relatives, and, almost by definition, their mundane daily activities are little entwined with those of close kin. They have 'middle-class' (or more highly educated) social networks, with more non-kin contacts than in a 'working-class' (or less educated) network, and close and mutually supportive contacts with close relatives – but not proximate residence, frequent visits or great amounts of time spent in shared activities. Some nonetheless have very close family relationships, with substantial exchanges of strategic advice and financial support: it is only the levels of day-to-day interchange and practical support that are low. Sudden breaks in this pattern occur, as when a child's marital estrangement or a grandchild's illness leads the migrant in Spain to return to their home northern country to provide more intensive instrumental help.

The 'young' age, nuclear form and independent attitudes and behaviour of northern European retirement migrant households in the southern countries are consistent with the widespread view that most will return to their native countries if they become sick, if their income substantially declines, or if they are bereaved of spouse. In both North America and Europe, however, the few studies of 'returns' of retirement migrations suggest that the probability of its occurrence is much exaggerated, and that many migrants develop strong attachments to their new homes, environments and social contacts. They resolve never to return, even if they are widowed or become frail.

How, then, are they supported, and do they cope? Above all, most retired migrants have assets and relatively good incomes and can draw support from their close relatives even if they reside in other countries. Most have private health insurance that covers at least elective hospital treatments. They are most disadvantaged in respect of their eligibility for domiciliary health and social services and for long-term residential care, either because these services are less well developed in their adopted than in their home country, or because the entitlements that they would have in their northern home country are not 'portable' to the south. Voluntary community associations can partly fill the gap. One of the longest established communities of northern European retirees in a Mediterranean country are the British in Malta (Warnes and Patterson, 1998). The community has established a British Residents' Association that provides welfare advice and low-level support, has fostered good relations between the expatriate and the host communities, and has negotiated with both the British High Commission and the Maltese government for improved entitlements and access to health and social services. It can be expected that, in other areas with a substantial number of foreign retired residents, similar associations will grow up and represent the interests of their members, as can already been seen on the Costa del Sol (O'Reilly, 2004).

The care resources of an international migrant without local kin are not simply a function of high income, even though in Spain and Malta it was found that a minority of frail northern European retirees employed domestic help. Only a very few, however, are not concerned about the possibility of having to enter a nursing home and about how to pay the fees – these concerns are not, of course, particular to migrants or created by the move to the south. Citizens of EU member states are entitled to emergency medical care in all member states. In Spain, many of the older retirees have registered as residents and *pensionistas,* and therefore are entitled to all of its National Health Service care. Many have some medical insurance, most often for elective hospital treatments. A common concern in southern Europe, however, is the scarcity of and ineligibility for domiciliary social and nursing services.

If these two groups of older migrants have been recognised by researchers and the media, and as 'special needs' groups among health and social service providers, other European older migrants have received less research, practice or policy attention; for example, the return labour migrants from northern Europe to Andalusia and southern Italy or from Great Britain to Ireland (King, 2002; Rodríguez et al, 2002). Among the British (and most likely the Germans and Dutch) aged 50 years or older who move across international borders, however, the majority are neither return labour migrants nor taking homes in the most visible sunbelt resorts or coastal strips. They move to live near (and some with) their close relatives, or partners or friends, in scattered destinations across Europe, the Americas, the Antipodes and south and east Africa. For example, many Germans go to Brazil (Table 10.2). Of the more than 820,000 UK state pensioners who receive their pensions overseas, nearly a quarter are in Australia and nearly two thirds in that country and in the US, the Irish Republic and Canada (Warnes, 2001). Moreover, there are a third more British pensioners in Germany than in Cyprus, Gibraltar, Greece, Malta and Portugal put together, while among German pensioners there are more in Switzerland and in Austria than in either Spain or in Italy, Portugal and Greece combined (Table 10.2).

Within all the major groups of older migrants, there are of course many nationalities and religions as well as a great diversity of educational, occupational, marital and fertility histories. These personal characteristics combine with facets of the economy, political and legal systems and social conditions of the country of residence to determine the migrant's resources or preparedness for old age. Variations in the resources that a migrant possesses arise in several ways. Aspects of a person's migration and family histories, particularly the ages at which they moved and took up permanent residence, and where they married and had children, influence the locations and affinity of their close and extended kin and therefore the availability of informal social and instrumental support. The migrant's personal history interacts with the national policy towards immigrants to determine their state welfare entitlements, as to pensions, income benefits, health and personal social services, and social or subsidised housing and long-term care (Burholt et al, 2000; Phillipson et al, 2000, 2003; Cylwik, 2002). As in the general population, a migrant's educational and occupational backgrounds correlate with their lifetime earnings and income and assets in

Table 10.2: German social insurance pensioners receiving their old-age benefits in foreign countries (1997)

	All		Men		Women	
	Number	%	Number	%	Number	%
USA	19,978	16.6	5,748	14.1	14,230	17.9
Austria	15,082	12.5	3,466	8.5	11,616	14.6
Switzerland	9,219	7.7	3,082	7.6	6,137	7.7
France	9,137	7.6	3,719	9.1	5,418	6.8
Australia	4,959	4.1	1,935	4.8	3,024	3.8
Spain	4,834	4.0	1,864	4.6	2,970	3.7
Argentina	3,895	3.2	1,177	2.9	2,718	3.4
South Africa	3,731	3.1	1,461	3.6	2,270	2.9
Brasil	3,221	2.7	1,098	2.7	2,123	2.7
Italy	2,963	2.5	914	2.2	2,049	2.6
Portugal	388	0.3	141	0.3	247	0.3
All	120,178	100.0	40,674	100.0	79,504	100.0

old age. The socioeconomic background also strongly influences the migrant's knowledge of the host country's welfare institutions and their ability to make use of the available services, especially through their language skills. These capacities are modified by information received from their relatives and friends, and by whether the migrant can turn to a group association for advice. Access to and utilisation of services will also be strongly influenced by the receptiveness of the country's housing, health and personal social services agencies and their staff to foreigners and cultural minorities. In short, for both labour and amenity-seeking older migrants, there are complex relationships between their migration history, current social position, national policies, and their access to social security, housing privileges and informal and formal care. More studies of local communities and of different migrant groups are required to inform local health and social service planners and practitioners.

Disadvantage and social exclusion among older migrants

The great majority of migrants are disadvantaged by living in a country in which they are culturally distinctive, non-native and not lifetime resident. Such disadvantages apply to all income groups, although higher income groups have greater capacity to overcome the disadvantages. The international labour migrants on the threshold of old age with the weakest family resources are those whose migration and life histories have been characterised by marked sex selection and low rates of marriage, family formation and fertility. One such group across western Europe are those from China and Hong Kong who worked in low-cost restaurants and the take-away catering trade (Yu, 2000; Chau and Yu, 2001; Hoeksma, 2004). Many of the men worked long and antisocial hours for very low wages, especially so if they were illegal migrants or irregular workers, and many remained unmarried and in old age are socially isolated. They were exposed to exceptional occupational hazards associated with poor hygiene and cramped working conditions, have high rates of morbidity, and weak social networks in both origin and adopted countries. The option of returning to the People's Republic of China or Hong Kong has either been closed or become unattractive, not least because of the very high cost of living in Hong Kong.

An equivalent group among European women moved when adolescent from the poorer southern and eastern countries to work in hotels, nursing homes, boarding schools and private homes as maids and carers. While for most this was a brief interlude in their lives, some continued in these occupations for decades, or returned to them after the breakdown of a relationship or marriage, while others fell into sex work or other insecure, hazardous and poorly paid occupations. A recent study found that among the unrecognised and neglected groups resident in London's hostels for single homeless people were older women from continental Europe who had worked as domestics and who lost tied accommodation when they were dismissed (Warnes and Crane, 2001). The recent growth in Greece, Italy and other European countries of the practice of employing illegal migrants as 'live-in' domestic servants to care for chronically sick and dependent older people may lead to a comparably disadvantaged group (Ungerson, 2004).

The diverse studies of older migrants that are becoming available across Europe also show that policy gaps and service deficiencies are widespread in creating income deprivation, social exclusion and unmet social support and healthcare needs (Blakemore, 1999). There is a widespread need and indeed obligation to develop culturally sensitive and responsive services, but the spread of such services is slow. Common problems are inadequate guidance on the prevalent problems and unmet needs, and too little sharing of experience, especially in approaches to the development of feasible and effective services. Many studies report not only the absence of interpreter services in health and welfare agencies and facilities, but also the unsympathetic reactions of 'frontline' staff, a consequence of the lack of both training and consciousness raising by employers (Askham et al, 1995; Pharoah, 1995; Ahmad and Atkin, 1996; Chau and Yu, 2000). Researchers and academics could do more to assist managers and clinicians gain an understanding of how new services can be successfully developed.

Conclusions

An inconsistency between policies that promote the movement of labour and national governments' practice of withholding full citizenship rights from legal immigrants is evident throughout the EU. As Bolzman et al (2004) show for Switzerland, governments and local authorities apply not only 'tax contribution records' but also nativity and local connection tests that amount to a continuing distinction between the eligible (deserving) and ineligible (undeserving) older population. Very few challenge this apparently common-sense and reasonable attitude, but it harbours a contradiction that should be exposed. If a state promotes the immigration of labour, or the sale of land and property to affluent retirees from other countries, then there is de facto recognition that the migrants play valued economic roles. Recognition should then follow that migrants will at times be sick, become old and have dependants, including children and older parents who may be frail. If a corporate employee is rewarded above the norm for undertaking a foreign 'tour', those who uproot their lives and face the challenge of making new lives in a foreign country deserve at least equal treatment with the host country citizen. Similarly, European national governments will increasingly find that their citizens who have moved abroad for retirement demand that the benefits and entitlements that they could receive in the home country should be exportable to their current country of residence, particularly within the EU.

It can already be seen that, during the coming century throughout the affluent nations, among the deep-seated problems for governments will be population and labour force decline, the compensatory immigration of people with relatively low education who are willing to take on low-wage menial jobs, and the increasing cultural and religious diversity of the resident population. To date, social gerontological research has responded little to these powerful trends and the changes they have brought about. Not even the innovative roles and activity patterns that the latest generations of affluent migrant older people are fashioning have attracted much research. Those on the threshold of old age who move abroad or circulate around two or more addresses in different countries, and those who successfully pursue new recreations and social opportunities while maintaining close involvement with their parents' and children's lives are pioneering positive approaches to contemporary old age. Recent research is beginning to assemble new evidence on these new lives and on the impacts they are having on our societies and national governments. It is hoped that they will both inform and stimulate much new research.

References

Ahmad, W.Q.I. and Atkin, K. (eds) (1996) *'Race' and community care*, Buckingham: Open University Press.

Annan, K. (2004) *A Europe open to well managed migration will be fairer, richer, stronger*, Address to the European Parliament, Brussels, 29 January, Press Release SG/SM/9134, New York, NY: UN (www.un.org).

Askham, J., Henshaw, L. and Tarpey, M. (1995) *Social and health authority services for elderly people from black and minority ethnic communities*, London: HMSO.

Blakemore, K. (1999) 'International migration in later life: social care and policy implications', *Ageing and Society*, vol 19, no 6, pp 761-74.

Bolzman, C., Fibbi, R. and Guillon, M. (2001) 'Emigrés-immigrés: vieillir et là-bas', *Revue Européenne des Migrations Internationales*, vol 17, no 1 (Special Issue), pp 7-198.

Bolzman, C., Poncioni-Derigo, R., Vial, M. and Fibbi, R. (2004) 'Older labour migrants' well-being in Europe: the case of Switzerland', *Ageing and Society*, vol 24, no 3, pp 411-29.

Burholt, V., Wenger, G.C., Scott, A., Yahya, B. and Roy, S. (2000) 'Bangladeshi immigration to the United Kingdom: older people's support networks in the sending and receiving countries', *Quality in Ageing*, vol 1, no 2, pp 18-30.

Carlin, J. (2004) 'All hail Berlusconi', *The Observer Magazine*, 18 January.

Casado-Díaz, M.A., Kaiser, C. and Warnes, A.M. (2004) 'Northern European retired residents in eight southern European areas: characteristics, motivations and adjustment', *Ageing and Society*, vol 24, no 3, pp 353-81.

Castles, S. and Miller, M.J. (2003) *The age of migration*, New York, NY: Guilford.

Chau, R. and Yu, S. (2001) 'Social exclusion of Chinese people in Britain', *Critical Social Policy*, vol 21, no 1, pp 103-25.

Cylwik, H. (2002) 'Expectations of inter-generational reciprocity among older Greek Cypriot migrants in London', *Ageing and Society*, vol 22, pp 599-613.

Fonseca, M.L., Caldeira, M.J. and Esterves, A. (2002) 'New forms of migration into the European south: challenges for citizenship and governance – the Portuguese case', *International Journal of Population Geography*, vol 8, no 2, pp 135-52.

Haug, W., Compton, P. and Courbage, Y. (eds) (2002) *The demographic characteristics of immigrant populations*, Population Study 38, Strasbourg: Council of Europe.

Hoeksma, J. (2004) 'The needs for care of older Chinese migrants in Rotterdam', in A.M. Warnes, M. Casado-Díaz and U. Lundh (eds) *Older migrants in Europe: Sources, case studies and a guide to research*, Sheffield: Sheffield Institute for Studies on Ageing.

Joppke, C. and Morawaska, E. (2003) *Towards assimilation and citizenship: Immigrants in liberal states*, Basingstoke: Palgrave Macmillan.

King, R. (2002) 'Towards a new map of European migration', *International Journal of Population Geography*, vol 8, no 2, pp 89-106.

King, R., Warnes, A.M. and Williams, A.M. (2000) *Sunset lives: British retirement migration to the Mediterranean*, Oxford: Berg.

Lie, B. (2002) *Immigration and immigrants 2002*, Oslo: Statistics Norway.

O'Reilly, K. (2000) *The British on the Costa del Sol: Trans-national identities and local communities*, London: Routledge.

O'Reilly, K. (2004) 'Older migrant adaptation strategies: patterns of association and social activities of British migrants in the Costa del Sol', in A.M. Warnes, M. Casado-Díaz and U. Lundh (eds) *Older migrants in Europe: Sources, case studies and a guide to research*, Sheffield: Sheffield Institute for Studies on Ageing.

Pérez, N.O. (2003) 'Spain: forging an immigration policy', (Country profile), Washington, DC: Migration Policy Institute (www.migrationinformation.org/Profiles/).

Petersen, W. (1975) *Population*, New York, NY: Macmillan.

Pharoah, C. (1995) *Primary health care for elderly people from black and minority ethnic communities*, Studies in Ageing, Age Concern Institute of Gerontology, London: HMSO.

Phillipson, C., Alhaq, E., Ullah, S. and Ogg, J. (2000) 'Bangladeshi families in Bethnal Green, London: older people, ethnicity and social exclusion', in A.M. Warne, L. Warren and M. Nolan (eds) *Care services for later life: Transformations and critiques*, London: Jessica Kingsley, pp 273-90.

Phillipson, C., Ahmed, N. and Latimer, J. (2003) *Women in transition: A study of the experiences of Bangladeshi women living in Tower Hamlets*, Bristol: The Policy Press.

Poulain, M. and Perrin, N. (2002) 'The demographic characteristics of immigrant populations in Belgium', in W. Haug, P. Compton and Y. Courbage (eds) *The demographic characteristics of immigrant populations*, Strasbourg: Council of Europe, pp 57-129.

Rodríguez, V.R., Egea, C. and Nieto, J.A. (2002) 'Return migration in Andalusia, Spain', *International Journal of Population Geography*, vol 8, no 3, pp 233-54.

Rodríguez, V.R., Casado-Díaz, M.A. and Huber, A. (eds) (2004) *Migración internacional de retirados en España* [*International retirement migrants in Spain*], Madrid: Consejo Superior de Investigaciones Cientificas.

Simpson, S. (1997) 'Demography and ethnicity: case studies from Bradford', *New Community*, vol 23, no 1, pp 89-107.

Spence, L. (2003) *Third country nationals living in London 2000/01*, Briefing Paper 2003/6, Data Management and Analysis Group, London: Greater London Authority.

Ungerson, C. (2004) 'Whose empowerment and independence? A cross-national perspective on "cash for care" schemes', *Ageing and Society*, vol 24, no 2, pp 189-212.

Warnes, A.M. (1992) 'Migration and the life course', in A.G. Champion and A. Fielding (eds) *Migration processes and patterns: Volume I: Research, progress and prospects*, London: Belhaven, pp 175-87.

Warnes, A.M. (1996) 'The age structure and ageing of the ethnic groups', in D.C. Coleman and J. Salt (eds) *Demographic characteristics of the ethnic minority populations. Volume 1* (Ethnicity in the 1991 Census Series), London: The Stationery Office, pp 151-77.

Warnes, A.M. (1997) *The health and care of older people in London*, London: King's Fund London Commission.

Warnes, A.M. (2001) 'The international dispersal of pensioners from affluent countries', *International Journal of Population Geography*, vol 7, no 6, pp 373-88.

Warnes, A.M. (2002) *Older people in Yorkshire and the Humber*, Sheffield: Sheffield Institute for Studies on Ageing, University of Sheffield.

Warnes, A.M. and Crane, M. (2001) *Single homeless people in London: Profiles of service users and perceptions of needs*, Sheffield: Sheffield Institute for Studies on Ageing, University of Sheffield.

Warnes, A.M. and Patterson, G. (1998) 'British retirees in Malta: components of the cross-national relationship', *International Journal of Population Geography*, vol 4, no 2, pp 113-34.

Willan, P. (2001) 'New law gets Berlusconi off the hook', *The Guardian*, 3 October.

Yu, W.K. (2000) *Chinese older people: A need for social inclusion in two communities*, Bristol/York: The Policy Press/Joseph Rowntree Foundation.

ELEVEN

Transnational communities, migration and changing identities in later life: a new research agenda

Chris Phillipson and Nilufar Ahmed

Key points

- Transnational migration is a major feature of global societies.
- Global migration produces great diversity in respect of the social networks within which old age is shaped and managed.
- Migrant groups are likely to experience discontinuous and disordered lifecourse transitions.
- Elderly migrants may represent a new 'urban underclass', marginalised from essential support services as well as dominant social and cultural institutions.

Key readings

Gardner, K. (2002) *Age, narrative and migration*, Oxford: Berg
Levitt, P. (2001) *The transnational villagers*, Berkley, CA: University of California Press.
Phillipson, C., Ahmed, N. and Latimer, J. (2003) *Women in transition: A study of the experiences of Bangladeshi women living in Tower Hamlets* (A report for the Nuffield Foundation), Centre for Social Gerontology, University of Keele, Bristol: The Policy Press.
Warnes, A.M., Freidrich, K., Kellaher, L. and Torres, S. (2004) 'The diversity and welfare of older migrants in Europe', *Ageing and Society*, vol 24, no 3, pp 307-26.

Introduction

The relationship and interaction between globalisation and ageing has become the subject of extensive debate and discussion within gerontology, with contributions covering the field of pensions (Vincent, 2003), health and social care (Phillipson et al, 2000, 2003) and more general developments within social policy (Walker and Deacon, 2003). The concern of this chapter is to place on the agenda one facet of globalisation that, as the 21st century unfolds, will increase in importance in shaping nation states – the development of what may be termed 'transnational communities'. Transnational communities may be said to arise from a context in which those who leave a country and those who stay may remain connected through social and symbolic ties, these maintained over time and across space in complex patterns of exchange and support (Faist, 2000).

For societies in the 21st century, communities of families and relations sustained across wide geographical distances are likely to play an increasingly influential role in daily life. The American demographer Douglas Massey (2000, p 134) argues that, barring some calamity or a radical shift in family-planning trends, "migration will play a greater role than reproduction in determining the strength and tenor of our societies". And the Population Division of the UN indicates that, at current birth and death rates, the EU would need 1.6 million immigrants a year to keep its working-age population stable in the next 50 years (CEPR, 2001).

Transnational communities are themselves linked to the changes associated with the emergence of globalisation. Beck (2000) has defined globalisation as "denoting the process through which sovereign national states are criss-crossed and undermined by transnational actors with varying prospects of power, orientations, identities and networks". Part of what Bauman (1998) refers to as the 'human consequences of globalisation' concerns the resurgence of international migration in various forms and the maintenance of dense social ties over time and across space. The formation of communities arising from such ties produces, it is argued in this chapter, important issues for gerontologists to consider when undertaking research on older people in general and minority ethnic groups in particular.

The chapter reviews, first, issues relating to the theme of transnational migration and community, drawing on a selection of the research in this area. This is then illustrated through findings from an empirical study of Bangladeshi women living in the London Borough of Tower Hamlets, with a particular focus on experiences of care and support provided by the women both in the UK and Bangladesh. The chapter then concludes with an assessment of what transnationality entails for the study of research in gerontology, particularly in relation to questions of social policy.

Globalisation and transnational communities

Peggy Levitt (2001, p 4) suggests that the rise of the transnational community reflects "how ordinary people are incorporated into the countries that receive them while remaining active in the places they come from". Basch et al (1994, p 6) further define this relationship as follows:

> ... transnationalism [is] the process by which immigrants forge and sustain multi-stranded social relations that link together their societies of origin and settlement. We call these processes transnationalism to emphasize that many immigrants build social fields that cross geographic, cultural and political

borders ... an essential element is the multiplicity of involvements that transmigrants sustain in home and host societies.

Portes and Bach (1985) have described migration as a process of network building, "which depends on and in turn reinforces social relations across space linking migrants and non-migrants" (p 10). This approach draws out the dynamic nature of the ties maintained through different stages of migration. Westwood and Phizacklea (2000, p 7) emphasise:

> [the] active decision-making processes of migration and the ways in which economic and cultural phenomena are creatively reinscribed in new settings and the ways in which the diasporic feeds economically and culturally back into the homeland, for instance, through remittances.

Much of the literature on transnational migration, as Papastergiadis (2000) has argued, has tended to assume a model either of family migration led by men, or of male pioneers followed by female and younger dependants. However, female migrants may in fact occupy a distinctive position within transnational communities. Khanum (1994) highlights their social and economic role in strengthening kinship ties, often to the detriment of their own social and economic needs. Drawing on her fieldwork in Bangladesh, she observes that:

> [The] kinship tie demands that women send money to the poor relatives of their husbands in Bangladesh. Apart from these cases, women also have to contribute to relatives living in the UK even when they are supported by [income support] or from their own earnings, simply because of the prevailing norms. (Khanum, 1994, p 296)

Women may also play a significant role in the construction of what Hochschild (2000) refers to as 'global care chains', these representing the "personal links between people across the globe based on the paid or unpaid work of caring" (p 131). However, migration may also bring major new opportunities for women. Westwood and Phizacklea (2000, p 108) refer to it as providing an economic and social escape route. And DeLaet (1999, p 2) poses the question:

> Does international migration provide women with an opportunity for liberating themselves from subordinate gender roles in their countries of origin, or are traditional gender roles perpetuated in the host societies?

Following this, the development of transnational communities may be said to reflect both the growth of a global economy, and the impact this has produced on the construction of family and community ties. Estes and Associates (2001) have argued that at the ideological level, globalisation has assumed a power and force of its own, and that it has been especially important for promoting the inevitability of competitive global forces and the policies developed by corporations. A globalised, corporate-driven, capitalist economy has clearly had a significant impact on agendas and challenges in respect of achieving security in old age, as Vincent (2003) and others have noted (Estes and Phillipson, 2002). Increasingly, the sovereignty of nation states is viewed as being influenced to a greater or lesser extent by different kinds of transnational actors. Older people live in a global even more than a national society, and are increasingly contributing to, as well as depending upon, transnational chains of paid and unpaid labour.

This new political economy is also creating what may be described as 'global families' – these arising from the communities that emerge from international migration. Arlie Hochschild (2000) makes the point that most writing about globalisation focuses on money, markets and labour flows, with scant attention to women, children and the care of one for the other. However, older people are clearly a significant group to add to this list. Elderly people are now an important part of the global flow of women and men moving across and within continents. The largest group comprises those who came as labour migrants (or as the wives thereof) to countries such as Britain and who have subsequently 'aged in place' (Warnes et al, 2004). Many of these, however, even among the poor, and especially among the first generation of migrants, may return at regular intervals to their country of origin (Gardner, 1995). As a consequence, globalisation is producing a new kind of ageing in which the dynamics of family and social life may be stretched across different continents and across different types of societies (Castells, 1996).

Globalisation and structured dependency

Global migration is also producing considerable diversity in respect of the social networks within which growing old is shaped and managed. Typically, older people's networks have been examined within national borders, and their experiences of care and support assessed within this context (Phillipson, 1998). However, migrants bring important variations with responsibilities that may cover considerable physical as well as cultural distances. This is likely to be a particular issue for women and men migrating in search of work or for women who leave home for a new country.

Such developments may create forms of 'structured dependency' (Townsend, 1981) that play differently in a global as opposed to a national context. Structured dependency theory in critical gerontology has been criticised from a number of perspectives: for playing down human agency on the one hand, and for undue emphasis on social inequality on the other (arguments developed most recently in a British context by Gilleard and Higgs, 2000). Yet in a global context it may be that a reformulated structured dependency argument has much to offer in addressing the widening inequalities between nation states and the crisis this generates in the communities supporting older people.

The structured dependency argument is especially significant when related to gender and the problems facing women within different transnational settings.

A major aspect of globalisation has been its impact on women who stay behind in the villages and cities of less-developed countries, and those uprooted through international migration. Gulati's (1993) study, *In the absence of their men: The impact of male migration on women*, is one of the few investigations to examine the lives of those who remain in their countries of origin. Gulati studied male migration from the Indian state of Karala to west Asia, noting the challenges facing women coping with managing alone with a new family, but with a long period of separation from a husband to whom they may have been married for just a few weeks. Conversely, the arrival of women through family migration has been an important aspect of migration trends in Europe over the past two decades, one that has posed significant issues both for the women and the communities in which they settle (Warnes et al, 2004).

A research study undertaken in the Bangladeshi community living in London's East End examined the pressures experienced by women who travel thousands of miles to set up hew homes, often in neighbourhoods struggling with the effects of economic deprivation and racism towards minorities (Phillipson et al, 2003). The research investigated the family life of 100 migrant women aged 35-55 who had come to Britain in the 1970s and 1980s (a detailed account of the methodology of study can be found in Phillipson et al, 2003). The study was concerned with examining issues about inter-generational as well as transnational support, with a particular focus on a group of women caring for older husbands (in many cases aged 60+) as well as very young children (often aged 12 or younger).

Most of the women interviewed had well-established family and social networks within their villages in Bangladesh. For them, migration was an economic gamble but it had social and cultural dimensions as well. Gardner (1995) argues that migration can be seen as "part of wider project in which individuals and households strive to reinvent themselves". But for groups such as women – who may be the least powerful within their communities – this can be a daunting experience.

In terms of the demography of our sample of women, 76% were married, 17% were widowed and 7% were divorced or separated. Census data have confirmed the relatively large household size of Bangladeshi households – 4.5 persons in the 2001 Census (compared with 2.4 for the average household). Over 60% of Bangladeshi households were of five persons or more. In our study, average household size was 6.6, and 87% of households comprised five or more persons: findings that reflect the particular age group targeted for the research. We should also note the 7% of households with 10 or more persons; in contrast there was just one single-person household. The average number of children was 5.2, with just 8% of women having two children or less (two women were childless). Two thirds of respondents had five or more children.

Bangladeshi women: patterns of intergenerational support

During the interview the women were asked to first describe a 'typical' day in their life, and second, to think about this day in comparison with the one they might have had if they were still living in Bangladesh. Taking the former, coding of the replies brought out the centrality of household tasks (mentioned by 83%) and care within the home (76%), followed by religious activities (61%) as a third major strand; leisure-related activities were listed by 28%. Here are accounts from three women about a typical day in their life:

> "In the morning I get the children ready for school, dress them, feed them breakfast, then drop them off. Then at home I have my youngest and he needs looking after. I do the cooking and cleaning ... that needs to be done every day. I pray at prayer times. Then I go and pick up the children from school at 3.30. Then at 4.30 I drop them off to Bangla School and pick them up at 6. At 7 they go to Arabic classes and come home at 9. They go to Arabic on Thursday, Friday and Saturday, and Bangla classes Monday to Thursday." (Nuresa, married with four children)

> "My whole day goes with my housework." (Waheeda, married with five children)

> "I get up in the morning and I pray. Then I wake the children up, get them ready and take them to school. When I come home I cook and watch TV. If I need to I go out and do some shopping. Then I pick up the children from school. When I bring them home it is a bit of a rush to feed them and get them ready for their Arabic classes. They can go all together by themselves, but I pick them up because it gets late." (Nazia, separated, seven children)

Other women reported a wider range of activities running alongside or replacing certain types of care work:

> "I'm doing a course from this September. It's a three-month course. It should help me pass my time too when the children are in school and I'm alone in the house." (Saika, married with five children)

> "Two days a week I go to the gym for exercise and two days a week I go to language classes." (Habiba, married with four children)

> "I always feel so hurried. I get really fed up! After I do everything then I get ready for college. I go to [English] classes on Monday and Tuesdays 10-12, then I do IT [Information Technology] from 1-3. I do IT five days a week. On Fridays I [have another class]. I only do that on Fridays, but I have to do so much for it – it is a lot of hard work! There is so much coursework!" (Asma, married with three children)

"I go to my English class three days a week – Monday, Tuesday and Wednesday."
(Nazma, widowed, one child)

Caring for school-age children was a major focus of everyday life for the majority of women. However, coping with the ill health of their husband (many of whom were in their 60s and early 70s) was also highly significant for those interviewed. Thirty-two per cent of the women reported currently providing personal care to someone in the home, the majority of those being partners with chronic health problems:

"He can't do anything for himself. When I go to college I put his meal in the microwave and set the timer so all he has to do is press start. I go at one and come back at three. In that time he prays and eats. He is always in a lot of pain, so I have to spend as much time with him as I can, in case he needs anything. I worry about him all the time." (Rohima, five children)

"We can't do anything together, he is very ill. He has had five heart attacks. He has diabetes, high pressure, skin disease all over his body, and psychiatric problems. Some days he is very ill, other days it's not too bad ... I am just kept busy by him. Give him this, give him that, he wants to eat this, then he doesn't, this is good, then it's not. That takes up my whole day.... They were going to give us a nurse to look after him at home, but he doesn't want that – he can't think properly, and he just says that he doesn't want a nurse, he wants me to do everything. And we just want to do whatever keeps him happy, so we haven't got a nurse." (Salma, six children)

"I have to give him medicine. I have to watch him all night because he could choke. He is fitted to machine to help him breathe. I can't sleep because I am worried about him and because my sugar levels get high and I get dizzy." (Jannat, four children)

"He has had three operations on his leg. I have to bathe him, get his food ready. Help him dress. He has diabetes and so he needs special food. It is very difficult getting him in and out of the bath. I have heard that people can have bars fitted to help them get into the bath. But we haven't got anything." (Sani, six children)

How did the women compare daily life in Bangladesh with the kind of life that they had now living in a deprived inner London borough? Following on from the earlier discussion in this chapter, we find 39% mentioning that they might have had more help around the home if they were in Bangladesh instead of living in Britain. In some cases these would be members of the women's own family network, but they might in addition be servants (often an unmarried or widowed woman with a child of her own) who would be employed to provide help around the home:

"In Bangladesh it would be easier, there are people around to help, and you have all your family there. If I had one or two of my sisters here, it would be much easier for me. My mother would have shared her time between us." (Toslima, divorced with four children)

"In Bangladesh it would be different. There are lots of people around. I would have my mother-in-law and sisters-in-law to help. Everyone would be together. Their uncles could take them to school. I wouldn't have to do that duty." (Khadija, married with four children)

"It is much harder in this country. Here we have to take them to school, bring them home, they need so many things. It was never like this in Bangladesh. In Bangladesh I would have more help. In this country I am on my own. I have to do everything. I have been cleaning the house since this morning. Children in this country aren't very good at cleaning, are they? So I have to do it all myself." (Rafeya, married with five children)

"If I was in Bangladesh then it would have been comfortable because I would have had people to help me. What I'm doing now ... it's more than I can manage ... because there's only one of me in the house looking after six children. My husband is ill and I have to look after him too. It's too much for me. But if I was in Bangladesh, I would have had a helper. I wouldn't have had to work so hard. Everyone wants a bit of rest for themselves." (Feroza, married with six children)

At the same time, most of the women did not view returning to Sylhet as an obvious solution to their problems. Indeed, most of the women, at various points of the interview, emphasised the advantages of migration – for themselves as well as their children:

"In Bangladesh it would be very different. There aren't these kind of opportunities, are there? Or there might be, but they would only be in the towns, not in the villages. There I would just be at home all day. Here I can go out more." (Alima, married with one child)

"I wouldn't have had all these opportunities, and I would have never known what these opportunities were! But I am glad I am here because I am learning new things, and meeting new people. I meet different people, I have one group of friends in my ... classes, and another in my childcare. Last year I registered as a childminder. I think it is good that I have learnt all these things and I can do something for myself now." (Asma, married with three children)

"It would have been harder in Bangladesh. There would be more worries. There is more work to do there. In this country you don't have to worry about harvests and crops, in Bangladesh you do. There is a lot of outdoor work. Here it is all indoors." (Sadika, married with six children)

Contact with mothers

Thompson and Bauer (2001), in a study of Jamaican families, emphasise that "transnationalism is not a figment of the social scientist's imagination, but a reality both in the mind and in practice" (p 14). Reflecting this point, the women in our study maintained a variety of ties with Bangladesh. The majority (79%) had returned for visits to Bangladesh, these often stretching for substantial periods of time (49% reported stays lasting between two and four months; 11% had stayed for a period of 10 months or more). The longest visits often tended to be around the time when children were of pre-school age. Keeping in touch with relatives, getting children married, or seeing a family member who was ill (often a mother or father) were identified as the main reasons for returning to Bangladesh. Contact would also be sustained through regular telephone calls and in some cases e-mail. Many of the women mentioned financial or other obstacles preventing them from returning to Bangladesh as often as they would like:

"My mother always cries for me to go to Bangladesh all the time. I am the only one of her children in this country. My youngest brother got married a few weeks ago. I couldn't go – how could I go? I can't afford to take them all and they are all studying." (Neefa)

"I would like to go to Bangladesh again but I don't know if I will. My whole family is there, my parents and brothers and sisters. I am the only one here. But I can't afford to take my children and I can't leave them behind either." (Rong)

"I would like to go back but you need money to go back. Where would I get the money from? I don't even have enough money to pay the bills and eat. How can I go back to Bangladesh?" (Sani)

"I do feel a tug to go back, but how can I go, with so many children? I can't leave them and I can't take them either – where would I get the money from? How much would the fares cost?" (Rupa)

Contacts with mothers were an important part of these transnational ties. The majority of the women (71%) still had an elderly mother living (in the majority of cases) in Bangladesh. Twenty-six of the women reported that their mother's health was 'very good or good', but 31 said it was 'poor or very poor'. A number of the women reported on the tensions created by trying to maintain ties with their mothers:

"After I came here I couldn't keep in touch with her very much. Every four or five months we would write letters. But we never spoke on the phone. I never heard her voice again after leaving Bangladesh [respondent cries]." (Sani)

Interviewer: "Where does your mother live?"

"America. She lives with my brothers there. She has been there for four years." (Sabera)

Interviewer: "Has she come here?"

"Yes. But she didn't like being in the house all day. In Bangladesh there are more open spaces and it is not like that here. She liked it because we are here, but she didn't like being in the house all day." (Sabera)

"She came and stayed when she was doing her Hajj [pilgrimage to Mecca]. But she didn't like it here. It isn't as free as our country is it? You have to rely on other people if you want to go anywhere. So she didn't like staying here." (Asma)

"She lived between this country and Bangladesh. She would go to Bangladesh because she missed my brother's children, but when she was there she would miss us and come back. And when she came back she would start missing them and want to go back again. She didn't have peace in either country. While she was there she missed us, but she couldn't stay a year here before wanting to go back. She died in this country, but we sent her body back to Bangladesh." (Shipa)

There was some evidence from our study of the maintenance of remittances from the women to mothers and close family members in Bangladesh. Gardner (1995) suggests that financial flows from London to Sylhet were important in the 1960s and 1970s, when wives and children had yet to migrate. With their arrival, however, financial support was gradually reduced. Our research suggested that while generally the case, the pressure to send money home was still an issue for some families. Shuara comments that:

"I occasionally send some money. My heart can't bear it – I always wonder if they are going without: are they eating properly? what are they eating? If I hear they are ill I don't know what to do. I don't have much to give myself. If only I could speak the language I could work. Then I could open the letters from Bangladesh with a light heart, and write back to them and make them happy. Even if I do write to them they are upset – if you don't give them money they don't like you." (Shuara)

Others continued to maintain some support, especially to their mothers:

"If we can we give a bit of money to help with medicines. Sometimes we send money over for her medication or so that they can buy her nice food." (Ruji)

"Sometimes I would send a little money for her." (Yasmeen)

"I send money as often as I can." (Poroush)

How did the women we interviewed see their lives unfolding? Now established in Britain and with the second half of their lives ahead of them, what hopes did they have for the future? Of the 97 answering this question, 61 (63%) focused on hopes for the future success of their children. The following comments are representative:

"I don't have any hopes for myself. I just want to be able to raise the children well and educate them and make them into decent people." (Shaira)

"That our children don't spend their lives on benefit like us." (Ranu)

"My children's hopes are now my hopes. As long as they are happy, I am happy." (Shipa)

Fourteen women were unable to identify any hope or aspiration for the future, some of these harbouring especially negative views about the way ahead:

"What hopes can I have? I have no hopes. I just hope that Allah gives me a quick death." (Shuara, aged 48)

"What hopes can I have – I am going to die soon anyway." (Monwara, age 39)

"Women's lives are over when they reach 35 or 40. What more of a life do I have?" (Sabina, aged 50).

"My days are going now – they are not coming any more are they? My days are getting shorter not longer!" (Nazma, aged 41)

These are striking comments for a group of people still comparatively young by western standards and reflect the way in which the women's lifecourse had already been marked by changes that would normally be spread over a longer period of time. For some of the respondents, marriage, childbirth, migration, divorce, widowhood and ill health had been compressed into a short span of time – two decades or less. Change was relentless and holding onto a sense of perspective about the direction in which life was taking them presented complex issues for many of the women interviewed.

Developing a transnational agenda in gerontology

A number of themes relevant to social gerontology are raised by the research discussed in this chapter. The first concerns the impact of change and movement over the lifecourse. For much of the previous century, gerontology – at least in its attention to older people in western societies – focused on the idea of an orderly lifecourse built around education, paid work and retirement. As Hoerder (2001, p 525) remarks:

> A so-called normal biography emerges which, however, excludes large segments of any population from consideration. First, lifecourse models based on remunerative production or administrative work are male orientated and thus neglect the other half of any society. Second, such linear lifecourse models exclude risks and assume similar access to social resources by men. Third, non-linearity, formerly called 'fate' needs to be introduced – that is, the disruption of lifecourses by natural catastrophes or war, or by illness or the sudden death of near kin.

Following the above, one conclusion from this chapter is that themes of 'discontinuity' and 'disorderliness' in lifecourse transitions are likely to become of greater significance in understanding patterns of adjustment in later life (Gardner, 2002). In the case of our sample of Bangladeshi women, a majority are likely to enter their 60s as widows, in many instances still caring for young children. More generally, they will have experienced what Papastergiadis (2000) refers to as the 'turbulence of migration', having biographies built around complex migrations across nation states. For such women (and for an increasing number of people in first as well as third world countries) the 'journey of life' (Cole, 1992) will be viewed as dictated by chance with a high degree of unpredictability in respect of outcome.

A major issue for gerontology concerns, then, how to assimilate personal experiences of disruption and disorder into theoretical models that typically assume stability and development. The challenge in studies of ageing will be to acknowledge the way in which the lifecourse may assume a 'non-linear' form, with features of 'normal ageing' occurring earlier or later in life depending upon a particular sequence of biographical events. By extension, an additional issue will be acknowledging greater variability in respect of images and definitions of ageing. In the context of complex migrations, the notion of what it means to grow old, when old age begins, and normative behaviours for old age, will all show wider variation in one society than has historically been the case. The new reality of ageing will pose a substantial challenge to social policies in areas such as income maintenance and care support, which may be based upon inaccurate assumptions about length of residence, household characteristics and self-defined needs. In conceptual terms, migration must be viewed as a significant part of the risk society, reflecting what Beck (1992, p 21) defines as the "hazards and insecurities induced and introduced by modernisation". As such, older migrants may move into what might be termed a 'zone of indeterminancy' marginal to work and welfare, but deprived at the same time of those biographical continuities that studies of ageing often take for granted (Estes et al, 2003).

Conclusions

Understanding ageing, it is argued in this chapter, increasingly needs to be located through the influence of transnational communities and the role of migration in reshaping nation states (Winder, 2004). In this context, if what might be called 'the first phase of ageing' (which lasted for much of the 20th century) was about growing old as a reinforcement of national identity and citizenship, the second phase will involve to a much greater extent the development of 'hybrid identities'. Growing old in the first phase – or ageing in the 20th century – was partly a celebration of community, or of lives lived within particular communities with particular histories (Estes et al, 2003). In the second phase, however, which we have now entered, belonging and identity is becoming detached from particular places. Beck (2000, p 169) argues that "People are expected to live their lives with the most diverse and contradictory transnational and personal identities and risks". And Albrow (1996, p 151) makes the point that:

> Under globalised conditions it becomes less easy for individuals to affirm their identity within the strict confines of nation, gender, age or any other categorical distinctions.

Clearly, there will be losers and winners in this process, but the increasing importance of migration and mobility is raising substantial questions for gerontological research in a global context. In conclusion, three illustrations might be made of this point. First, the processes associated with migration clearly raise the possibilities of additional forms of ageism affecting older people in the 21st century. Elderly migrants in particular may represent a new 'urban underclass', marginalised from key support services as well as dominant social and cultural institutions. This much is identified in the review by Warnes et al (2004), which examined the position of elderly migrants across a number of European countries. The authors confirmed the extent to which gaps in social policy were leading to social exclusion as well as failure to respond to social and healthcare needs. Common problems were summarised as

... inadequate guidance on the prevalent problems and unmet needs, and too little sharing of experience especially in approaches to the development of feasible and effective services. (Warnes et al, 2004, p 318)

Second, a world of greater mobility will in the long term bring benefits of cultural diversity. However, in the short term an increase in racism and associated forms of oppression also seems evident and may well create further divisions within the population of older people. Our research at Keele, spread over the period since the mid-1990s, has found significant conflict between white and black and Asian elders in certain geographical areas – to an extent that dispels ideas that age-based coalitions will be easy to achieve in the immediate future (Phillipson et al, 2001).

Third, transnational communities bring major issues for social policy with the development of groups holding together care tasks or financial responsibilities that may be strung across continents. Cross-cultural social networks will also continue to thrive, sustained through the expanded possibilities introduced by new technology (Vertovec, 2001). The key issue, however, is the extent to which these additional elements of citizenship are given due acknowledgement in the countries to which people migrate (Ackers and Dwyer, 2002). The argument here is that without such recognition new forms of social exclusion may appear and full participation in society compromised. Transnational communities do in fact promote social inclusion in a variety of ways – through generating new forms of social capital; through remittances; through paid and unpaid labour; and through the maintenance of strong social ties. All of these aspects may be highly positive for older migrants, especially in a context where the welfare state is withdrawing from significant areas of responsibility. Greater understanding of the meaning of new forms of community is both an important challenge for social policy, and a major issue for research into ageing to address.

References

Ackers, L. and Dwyer, P. (2002) *Senior citizenship?: Retirement, migration and welfare in the European Union*, Bristol: The Policy Press.

Albrow, M. (1996) *The global age*, Cambridge: Polity Press.

Basch, L., Schiller, N. and Blanc-Szanton, C. (1994) *Nations unbound: Transnational projects, post-colonial predicaments and de-territorialised nation-states*, Langhorne: Gordon and Breach.

Bauman, Z. (1998) *Globalisation*, Cambridge: Polity Press.

Beck, U. (1992) *The risk society*, London: Sage Publications.

Beck, U. (2000) *What is globalisation?*, Cambridge: Polity Press.

Castells, M. (1996) *The rise of the network society*, Oxford: Blackwell.

CEPR (Centre for Economic Policy Research) (2001) *Bulletin*, Spring, London: CEPR.

Cole, T.R. (1992) *The journey of life: A cultural history of aging in America*, Cambridge: Cambridge University Press.

DeLaet, D. (1999) 'Introduction: the invisibility of women in scholarship on international migration', in G. Kelson and D. DeLaet (eds) *Gender and immigration*, London: Macmillan, pp 1-24.

Estes, C. and Associates (2001) *Social policy and ageing*, Thousand Oaks, CA: Sage Publications.

Estes, C. and Phillipson, C. (2002) 'The globalization of capital, the welfare state and old age policy', *International Journal of Health Services*, vol 32, no 2, pp 279-97.

Estes, C., Biggs, S. and Phillipson, C. (2003) *Social theory, social policy and ageing*, Buckingham: Open University Press.

Faist, T. (2000) *The volume and dynamics of international migration and transnational social spaces*, Oxford: Clarendon Press.

Gardner, K. (1995) *Global migrants, local lives*, Oxford: Oxford University Press.

Gardner, K. (2002) *Age, narrative and migration*, Oxford: Berg.

Gilleard, C. and Higgs, P. (2000) *Cultures of ageing*, London: Prentice Hall.

Gulati, L. (1993) *In the absence of their men: The impact of male migration on women*, New Dehli: Sage Publications.

Hoerder, D. (2001) 'Reconstructing life courses: a historical perspective on migrant experiences', in V. Marshall, W. Heinz, H. Kruger and A. Verma (eds) *Reconstructing work and the life course*, Toronto: University of Toronto Press, pp 525-39.

Hochschild, A. (2000) 'Global care chains and emotional surplus value', in W. Hutton and A. Giddens (eds) *On the edge: Living with global capitalism*, London: Jonathan Cape, pp 130-46.

Khanum, S.M. (1994) 'We just buy illness in exchange for hunger: experiences of health care, health and illness among Bangladeshi women in Britain', Unpublished PhD thesis, Keele: University of Keele.

Levitt, P. (2001) *The transnational villagers*, Berkeley, CA: University of California Press.

Massey, D. (2000) 'To study migration today, look to a parallel era', *The Chronicle of Higher Education*, 18 August, pp B4-5.

Papastergiadis, N. (2000) *The turbulence of migration*, Cambridge: Polity Press.

Phillipson, C. (1998) *Reconstructing old age: New agendas for social theory and practice*, London: Sage Publications.

Phillipson, C., Ahmed, N. and Latimer, J. (2003) *Women in transition: A study of the experiences of Bangladeshi women living in Tower Hamlets*, Bristol: The Policy Press.

Phillipson, C., Al-Haq, E., Ullah, S. and Ogg, J. (2000) 'Bangladeshi families in Bethnal Green', in A. Warnes, L. Warren and M. Nolan (eds) *Care services for later life*, London: Jessica Kingsley, pp 273-90.

Phillipson, C., Bernard, M., Phillips, J. and Ogg, J. (2001) *The family and community life of older people*, London: Routledge.

Portes, A. and Bach, R. (1985) *Latin journey: Cuban and Mexican immigrants in the United States*, Berkeley, CA: University of California Press.

Thompson, P. and Bauer, E. (2001) 'Jamaican transnational families: points of pain and sources of resiliance', *Wadabagei: A Journal of the Caribbean and its Diaspora*, vol 3, pp 1-37.

Townsend, P. (1981) 'The structured dependency of the elderly: the creation of policy in the twentieth century', *Ageing and Society*, vol 1, no 1, pp 5-28.

Vertovec, S. (2001) *Transnational social formations: Towards conceptual cross-fertilization*, Center for Migration and Development Working Paper Series, Princeton: Princeton University Press.

Vincent, J. (2003) *Old age*, London: Routledge.

Walker, A. and Deacon, B. (2003) 'Economic globalization and policies on aging', *Journal of Societal and Social Policy*, vol 2, no 2, pp 1-18.

Warnes, A.M., Freidrich, K., Kellaher, L. and Torres, S. (2004) 'The diversity and welfare of older migrants in Europe', *Ageing and Society*, vol 24, no 3, pp 307-26.

Westwood, S. and Phizacklea, A. (2000) *Transnationalism and the politics of belonging*, London: Routledge.

Winder, R. (2004) *Bloody foreigners: The story of immigration to Britain*, London: Little, Brown & Co.

Section IV:
Structure and agency

TWELVE

Societal trends and lifecourse events affecting diversity in later life

Jenny De Jong Gierveld

Key points

- Developments started in the second half of the 20th century result in new demographic values and behaviour among young adults and among older adults. Standard life biographies are replaced by choice biographies involving diverse lifestyles and life strategies.
- Consequently, in addition to the current partner status, the partner history needs to be taken into account.
- Partner status and partner history together affect the social integration of older adults as far as children and the broader family are concerned. This is illustrated with empirical research among older adults in the Netherlands.
- Policy makers need to take into account the diversity in support needs as related to the aforementioned variety in social contacts of older adults.

Key readings

Coleman, M., Ganong, L. and Fine, M. (2000) 'Reinvestigating remarriage: another decade of progress', *Journal of Marriage and the Family*, vol 62, pp 1288-307.
De Jong Gierveld, J. and Dykstra, P.A. (2002) 'The longterm rewards of parenting: older adults' marital history and the likelihood of receiving support from adult children', *Ageing International*, vol 27, no 3, pp 49-69.

Introduction

In the context of the description, and investigation of the mechanisms behind late-life diversity, the lifecourse perspective is broadly accepted as a useful paradigm.

> [Lifecourse theory] locates people in a historical context and life stage, highlights the differential timing and connectedness of people's lives, and stresses the role of individuals in shaping their own lives. (Elder, 1995, p 47)

Two of the facets of the lifecourse theory will be addressed in this chapter: historical time and life events, both of which affect the individual's 'biography'.

The historical time underlines the importance of historical changes at the macro level for life patterns, opportunities and restrictions facing both younger and older adults. The severe economic problems of the Great Depression and the consequences of the Second World War are frequently mentioned as examples in this context. The effects of particular historical changes will vary in type and relative influence across the lifecourse, and might thus be different for younger and older adults. In this chapter, the demographic and social effects of changes in the socio-structural and socio-cultural components of society starting around 1968/70 in different regions of Europe will be addressed. Research up until now has pointed out that young adults are deeply affected by these trends: new types of demographic behaviour and attitudes can be seen (Van de Kaa, 1987; Lesthaeghe and Surkyn, 1988; Liefbroer, 1999). I intend to investigate if and to what extent, older adults' lives have also been affected by these more recent changes. In this chapter, I will briefly describe some of the macro-level trends, and in doing so I will try to answer the first research question:

• Are older adults' behaviour and attitudes affected and shaped by the socio-structural developments and the changing values and norms of the final decades of the 20th century?

Life events are related to how individuals move through life. Events (transitions, status passages) and trajectories (the phases of life delineated by the events that occur at given points in time) characterise the personal 'biography' (Dykstra and Van Wissen, 1999). In the second, micro-level section of this chapter, I would like to illustrate the relationship between specific characteristics (life events) of the persons' biography and diversity in later life. More specifically, I would like to investigate widowhood versus divorce, and living alone versus repartnering, as well as the consequences of these events for the social embeddedness and social well-being of older adults. Empirical investigation of ageing and social embeddedness has been approached almost exclusively from the perspective of the current marital status. In this chapter, I would like to illustrate that it might be important to take into account older adults' marital histories as well. So, the second research question is:

• Starting from the life events of widowhood, divorce and repartnering, what can be said about late-life diversity among older adults, and more specifically diversity as far as social embeddedness and social well-being are concerned?

Societal trends

The period starting around 1960/70 can be characterised as a period of in-depth societal changes in several countries of Europe. Behavioural patterns, norms and attitudes concerning fertility, and the formation and dissolution of unions that had been changing for several decennia already are from that point in time affecting the broader audience of (young) adults. These changes are caused and supported by in–depth socio-structural changes, cultural changes and technological innovations (Van de Kaa, 1987, 1994; Lesthaeghe and Surkyn, 1988; Liefbroer, 1998, 1999; Lesthaeghe and Neels, 2001).

Important facets of the socio-structural changes that have taken place are a general increase in wealth, social security programmes, and health provision for both younger and older persons. During the second half of the 20th century, educational advancement has improved substantially. More young male and female adults than ever before are continuing full-time education up to high school and university levels. These changes have contributed to the increase of young women and mothers participating in the labour force, and in an important change in the relationships between men and women, more particularly in the position of women in society. The prolonged period spent in education, in particular of women, has also affected patterns of union formation and fertility (Van de Kaa, 1987). In several countries, combining motherhood and employment is difficult due to shortages in day-care facilities and an unequal division of labour, including family responsibilities, between husbands and wives. The expectation that they will be confronted with these obstacles is the reason why in many countries women, especially the better educated, now prefer to postpone union formation, marriage and the birth of a first child (Liefbroer and De Jong Gierveld, 1993). At the beginning of the 21st century, the mean mother's age at first birth had risen to 29 years in the Netherlands, Switzerland and a number of their neighbouring countries.

Cultural changes that have taken place in Europe have influenced the system of norms and values cherished by young and older adults, and values matter for all-important choices in life (Lesthaeghe and Moors, 2000). The past few decades have seen a decline in normative control on the behaviour of young adults, enabling them to fulfil their wishes and preferences to a much greater extent than their peers were able to do in the past. The authority of existing normative institutions, the authority of parents and the authority of the church have been eroded. Not only has the authority to exert normative control declined in recent decades, but the wish to exert such control has diminished as well (Liefbroer, 1999). These changes are linked to processes such as secularisation (Lesthaeghe and Neels, 2001) and individualisation, which affect the opportunities of individuals to decide for themselves how they wish to organise their lives.

Standard biographies, which entail a fixed ordering of life events (leaving the parental home to marry, followed by childbirth, the mother taking care of children and the home, being married until the death of one of the partners and continuing life as a widow or widower, living alone or co-residing with one of the children) have been – to a certain extent – replaced by choice biographies (Du Bois-Reymond and De Jong Gierveld, 1993). Choice biographies include the dominance of personal preferences concerning one's life and lifestyle over traditional, standard pathways, a trend that set in at the beginning of the 1950s, gained a massive group of followers by the end of the 1960s, and still persists. Characteristic of choice biographies is the growing diversity in living arrangements and combinations of realised life events. A biography may include such events as leaving the parental home to start living independently, followed by unmarried cohabitation, end of the unmarried cohabitation and return to the parental home, leaving the parental home for the second time, unmarried cohabitation, marriage, postponement of parenthood, separation and divorce, and so on. Young adults will be the first to accept and follow these new behavioural patterns.

I would like to make a plea for the investigation of the preferences for personal decision making concerning one's life and lifestyle, and choice biographies, among older adults as well. A first indicator of an individualistic lifestyle among older people is living independently in a one-person household after widowhood, in contrast to co-residence, the latter being connected to lifestyles that favour traditional patterns of family life. In the Census round 1990/91, it is pointed out that by far the majority of widowed men and women aged 50-80 years in northern, western and southern Europe are living in a one-person household (De Jong Gierveld et al, 2001).

The most influential technological innovation that triggered the new societal trends in European demographic behaviour was the introduction and widespread distribution of reliable contraceptives during the 1960s. The general availability of these products has enabled couples and individuals to regulate the number, timing and spacing of their children. Moreover, the influence of TV in the same period over the lives of people has further enhanced the acceptance of new lifestyles and informed younger and older people about new ways of life (Van de Kaa, 1994; Liefbroer, 1999).

The three broad sets of macro factors – socio-structural changes, cultural changes and technological innovations – together influenced the personal values, norms and preferences of broad layers of society. In addition, people had the possibility to actually realise their preferences during the course of their lives, so new biographies became an option for an ever-increasing proportion of the European population.

Empirical research by Liefbroer and Dykstra (2000) pointed out that in this context the year 1970 is indeed to be considered as a 'watershed' between the demographic attitudes and behaviours in the Netherlands before and after 1970. Based on several aspects of life (such as labour market participation of young mothers and divorce rates), the crucial developments of the 1960s and 1970s are illustrated.

Young adults in particular were affected by these developments, in that they re-evaluated union formation and marriage and postponed life decisions resulting in non-reversible outcomes such as childbearing. Investigation has yet to be carried out as to whether older adults were also affected by these developments. We hypothesise that ideas about marital and partner status – divorce, followed by living alone, remarriage, unmarried cohabitation or living apart together (LAT) – are being widely reconsidered among older people in Europe (De Jong Gierveld, 2002).

Lifecourse differentiation among older adults

A fairly large proportion of current older adults has been confronted with life events that were rather uncommon during their younger, formative years. Either as a consequence of their own or others' decisions, many older adults nowadays follow pathways other than those laid down in the standard biography. Divorce is one of the central life events in the non-standard biography. In addition, widowhood is postponed to higher ages, both for women and men. Older adults are well aware that living alone after divorce or widowhood increases the risk of loneliness (Walker, 1993), and that repartnering might provide them with a strong emotional bond and alleviate loneliness (De Jong Gierveld, 1998). Finding a new partner is a course that might especially attract men who feel deprived of the taken-for-granted sentient activities carried out for them by their former wives (Dykstra, 1990; Mason, 1996). Others, especially widows who might have cared for ailing former spouses, will hesitate to relinquish their new-found freedom and independence (Pyke, 1994; Lopata, 1996). The demographic imbalance in sex ratio favours men in finding a new partner at an advanced age, and for women the pool of suitable men diminishes as they age. This is intensified because males at higher ages tend to prefer females who are significantly younger than them (Morgan and Kunkel, 1998). When considering whether to take a new partner, the widowed or divorced woman or man has to weigh the pros and cons carefully. One of the issues to be considered is type of living arrangement: remarriage, unmarried cohabitation or LAT (Chevan, 1996; Davidson, 2002; Stevens, 2002; Peters and Liefbroer, 1997; Coleman et al, 2000; Karlsson and Borell, 2002).

Most older adults who adhere to traditional values will opt for remarriage, and those who incorporate more individualistic ideas will favour a consensual union or LAT (De Jong Gierveld and Peeters, 2002). Research has pointed out the financial and social consequences of divorce and subsequent repartnering, mostly concentrating on younger or middle-aged adults. The long-term consequences of divorce and repartnering on the social aspects of life, social embeddedness and well-being of older adults has not yet attracted much research. Moreover, the phenomenon has been approached almost exclusively from the perspective of the current marital status. Wolf et al (1997), for example, have shown that the children of widows and widowers 'step in' when their parents need help. In this chapter, I would like to illustrate that it might be important to take into account older adults' marital histories as part of their individual lifecourses because it might help elicit several facets of diversity in later life. In doing this, I have chosen to elaborate on some outcomes of survey research among older adults in the Netherlands.

Design of empirical research

This section makes use of data from the *Living arrangements and social networks of older adults* survey (Knipscheer et al, 1995). In 1992, face-to-face interviews were conducted with 4,494 men and women aged 55-89 years. The response rate was 62%. The sample can be considered as representative for the Dutch population aged 55+ (Broese van Groenou et al, 1995). Considering the non-response problems when interviewing an elderly population, the results are satisfactory, too. The sample was stratified according to sex and year of birth. Names and addresses came from the registers of 11 municipalities in the Netherlands: the city of Amsterdam and two rural communities in the western part of the country; one city and four rural communities in the north-eastern part; and one city and two rural communities in the south.

For this specific analysis, 10 subgroups of respondents were selected:

* women and men still in first marriage;
* women and men ever been widowed and never divorced, living alone;
* women and men ever been widowed and never divorced, repartnered;
* women and men ever having been divorced and live alone;
* women and men ever having been divorced, repartnered.

We refrained from introducing older adults' official marital status, because this is no longer a reliable indicator of their partner status and living arrangements.

Based on the principle of the lifecourse, various details were requested about the beginning, the continuation and the dissolution of each of the partner relationships in his or her life. Current partner status is asked:

1. Are you currently living with someone (= person of the opposite or the same sex) whom you consider to be a partner? In the Netherlands, as in more European countries, the partner in this context is explicitly meant and understood as an intimate, (potential) sexual relationship.
2. Is there someone with whom you do not share living quarters but do consider being a partner?

A second selection criterion was the availability of data about social network and social well-being. Respondents who did not answer these questions, and respondents without living children, have been omitted from this analysis. This provided us with a subsample of 3,325 men and women. In one of the sections of this study, we concentrate on repartnering at 50+, omitting those repartnered before the age of 50. This reduced the subsample to 3,204 respondents.

The number of surviving children is the first of the social network characteristics used in this study. Second, for each of the surviving children, we asked the respondents whether they were in touch with them regularly and whether they were important to them. Third, we asked the respondents to indicate the frequency of contact (face-to-face, by telephone or otherwise) with each child on a scale ranging from daily to several times per year.

Loneliness is defined as an unpleasant or inadmissible lack of (quality of) certain relationships. Loneliness includes situations where the number of existing relationships is smaller than desirable or acceptable, as well as situations where the intimacy wished for has not been realised (De Jong Gierveld, 1998). Loneliness is measured by the De Jong Gierveld Loneliness Scale (De Jong Gierveld and Kamphuis, 1985; De Jong Gierveld and Van Tilburg, 1999). The 11-item scale includes positively and negatively formulated items and has good psychometric properties (Van Tilburg and De Leeuw, 1991). The scale ranges from 0 (not lonely) to 11 (ultimately lonely). Respondents with a scale score of three or more are lonely.

The sample

Table 12.1 shows the respondents' demographic and social statistics. Men aged 55-89 are more frequently in first marriage and women are less frequently in first marriage but over-represented among the widowed living alone. Differences in life expectancy between men and women and differences in age at first marriage are the most important determinants of this finding. Of the ever-

Table 12.1: Descriptive statistics of the respondents by sex and lifecourse types

	n	**Mean age**[1]	**Mean number of children alive**[2]
Men			
First marriage	1,185	70.6[b]	3.2[a,b]
Widowed, alone	237	80.4[d]	3.4[a,b]
Widowed, repartnered	113	75.5[c]	3.6[b]
of which repartnered after 50	72	76.8	3.6
Ever divorced, alone	41	70.1[b]	3.1[a,b]
Ever divorced, repartnered	85	69.8[b]	2.7[a]
of which repartnered after 50	44	70.2	2.6
Women			
First marriage	808	66.7[a]	3.2[a,b]
Widowed, alone	699	77.0[c]	3.5[b]
Widowed, repartnered	40	69.3[b]	3.5[b]
of which repartnered after 50	21	72.3	2.9
Ever divorced, alone	81	69.8[b]	3.2[a,b]
Ever divorced, repartnered	36	65.3[a]	3.3[a,b]
of which repartnered after 50	16	66.9	4.3

Notes: *n*=3,325.

[1] Anova: $F_{(3325, 9)}$ =92.087, $p < 0.001$. Results from Waller-Duncan tests for the 10 main subgroups are provided. Not overlapping letter codes per column indicate significant differences between the subgroups, for example, women in first marriage (indicated by 'a') are significantly younger than ever-divorced women living alone ('b'), and both subgroups are significantly younger than widows living alone ('c').

[2] Anova: $F_{(3325, 9)}$ =2.306, $p < 0.05$. Results from Waller-Duncan tests for the 10 main subgroups are provided. Not overlapping letter codes per column indicate significant differences between the subgroups.

widowed men in this sample, 32% have repartnered, compared with only 5% of the widows. Repartnering is a characteristic of all age groups, but in Table 12.1 shows that half or more of the repartnering widowed men and women start a new partner relationship after the age of 50.

Ever having been divorced intensifies the heterogeneity and diversity in older adults' biographies compared with their peers some decades ago. The majority of the ever-divorced men (67%) have repartnered, compared with a minority of ever-divorced women (31%). Although the age at which people are confronted with the death of the partner is in general higher than the mean age at divorce, the portion of respondents who started a new partner relationship after age 50 is still around 45% or 50% of all the divorced repartnering in this sample.

Mean age of the respondents differs significantly when comparing men and women in the various lifecourse types: widowers living alone are by far the oldest group, followed by widows living alone, and women either in first marriage or repartnered after divorce belong to the youngest age groups.

The mean number of children varies significantly from relatively low for ever-divorced and repartnered men, to high for widowed men and women. These differences might be related to the age structure of the sample, widows and widowers being among the oldest groups of respondents and having formed a family at a time when having several children was the social norm. In the following sections I take this into account by controlling phenomena for age differences in the sample.

Results

Interconnectedness with children

In this section, I concentrate on the interconnectedness with children and, in doing so, select from the repartnered those who started the current partner relationship relatively recently, for example, after age 50. Table 12.2 shows that after controlling for differences in age between the respondents, the variations in mean number of living children are not significant for the subgroups of lifecourse types and gender. However, the differences in the mean numbers of children mentioned in the social network proved to be significantly different for the older adults in the various lifecourse types, for example, men in first marriage and widowers have significantly higher average numbers of children in their social network than divorced men. Moreover, Table 12.2 shows that the mean numbers of children contacted on a weekly basis or more frequently differs significantly: widows living alone are at the top of the list with a mean number of 2.3 children contacted at least weekly.

Men and women still in first marriages and widowers living alone follow with 2.2 and 2.1 respectively as mean numbers of children contacted at least weekly. Other subgroups lag behind; this is especially so for the ever-divorced men. For this group, living alone or being repartnered does not make much difference; the mean number of children contacted weekly is 1.0. And, although the number of living children for widowers alone (3.2) and divorced men alone (3.1) is only marginally different, the number of weekly contacts with children differs enormously between widowers alone (2.1), and divorced men alone (1.0). Although the mean number of living children for older widows living alone as well as for divorced women alone is high, the differences elicited in Table 12.2 for mean number of children contacted at least weekly differs significantly between 2.3 for widows alone and 1.5 for divorced women living alone.

Older adults and loneliness

According to the data of Table 12.2, respondents of several lifecourse types have a mean loneliness score that is 3.0 or higher, indicating moderate or extreme loneliness: widowers living alone (3.6), ever-divorced men living alone (4.3), and ever-divorced women living alone (3.8). Those in first marriage form the most important subgroups with lower mean loneliness scores.

Table 12.2: Interconnectedness with children, and loneliness of older adults with at least one child alive, corrected for differences in age; by sex, and lifecourse types; results of Multiple Classification Analyses

	n	Number of children alive[1]	Number of children in network[2]	Number of children contacted weekly d[3]	Loneliness score[4]
Men					
First marriage	1,185	3.3	2.8	2.2	1.6
Widowed, alone	237	3.2	2.6	2.1	3.6
Widowed, repartnered after 50	72	3.5	2.9	1.7	2.2
Ever divorced, alone	41	3.1	2.4	1.0	4.3
Ever divorced, repartnered after 50	44	2.6	1.7	1.0	2.9
Women					
First marriage	808	3.3	2.7	2.1	1.7
Widowed, alone	699	3.4	2.8	2.3	2.9
Widowed, repartnered after 50	21	2.9	2.3	1.7	2.7
Ever divorced, alone	81	3.2	2.2	1.5	3.8
Ever divorced, repartnered after 50	16	–	–	–	–

Notes: n=3,204.
[1] $F_{(3204, 8)}$ =1.825, p = 0.059, not significant
[2] $F_{(3199,8)}$ =3.484, p <0 .001
[3] $F_{(3199, 8)}$ =10.145, p < 0.001
[4] $F_{(3199, 8)}$ =29.813, p <0 .001

Conclusions

The aim of this study was first, to present the leading characteristics of the social and demographic changes that started around 1960/70 all over Europe. Socio-structural and cultural changes have had a major impact on the demographic attitudes and behaviour of young adults, but they have also affected the living conditions of older adults. These societal trends were illustrated in the first section of this chapter. The second section addressed the effects of the aforementioned trends on diversity in later life. Here, I differentiated older adults in 10 subgroups according to gender, current partner status, and partner history. Detailed characteristics of the start, the continuation and the dissolution of (each of the) partner relationships of the respondents were used to investigate their social embeddedness within the family.

The results of the study underscore the importance of looking at the diversity of the biographical history to understand the variations in familial embeddedness of older adults and the likelihood of being confronted with loneliness. Social embeddedness within the familial network as measured via the frequency of contacts with children is high among women and men in first marriage. Reciprocity in support giving and receiving between the older parental couple and their adult children is mentioned by Klein Ikkink et al (1999) as a driving mechanism in this context. Moreover, the number of children contacted on at least a weekly basis is high among widows and widowers living alone. Apparently children step in to provide instrumental and emotional support when older parents are becoming widowed (Lopata, 1996; Wolf et al, 1997).

The mechanisms mentioned for parental first-marriage couples in frequent contact with their children is not recognisable in the relationship of adult children and their widowed and subsequently repartnered parents. The repartnered parents are characterised by less frequent contact with children than those in first marriages. Embeddedness after repartnering might be affected by a confusing readjustment process. First, the repartnering may be a stressful event for both partners (Henry and Lovelace, 1995), because many changes have to be faced, such as moving to a new home and adapting to new household rules. Repartnered older adults require time and energy to 'invest' in each other, which may result in their having less time for their children and grandchildren (Spitze and Logan, 1992). Second, people who start a new partner relationship at an older age are confronted with a lack of social norms and guidelines regarding their role. Older partners may be unsure about how to relate to married stepchildren and their families (Coleman et al, 2000). One also has to take into account that the repartnering of a parent may profoundly affect any children in the new relationship. A child may feel distressed when someone takes the special place of a deceased father or mother. And a neglected aspect of the reaction of adult children towards their parent and a new partner is the resentment associated with the use of the family home by the new partner, and uncertainty about the future. What about the inheritance, for example? This may lead to ambiguous feelings.

The subgroups of divorced older adults are worth investigating separately. Here the gender differences are very prominent: divorced fathers (be they living alone or repartnered) score lowest in frequency of contact with children – much lower than divorced women.

The pattern of social embeddedness of older adults according to lifecourse patterns is also reflected in the patterns of loneliness registered.

Future policies should take into account not only older adults' situation of currently living with a partner versus living alone, but also the diversity in social embeddedness as related to the more detailed partner history of older adults.

Acknowledgement

This chapter is based on data collected in the context of the research programme *Living arrangements and social networks of older adults*. This research programme is being conducted at the Departments of Sociology and Social Gerontology and the Department of Social Research Methodology, Faculty of Social Sciences of the Vrije Universiteit in Amsterdam, and at the Netherland's Interdisciplinary Demographic Institute in the Hague. The research is supported by a programme grant from the Netherland's Programme for Research on Ageing (NESTOR), funded by the Ministry of Education and Science and the Ministry of Welfare, Health, and Cultural Affairs.

References

Broese Van Groenou, M., Van Tilburg, T.G., De Leeuw, E. and Liefbroer, A.C. (1995) 'Data collection', in C.P.M. Knipscheer, J. De Jong Gierveld, T.G. Van Tilburg and P.A. Dykstra (eds) *Living arrangements and social networks of older adults*, Amsterdam: VU University Press, pp 185-97.

Chevan, A. (1996) 'As cheaply as one: cohabitation in the older population', *Journal of Marriage and the Family*, vol 58, pp 656-67.

Coleman, M., Ganong, L. and Fine, M. (2000) 'Reinvestigating remarriage: another decade of progress', *Journal of Marriage and the Family*, vol 62, pp 1288-307.

Davidson, K. (2002) 'Gender differences in new partner choices and constraints for older widows and widowers', *Ageing International*, vol 27, no 4, pp 43-60.

De Jong Gierveld, J. (1998) 'A review of loneliness: concept and definitions, determinants and consequences', *Reviews in Clinical Gerontology*, vol 8, pp 73-80.

De Jong Gierveld, J. (2002) 'The dilemma of repartnering: considerations of older men and women entering new intimate relationships in later life', *Ageing International*, vol 27, no 4, pp 61-78.

De Jong Gierveld, J. and Kamphuis, F. (1985) 'The development of a Rasch-type loneliness scale', *Applied Psychological Measurement*, vol 9, pp 289-99.

De Jong Gierveld, J. and Peeters, A. (2002) 'Partnerpaden na het vijftigste levensjaar [Partner paths after the age of 50]', *Mens en Maatschappij*, vol 77, no 2, pp 116-36.

De Jong Gierveld, J. and Van Tilburg, T.G. (1999) *Manual of the loneliness scale*, Amsterdam, Vrije University, Department of Social Research Methodology.

De Jong Gierveld, J., De Valk, H. and Blommesteijn, M. (2001) 'Living arrangements of older persons and family support in more developed countries', *Population Bulletin of the United Nations* (Special Issue), nos 42/43, pp 193-217.

Du Bois-Reymond, M. and De Jong Gierveld, J. (1993) 'Van een standaardlevensloop-model naar een geïndividualiseerde keuzebiografie [From a standard biography towards a choice biography]', *Mens en Maatschappij*, vol 68, pp 7-16.

Dykstra, P.A. (1990) *Next of (non)kin: The importance of primary relationships for older adults' well-being*, Amsterdam: Swets and Zeitlinger.

Dykstra, P.A. and Van Wissen, L.J.G. (1999) 'Introduction', in L.J.G. Van Wissen and P.A. Dykstra (eds) *Population issues: An interdisciplinary focus*, New York, NY: Kluwer Academic/Plenum Publishers, pp 1-22.

Elder, G.H. Jr. (1995) 'Life trajectories in changing societies', in A. Bandura (ed) *Self-efficacy in changing societies*, New York, NY: Cambridge University Press, pp 46-68.

Henry, C.S. and Lovelace, S.G. (1995) 'Family resources and adolescent family life satisfaction in remarried family households', *Journal of Family Issues*, vol 16, pp 765-86.

Karlsson, S.G. and Borell, K. (2002) 'Intimacy and autonomy, gender and ageing: living apart together', *Ageing International*, vol 27, no 4, pp 11-26.

Klein Ikkink, K., Van Tilburg, T. and Knipscheer, C.P.M. (1999) 'Perceived instrumental support exchanges in relationships between elderly parents and their adult children: normative and structural explanations', *Journal of Marriage and the Family*, vol 61, pp 831-44.

Knipscheer, C.P.M., De Jong Gierveld, J., Van Tilburg, T.G. and Dykstra, P.A. (eds) (1995) *Living arrangements and social networks of older adults*, Amsterdam: VU University Press.

Lesthaeghe, R. and Van de Kaa, D.J. (1986) 'Twee demografische transities? [Two demographic transitions?]', in R. Lesthaeghe and D.J. Van de Kaa (eds) *Groei of Krimp? Mens en Maatschappij*, vol 61, pp 9-24.

Lesthaeghe, R. and Moors, G. (2000) *Life course transitions and value orientations: Selection and adaptation*, Interuniversity Papers in Demography, Working Paper 2000-7, Brussels: Vrije Universiteit.

Lesthaeghe, R. and Neels, K. (2001) *From the first to the second demographic transition: An interpretation of the spatial continuity of demographic innovation in France, Belgium and Switzerland*, Paper prepared for the Euresco Conference 'The Second Demographic Transition in Europe', Bad Herrenalb, Germany, 23-28 June.

Lesthaeghe, R. and Surkyn, J. (1988) 'Cultural dynamics and economic theories of fertility change', *Population and Development Review*, vol 14, pp 1-45.

Liefbroer, A.C. (1999) 'Life-planning during young adulthood: do intentions about the timing of family–life events come true?', Paper at the European Population Conference, The Hague, the Netherlands, 30 August-3 September.

Liefbroer, A.C. (1999) 'From youth to adulthood: understanding changing patterns of family formation from a life course perspective', in L.J.G. Van Wissen and P.A. Dykstra (eds) *Population issues: An interdisciplinary focus*, New York/Dordrecht: Kluwer Academic/Plenum Publishers, pp 53-85.

Liefbroer, A.C. and De Jong Gierveld, J. (1993) 'Veranderingen in de overgang van jeugd naar volwassenheid: een vergelijking van cohorten geboren tussen 1903 en 1965 [Changes in the transition from youth to adulthood: a comparison of cohorts born between 1903 and 1965]', *Mens en Maatschappij*, pp 17-35.

Liefbroer, A.C. and Dykstra, P.A. (2000) *Levenslopen in verandering; een studie naar ontwikkelingen in de levenslopen van Nederlanders geboren tussen 1900 en 1970 [Life courses in transition: A study into changes in the lifecourses of Dutch men and women born between 1900 and 1970]*, The Hague: Sdu Uitgevers.

Lopata, H.Z. (1996) *Current widowhood: Myths and realities*, Thousand Oaks, CA: Sage Publications.

Mason, J. (1996) 'Gender, care and sensibility in family and kin relationships', in J. Holland and L. Adkins (eds) *Sex, sensibility and the gendered body*, London: Macmillan, pp 15-36.

Morgan, L. and Kunkel, S. (1998) *Aging the social context*, Thousand Oaks, CA: Pine Forge Press.

Peters, A. and Liefbroer, A.C. (1997) 'Beyond marital status: partner history and well-being in old age', *Journal of Marriage and the Family*, vol 59, pp 687-99.

Pyke, K.D. (1994) 'Women's employment as a gift or burden? Marital power across marriage, divorce, and remarriage', *Gender and Society*, vol 8, pp 73-91.

Spitze, G. and Logan, J. (1992) 'Helping as a component of parent–adult child relations', *Research on Aging*, vol 14, pp 291-312.

Stevens, N. (2002) 'Re-engaging: new partnerships in late-life widowhood', *Ageing International*, vol 27, no 4, pp 27-42.

Van de Kaa, D.J. (1987) 'Europe's second demographic transition', *Population Bulletin*, vol 42, pp 1-47.

Van Tilburg, T.G. and De Leeuw, E. (1991) 'Stability of scale quality under various data collection procedures: a mode comparison on the De Jong-Gierveld Loneliness Scale', *International Journal of Public Opinion Research*, vol 3, no 1, pp 69-85.

Walker, A. (1993) *Age and attitudes: Main results from a Euro-barometer survey*, Brussels: European Commission.

Wolf, D.A., Freedman, V. and Soldo, B.J. (1997) 'The division of family labor: care for elderly parents', *The Journals of Gerontology* (Special Issue), 52B, pp 102-9.

THIRTEEN

Quality of life and social inequality in old age

Andreas Motel-Klingebiel

Key points

- Quality of life is a core outcome of unequally distributed access to social assets and/ or social positions that results in restricted or favoured life chances.
- The life domains relevant to overall quality of life vary considerably between age groups, with shifts from the outside world to inner life with increasing age.
- Quality of life is significantly lower but more divergent among older people.
- The results are in essence similar for all the countries included in the analyses (Norway, England, Germany, Spain and Israel), and point towards general patterns and relationships.

Key readings

Baltes, P.B. and Mayer, K.U. (eds) (1999) *The Berlin Aging Study: Aging from 70 to 100*, New York, NY: Cambridge University Press.

Motel-Klingebiel, A., Tesch-Römer, C. and von Kondratowitz, H.-J. (2003) 'The role of family for quality of life in old age – a comparative perspective', in V.L. Bengtson and A. Lowenstein (eds) *Global ageing and challenges to families*, New York, NY: de Gruyter, pp 323-54.

O'Rand, A.M. (1990) 'Stratification and the lifecourse', in R.H. Binstock, and L.K. George (eds) *Handbook of ageing and the social sciences*, San Diego, CA: Academic Press, pp 130-48.

Introduction

The ageing of societies is increasingly becoming a global phenomenon, thereby presenting a challenge to societies as we know them. For modern societies, especially in Europe, these rapid changes are intertwined inter alia with the combined tendencies of globalisation, European integration, new needs for occupational flexibility, migration and regional mobility. For central and eastern European countries, processes of transition to market societies must be added to this list. These developments not only influence the level of individual life nochances, behaviour, beliefs and preferences; they also impact significantly on the level of family and wider social networks and on the macro level of societal institutions, as well as on social structure in general. Thus, one faces a multilevel phenomenon that has to be covered by sociological and social policy analysis.

These developments may serve as a backdrop for the promotion of research on ageing and living conditions in old age as well as developments and markers of diversity and inequality between age groups and within cohorts. The analysis of quality of life plays an important role in this case as the concept includes objective and subjective dimensions of life situations that can be defined as outcome variables of continuous and complex multi-level processes of advantages and difficulties that take place in different but interrelated life domains.

This chapter connects the analysis of quality of life and of social inequality in a gerontological perspective and consists of three components. In the first, gerontological perspectives on quality of life and inequality will be introduced and the corresponding main hypotheses discussed. The second component briefly introduces measurement concepts and the database used by the analyses. In the third part, also the most comprehensive, analyses of quality of life based on the preceding theoretical remarks will be presented. The main emphasis will be on the hypotheses on social inequality and age discussed before. Finally, some conclusions will be drawn.

What does social inequality mean with respect to quality of life for older age groups? This chapter considers social inequality as given if access to available and desirable social assets and/or social positions is constrained – with limited and/or favoured opportunities for individuals, groups or societies evolving from that (see Kreckel, 1992). Such a broad definition goes beyond simple variability, conceptually includes the normative aspects of inequality and is directly connected to classical theoretical concepts of social inequality (Sen, 1973; Bolte et al, 1975; Atkinson, 1983). As access and restrictions may vary over the individual lifecourse with its different institutionalised stages (Kohli, 1985), between age groups and birth cohorts, this definition is sufficiently sensitive to analyse the interaction between age and social inequality. Quality of life emerges as a useful category in this perspective since quality of life as a desirable asset in itself can be defined as a significant outcome of unequally distributed living conditions and opportunities for people at different stages of their lifecourse and born at different historical times. This is independent of the differences in the concepts of quality of life itself (see Allardt, 1975; Smith et al, 1996; Noll and Schöb, 2002), which are discussed separately later in this chapter. The results of unequal access may differ by society and age groups, or social strata and other indicators that may vary over the lifecourse. Based on the hypotheses of continuity, differentiation, levelling and age dependency of social inequality in later life, this chapter discusses the distribution of overall quality of life according to age group and its association with different life domains.

Conceptual assumptions

The analyses in this chapter are driven by more than a mere descriptive urge. The question of how inequality is related to age is also important in a theoretical perspective that explores social inequality in a lifecourse perspective and seeks evidence for the conceptual assumptions of continuity, homogenisation, differentiation or age dependency. The exploration of the development of social inequality is relevant for evidence-based social policy intervention as well as a contribution to age-sensitive research on social inequality as one of the key issues in sociology (see, for example, Weber, 1976; Streib, 1985; O'Rand, 1990; Mayer and Wagner, 1996).

An assumption of unbroken continuity of inequality over the later lifecourse appears to 'solve' the problem by simply ignoring it. From a gerontological point of view, it should be stated that the hypothesis of continuity consistently disregards the inequality relevance of the age structure of societies and the discrimination between different stages of the lifecourse as such. A purely employment-oriented definition of social inequality, as still found in contemporary research, does not aspire to include old age in inequality analyses at all (Kohli, 1990). This may be problematic since individual dynamics of inequality positions over the later lifecourse are well documented (for income dynamics in old age, see Wagner and Motel, 1998). Hence, one has to seek alternatives that on the one hand are plausible from a theoretical point of view, and on the other hand can be tested empirically.

Beyond plain continuity, one can, first, formulate a hypothesis of homogenisation or destructurisation. The assumption of homogenisation applies to the standardisation of social positions. This may occur because of the relevance of institutional regulations that relatively favour those in lower positions. They offer social protection against the hazards of life and may, to a certain degree, level out the inequalities of working life. At the same time, more or less unsystematic differentiation may be found because of arbitrary inter-individual heterogeneity. This process is assumed to overlay initial social belonging and social differentiation.

Second, one can find arguments for differentiation and cumulation of diversity and therefore a reinforcement of social inequality. The differentiation hypothesis assumes that inequalities intensify in later life as a cumulation of earlier advantages and deprivations. Former material and social conditions determine – or at least influence – the process of ageing, they are correlated with the resources that are available to the individuals and their impact snowballs. In addition to this, institutional regulations not only secure living conditions against deterioration in old age, but they may also prevent an active improvement of material conditions in later life – and as a result stabilise basic inequality structures. Even if this is primarily the case for the income situation of the elderly as a basic condition in modern societies, it seems that it could also be relevant for other life domains such as health and social participation.

And third, in addition, the hypothesis can also be formulated of the age dependency of inequality structures and their basis, arguing that vertical intra-cohort distinctions, for example, differences between social strata or socio-economic status (measured by occupational positions, levels of education, income and/or assets), are replaced in the process of ageing by age-specific (such as health-related) differentiations, which then primarily determine the social position of individuals.

Theoretical assumptions may also simplify social reality by reducing social complexity to a set of mutually exclusive concepts that may be inadequate for the understanding of real life. It may be more pertinent to assume a mix of continuities and discontinuities of inequality positions in the specific life domains with a possibility for age-specific relevance of the domains.

Hence, it is theoretically unclear how social inequality develops over the later lifecourse and it needs empirical data and analyses to test the discussed hypothesis. But what form should this take? This chapter studies the problem by analysing overall and domain-specific quality of life in a comparative perspective. This will open the way to discussing the differences of social inequality between age groups as well as the distinctiveness of developments between life domains and the changes of their relative importance at different stages of the lifecourse. Based on this, the following questions will be addressed:

- What is the distribution of quality of life in old age?
- Can a highly unequal distribution within the group of the elderly be found?
- What are the differences between the age groups?
- Do we find similar or distinctive distributions according to age in different life domains?
- Which life domains are relevant for overall quality of life?
- Are there differences in the relevance of life domains between the different stages of the lifecourse?
- Are these patterns similar in different societies, so that it may be assumed that age effects are to a certain extent general development patterns?

The comparative perspective plays an important role even though this chapter does not apply a conventional welfare state comparative attitude. While cross-cultural comparisons are driven mainly by the search for generalities and distinctiveness as a result of similar structural necessities or different societal environments, this chapter explores possible similarities that can be interpreted as an indication of similar structural age patterns. Such matches between societies would point to unique lifecourse effects. If cultural embeddedness in different societies does not effect the age figures, this would support the argument against simple divergence between societal generations (Mannheim, 1964) in the analysis of cross-sectional data.

Theory and measurement of quality of life

Quality of life is a multidimensional construct and includes material and non-material, objective and subjective, individual and collective aspects (Motel-Klingebiel et al, 2003a). In relevant literature, two main traditions for the conceptualisation and measurement of quality of life can typically be observed (see Noll, 1999). One is the 'level of living' approach, which comes from the Scandinavian research tradition and is based on a resource concept (Erikson, 1974). The second approach, widely employed in Anglo–American research on well-being, focuses on the subjects' interpretations and their evaluation of living situations. The analyses presented in this chapter will focus on subjective representations by applying the WHO quality of life scale (see WHOQOL Group, 1994) in the short format of the scale (WHOQOL-Bref) as it is used in the OASIS study ('Old age and autonomy: the role of service systems and intergenerational family solidarity') (see Tesch-Römer et al, 2000). Quality of life is here seen as the individual's interpretation of the current living situation under the conditions of their respective culture, norms and values compared with their goals, expectations, standards and interests.

Basically, the WHOQOL-Bref instrument concentrates on four major life domains that are defined to cover the entire living situation of the respondents. Domain scores are computed as individual means in the areas 'physical health', 'psychological health', 'social relationships' and 'environment' (see Table 13.1) that are highly correlated with the complete WHOQOL measures (see WHO, 1996; WHOQOL Group, 1998). In addition, there are two single items on overall quality of life and life satisfaction measured on a five-point Likert scale, used as a semantic differential. The instrument is composed in order to be employed in international comparative research settings. The analyses here apply the hierarchical structure of the WHOQOL-Bref instrument. The study applies the combined measurement on the overall and domain level to investigate the relation between both, which is assumed to be age-related.

Database

The study is based on data of the OASIS project. The project was carried out between 2000 and 2003 and is linking representative data from the urban areas in Norway, England, Germany, Spain and Israel (Lowenstein and Ogg, 2003). It combines qualitative and quantitative approaches and allows a triangulation of research methods. This project basically offers two different sources of information: the OASIS survey sample and a qualitative OASIS sample. The OASIS survey sample, with data from 6,106 persons, is disproportionately stratified by age group and country. About 1,200 persons living in private households were interviewed in each country, with two thirds of age 25-74 and one third of age 75+. Even supposing participation rates are characteristically low in urban areas, the sample is representative for the target population with no survey-specific selectivity problems (Motel-Klingebiel and

Gilberg, 2002; Motel-Klingebiel et al, 2003b). The qualitative sampling is based on the survey sample. Older people of age 75+ at risk of becoming dependent (with low values on the SF-36 physical health subscale; see Ware and Sherbourne, 1992; Ebrahim, 1995; Gladman, 1998) were re-interviewed with a semi-structured instrument. Additionally, one of their adult children was interviewed, so that dyadic qualitative information is available. (For more information on the qualitative information, which will not be used in this chapter, see Phillips and Ray, 2003.)

Empirical results

In what follows, empirical results on the distribution of quality of life according to age and on the importance of the different life domains for overall quality of life in the five countries are introduced. The analyses presented are guided by four research hypotheses on the development of social inequality in the process of ageing and by the research questions outlined earlier.

Variations in quality of life

As a first step, the distribution of overall quality of life according to age group is analysed. In order to do this, the information from all the countries is condensed for the computations presented graphically in Figure 13.1 and later. As can be seen, there is a clear effect of age groups in the distribution of overall quality of life. While nearly 25% of the youngest rate their current quality of life as 'very good' and around 80% rate it at least as 'good' on a five-point scale ranging from 'very good' to 'very poor', these proportions are much lower in older age groups. Among those of age 85+, some 10% rate their overall quality of life as 'very good' and less than 60% at least as 'good'. Even if this is still impressively high compared with widespread common beliefs about living situations of older people, these values are substantially lower than in the younger age groups (Figure 13.1).

An analogous effect can be shown for all domains of quality of life if age-specific means of the domain scores are compared (Figure 13.2). Here, clear decreases according to age groups can be identified for the overall measure already explored in Figure 13.1 as well as for most of the domain-specific markers. 'Environment' (domain 4) is an exceptional case, decreasing only slightly among those aged 75+. This effect was expected, taking into account the indicators behind the construct (see Table 13.1).

This global picture that combines country-specific information from Norway, England, Germany, Spain and Israel can be confirmed when analysing the subject separately for each of the countries. Here fairly similar patterns in each of the countries can be identified. A structural difference regarding the culture of evaluations can be found when comparing overall and specific quality of life: while in Germany and to some extent in Israel the overall measure gives lower values than the domain scores, the opposite is the case for the other

Figure 13.1: Overall quality of life and age (all countries)

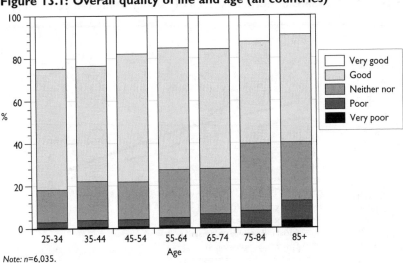

Note: n=6,035.
Source: OASIS (2000)

Table 13.1: Quality of life – the WHOQOL-Bref instrument

Domain 1 Physical health	Domain 2 Psychological health	Domain 3 Social relationships	Domain 4 Environment and living conditions	Overall measures Single indicators
• Activities of daily living • Energy and fatigue • Dependence on medicinal substances and medical aids • Mobility • Pain and discomfort • Sleep and rest • Work capacity	• Bodily image and appearance • Negative feelings • Positive feelings • Self-esteem • Spirituality, religion and personal beliefs • Thinking, learning, memory and concentration	• Personal relationships • Sexual activity • Social support	• Financial resources • Freedom, physical safety and security • Health and social care (accessibility, quality) • Home environment • Transport • Participation in and opportunities for recreation and leisure activities • Physical environment (pollution, noise, traffic, climate) • Opportunities for acquiring new information and skills	• Overall quality of life • Overall life satisfaction

Figure 13.2: Means of domain scores of quality of life (all countries)

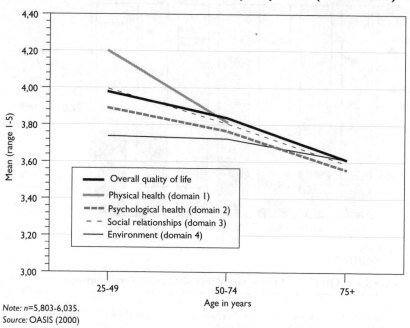

Note: *n*=5,803-6,035.
Source: OASIS (2000)

countries. This may result from cultural-specific evaluations, but in general, the same tendency according to age group can be found in all the five countries.

Since inequality may not only exist as mean differences between certain age groups but also within groups of people at different or similar stages of the lifecourse, it is also necessary to look at the variation and its development according to age. With respect to the variation of quality of life within the population, an increase can be noted (Figure 13.3). This is mainly the case for the overall measure and the health indicators. The coefficient of variation (standard deviation divided by mean level) for 'social relationships' (domain 3) and 'environment' (domain 4) seems to be quite stable. Again, this picture is confirmed for each country if analysed separately. One can find an overall tendency for a substantial increase of variation – and therefore inequality – in each country. In some of the countries, 'social relationships' (domain 3) and 'environment' (domain 4) are exceptions, with similar values in different age groups or only minor age differences. The diversity of health measures and the overall quality of life is highest in upper age groups. The coefficient of variation increases with age. 'Social relationships' show different effects in the societies analysed, while in the 'environment' domain no age-group differences are found. Israel is an exception, with increases for both, relationships and environment.

A special position for the environment measure can be observed, which is explained with reference to the indicators behind that domain. On the one hand, it includes the economic positions secured by public pension schemes

Figure 13.3: Coefficients of variance of domain scores of quality of life (all countries)

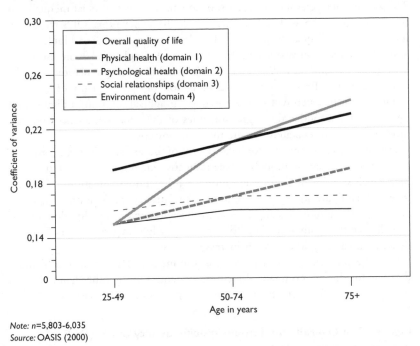

Note: *n*=5,803-6,035
Source: OASIS (2000)

that obviously work quite well. On the other hand, there is the housing environment – an aspect that also should not change dramatically as long as the individuals stay in their private households and avoid institutionalisation. The aspect of security may be an exception in this case.

Summarising, one finds lower levels of quality of life but higher variation in older age groups in particular with respect to health. This corresponds with results from the Berlin Aging Study (see Borchelt et al, 1996; Helmchen et al, 1996; Steinhagen-Thiessen and Borchelt, 1996) and other studies (Künemund, 2000; Jacobzone et al, 1999).

The distribution of quality of life in the 'social relationships' and 'environment' domains is more similar between age groups – age differences in means and in the coefficients of variation are smaller. Therefore, no overall statements regarding changes in inequality measures according to age group can be made. Instead it must be carefully specified which life domains are involved when discussing empirical results and testing theoretical hypotheses.

Summing up the outcomes, with only minor effects for external dimensions but marked effects for internal health-related measures, these descriptive results in some way support the assumptions of differentiation and specificity of inequality structures in old age as a general pattern in modern societies – at least in those countries included in the analyses presented here.

The relevance of life domains for overall quality of life

The age-specific relevance of each sub-domain for overall social inequality is the next issue to be analysed and discussed. To achieve this, OLS-regression models of overall quality of life on life domains are estimated (Table 13.1). This will be done on two levels. In the first step, simple models are estimated for three age groups (25-49, 50-74 and 75+) and the total population with the four WHOQOL-Bref life domains as predictors of overall quality of life. The results of that first step will be presented as a graphical solution in Figure 13.4 by estimating second-order regression lines of the beta coefficients from the models estimated separately for the three age groups.

Figure 13.4 shows the relative beta weights of the age-specific OLS (ordinary least squares) regression models for the respective life domains (adjusted for the beta weights of the OLS regression model for the entire population). The lines given in that figure are regression lines of the relative coefficients on age groups. A positive slope indicates an increase in the relevance of this life domain for overall quality of life according to age group, while negative slopes indicate declines in the importance with increases in age.

One the one hand, a clear increase in the impact of 'physical health' and a decrease for the 'environment' domain is evident. On the other hand, there is no significant effect on the life domains 'psychological health' and 'social

Figure 13.4: Overall and domain-specific quality of life (OLS regression, all countries)

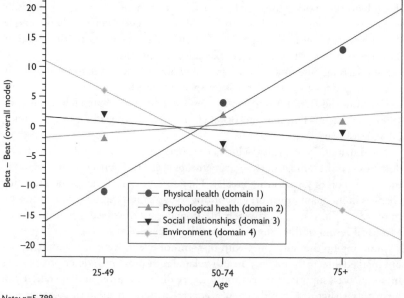

Note: n=5,789.
Source: OASIS (2000)

relationships' in the models that condense data from all five countries. The results broadly document a shift from the outside to the inner world with increasing age. This is demonstrated even more strikingly in Table 13.1. This shows the absolute beta coefficients for the three age groups and the total population in the five countries researched by OASIS. There is a clear picture of an increase for 'physical health' (domain 1) and a decrease for the 'environment' (domain 4) according to age group, with quite stable effects for 'psychological health' (domain 2) and 'social relationships' (domain 3) that were also documented graphically in Figure 13.4.

The total model (Table 13.1) indicates that the overall impact of three dimensions (domains 1, 2 and 4) is similar and quite high, while domain 3 (social relationships) is an exceptional case with only a small but still significant direct impact on overall quality of life. The minor exploratory power of domain 3 is reasonable, since this domain is measured by only three items in the WHOQOL-Bref and it therefore offers only limited variance. Nevertheless, from a theoretical perspective, the analyses do not focus on the strength of single domains but on their development according to age. In this respect, the domains behave differently, as documented earlier.

In a second step, the OLS regression models that have been estimated for each age group separately and for the total population, will be extended by interaction effects of life domains by age to test the effects simultaneously. This will be done by including age as a predictor variable ('Total (b)', Table 13.2). The final move on the overall level will be to estimate a full model including

Table 13.2: Overall and domain-specific quality of life (OLS regression, all countries)

	25-49	50-74	75+	Total (a)	Total (b)	Total
Physical health (domain 1)	0.09**	0.24**	0.33**	0.20**	0.19**	0.20**
Psychological health (domain 2)	0.22**	0.26**	0.25**	0.24**	0.24**	0.23**
Social relationships (domain 3)	0.10**	0.05*	0.07**	0.08**	0.07**	0.08**
Environment (domain 4)	0.26**	0.16**	0.06*	0.20**	0.20**	0.19**
Physical health (domain 1) by age	–	–	–	–	–	0.09**
Psychological health (domain 2) by age	–	–	–	–	–	0.03
Social relationships (domain 3) by age	–	–	–	–	–	–0.01
Environment (domain 4) by age	–	–	–	–	–	–0.09**
Age (years)	–	–	–	–	–0.01	–0.01
n	2,194	1,719	1,876	5,789	5,789	5,789
R^2	0.31	0.36	0.38	0.36	0.36	0.37

Notes: standardised coefficients beta, * $p<0.05$; ** $p<0.01$
Source: OASIS (2000)

'age' as well as the interactions of 'age*domain 1', 'age*domain 2', 'age*domain 3' and 'age*domain 4' as predictors ('Total'). This is done to analyse the interaction between the domain indicators and chronological age in more detail and to examine whether there is a statistically significant decline or increase in the importance of certain domains. As expected from the graphical analyses presented earlier, a strong and significant positive effect of the interaction between physical health and age and a substantial negative effect of the interaction between the environment dimension and age can be traced. The effects of the other interactions are negligible and of no significance. The main effects are not significantly influenced by the interactions added in this step and remain unaffected by the integration of the terms.

The changes in the predictors over age groups shown graphically earlier are confirmed in a complex multivariate analysis. This result can be illustrated more strikingly if one concentrates on the ranking of life domains by size of beta coefficients. Establishing a ranking of life domain makes the point clearer: there is no stability in the relative impact of the life domains on overall quality of life. There is, however, an essential and statistically significant relative increase of the importance of 'physical health', which advances from position four in the youngest age group to position one in the oldest, and a relative decrease of 'environment' factors that moves downwards respectively in the hierarchy of predictor dimensions.

The final step in the analyses will be the introduction of a comparative perspective. This means estimating the models separately for each of the countries. To cut a long story short, only the final models are presented in Table 13.3. This tabulation distinguishes the OLS regression models of overall quality of life on domain indicators by country with chronological age, the four life domains and the interaction between life domains and age included in the estimation. What can be seen here is similar to what was demonstrated for the overall model in more detail. Patterns in the countries look quite similar, on the whole indicating a shift from the outer to the inner life. The models for Norway, England and Germany show very similar effects as known from the overall model: relative increases for 'physical health' according to age with some type of relative decreases in the significance of external dimensions.

Spain and Israel are exceptions in one way or another; for Spain no significant effects can be observed, even though there is some mild decline in the effects of relationships according to age. This may be a result of cohort effects with the current Spanish urban population but there is no conclusive and satisfactory explanation. Israel shows quite similar patterns to the specified European societies, but 'physical health' seems to be replaced by 'psychological health' as a distinctive feature of this society: 'psychological health' obviously takes over the role of 'physical health' in the models for Norway, England and Germany.

Table 13.3: Overall and domain-specific quality of life (OLS regressions by country)

	Norway	England	Germany	Spain	Israel	Total
Physical health (domain 1)	0.25**	0.20**	0.24**	0.22**	0.1**	0.20**
Psychological health (domain 2)	0.42**	0.26**	0.30**	0.14**	0.14**	0.23**
Social relationships (domain 3)	0.00	0.06*	0.11**	0.07*	0.05	0.08**
Environment (domain 4)	0.05	0.20**	0.10**	0.23**	0.34**	0.19**
Physical health (domain 1) by age	0.07[a]	0.14[b]	0.14[b]	0.00	0.03	0.09[b]
Psychological health (domain 2) by age	−0.02	0.04	0.01	0.05	0.07*	0.03
Social relationships (domain 3) by age	-0.06*	−0.05	−0.05*	−0.05	0.03	−0.01
Environment (domain 4) by age	−0.09**	−0.01	−0.05*	−0.01	−0.10**	−0.09**
Age (years)	0.05	0.06	−0.04	0.05	0.03	−0.01
n	1,176	1,171	1,277	1,142	1,023	5,789
R^2	0.36	0.40	0.45	0.27	0.35	0.37

Notes: Standardised coefficients beta, $*p<0.05$; $**p<0.01$
Source: OASIS (2000)

Conclusions

Quality of life can be understood as an outcome of unequally distributed access to available and desirable social assets or positions, with restricted or favoured opportunities evolving from that. Quality of life is based on objective resources and conditions as well as on subjective evaluations. It is present on the individual as well as on the societal level.

Based on the subjective aspects on the individual level, this chapter introduces quality of life as a multidimensional and multilevel construct that can be measured overall and in four separate life domains according to the short version of the World Health Organisation quality of life scale (WHOQOL-Bref). This instrument was developed for comparative purposes during the 1990s. With respect to social inequality and ageing, four different hypotheses have been discussed and tested: continuity, homogenisation, differentiation and age dependency of inequality structures. These theoretical concepts guided the empirical analyses of quality of life and social inequality in later life.

The analyses demonstrate that lower levels of quality of life in old age can be found in all the participating countries. At the same time, there is a significantly higher degree of variation in older age groups than in the younger population. The 'environment' – and for some of the countries the 'social relationships' – are an exception in this case. 'Physical health' is the most important single domain for overall quality of life in old age. There is a shift of relevance of life domains for the overall quality of life according to the different age groups from the external, social spheres to the psychological and physical aspects of life. The external world is obviously less important for the oldest compared with the inner world. These findings are common in all five countries: analysed stability in the cultural comparative perspective allows the assumption that lifecourse and not just cohort effects are to be found.

The assumption of destructuring or homogenisation according to age group is not supported by the results. The increase in the inequality of the distribution of quality of life attests that there are significant processes of differentiation. The age differences in the structure of the predictors of overall quality of life support the hypothesis of age dependency of inequality structures. Social relations (including family) lose importance for the perceived quality of life among older people, while health-related dimensions – especially physical health – are the most relevant in later life. This is certainly the most significant result of the analyses presented in this chapter. Further analyses must provide evidence of how moderating or supplementary an effect certain other factors, such as need for care or social class, have on these results.

Acknowledgement

The analyses reported were conducted in the context of the OASIS project, carried out by the German Centre of Gerontology, Norwegian Social Research, the University of Keele, the University of the Basque Country and the University of Haifa (coordinator). The project was funded within the 5th Framework Programme of the European Commission (Contract No QLK6-CT-1999-02182). See Tesch-Römer et al, 2000; Lowenstein and Ogg, 2003; Phillips and Ray, 2003.

References

Allardt, E. (1975) *Dimensions of welfare in a comparative Scandinavian study* (Research reports), Helsinki: Research Group for Comparative Sociology.

Atkinson, A.B. (1983) *The economics of inequality*, Oxford: Clarendon.

Bolte, K.M., Kappe, D., and Neidhardt, F. (1975) *Soziale Ungleichheit*, Opladen: Leske + Budrich.

Borchelt, M., Gilberg, R., Horgas, A.L. and Geiselmann, B. (1996) 'Zur Bedeutung von Krankheit und Behinderung im Alter' ['On the significance of morbidity and disability in old age'], in K.U. Mayer and P.B. Baltes (eds) *Die Berliner Altersstudie*, Berlin: Akademie Verlag, pp 449-74.

Ebrahim, S. (1995) 'Clinical and public health perspectives and applications of health-related quality of life measurement', *Social Science and Medicine*, vol 41, no 10, pp 1383-94.

Erikson, R. (1974) 'Welfare as a planning goal', *Acta Sociologica*, vol 17, pp 273-8.

Gladman, J.R.F. (1998) 'Assessing health status with the SF-36', *Age and Ageing*, vol 27, no 3, p 3.

Helmchen, H., Baltes, M.M., Geiselmann, B., Kanowski, S., Linden, M., Reischies, F.M., Wagner, M. and Wilms, H.-U. (1996) 'Psychische Erkrankung im Alter' ['Psychiatric illness in old age'], in K.U. Mayer and P.B. Baltes (eds) *Die Berliner Altersstudie*, Berlin: Akademie Verlag, pp 185-219.

Jacobzone, S., Cambois, E., Chaplain, E. and Robine, J.-M. (1999) *The health of older persons in OECD countries: Is it improving fast enough to compensate for population ageing?*, Labour Market and Social Policy Occasional Papers 37, Paris: OECD.

Kohli, M. (1985) 'Die Institutionalisierung des Lebenslaufs – historische Befunde und theoretische Argumente' ['The institutionalisation of the life course – historical results and theoretical arguments'], *Kölner Zeitschrift für Soziologie und Sozialpsychologie*, vol 37, pp 1-29.

Kohli, M. (1990) 'Das Alter als Herausforderung an die Theorie sozialer Ungleichheit' ['Old age as a challenge for the theory of social inequality'], in P.A. Berger and S. Hradil (eds) *Lebenslagen, Lebensläufe, Lebensstile. Soziale Welt* (Sonderband 7), Göttingen: Schwartz, pp 387-408.

Kreckel, R. (1992) *Politische Soziologie der sozialen Ungleichheit* [*Political sociology of social inequality*], Frankfurt: Campus.

Künemund, H. (2000) 'Gesundheit', in M. Kohli and H. Künemund (eds) *Die zweite Lebenshälfte – Gesellschaftliche Lage und Partizipation im Spiegel des Alters-Survey* [*The second half of the life course – Results of the German Aging Survey on living conditions and participation*], Opladen: Leske + Budrich, pp 102-23.

Lowenstein, A. and Ogg, J. (eds) (2003) 'OASIS – Old age and autonomy: The role of service systems and intergenerational family solidarity', Final report, Haifa: University of Haifa (www.dza.de/forschung/oasis_report.pdf).

Mannheim, K. (1964) 'Das Problem der Generationen' ['The problem of generations'], in K. Mannheim (ed) *Wissenssoziologie. Auswahl aus dem Werk; eingeleitet und herausgegeben von Kurt H. Wolff*, Berlin, Neuwied: Luchterhand, pp 509-65.

Mayer, K.U. and Wagner, M. (1996) 'Lebenslagen und soziale Ungleichheit im hohen Alter' ['Situations in life and social inequality in old age'], in K.U. Mayer and P.B. Baltes (eds) *Die Berliner Altersstudie*, Berlin: Akademie Verlag, pp 251-75.

Motel-Klingebiel, A. and Gilberg, R. (2002) 'Zielsetzungen, Perspektiven und Probleme bei Surveybefragungen mit alten Menschen' ['Goals, perspectives and problems of survey research in the field of aging'], in A. Motel-Klingebiel and U. Kelle (eds) *Perspektiven der empirischen Alter(n)ssoziologie*, Opladen: Leske + Budrich, pp 133-53.

Motel-Klingebiel, A., Tesch-Römer, C. and von Kondratowitz, H.-J. (2003a) 'The role of family for quality of life in old age – a comparative perspective', in V.L. Bengtson and A. Lowenstein (eds) *Global aging and challenges to families*, New York, NY: de Gruyter, pp 323-54.

Motel-Klingebiel, A., Tesch-Römer, C. and von Kondratowitz, H.-J. (2003b) 'The quantitative survey', in A. Lowenstein and J. Ogg (eds) *OASIS – Old age and autonomy: The role of service systems and intergenerational family solidarity. Final report*, Haifa: Haifa University, pp 63-101.

Noll, H.-H. (1999) *Konzepte der Wohlfahrtsentwicklung: Lebensqualität und 'neue' Wohlfahrtskonzepte* [*Concepts of welfare development: Quality of life and 'new' concepts of welfare*], EuReporting Working Paper no 3, Mannheim: ZUMA.

Noll, H.-H. and Schöb, A. (2002) 'Lebensqualität im Alter' ['Quality of life in old age'], in Deutsches Zentrum für Altersfragen (ed) *Das hohe Alter – Konzepte, Forschungsfelder, Lebensqualität. Expertisen zum Vierten Altenbericht der Bundesregierung*, Band 1, Hannover: Vincentz, pp 229-313.

O'Rand, A.M. (1990) 'Stratification and the life course', in R.H. Binstock and L.K. George (eds) *Handbook of aging and the social sciences*, San Diego, CA: Academic Press, pp 130-48.

Phillips, J. and Ray, M. (2003) 'The qualitative phase', in A. Lowenstein and J. Ogg (eds) *OASIS – Old age and autonomy: The role of service systems and intergenerational family solidarity. Final report*, Haifa: Haifa University, pp 103-26.

Sen, A. (1973) *On economic inequality*, Oxford: Oxford University Press.

Smith, J., Fleeson, W., Geiselmann, B., Settersten, R. and Kunzmann, U. (1996) 'Wohlbefinden im hohen Alter: Vorhersagen aufgrund objektiver Lebensbedingungen und subjektiver Bewertung' ['Well-being in old age: estimations based on objective living conditions and subjective evaluation'], in K.U. Mayer and P.B. Baltes (eds) *Die Berliner Altersstudie*, Berlin: Akademie Verlag, pp 497-523.

Steinhagen-Thiessen, E. and Borchelt, M. (1996) 'Morbidität, Medikation und Funktionalität im Alter' ['Morbidity, medications and physical functioning in old age'], in K.U. Mayer and P.B. Baltes (eds) *Die Berliner Altersstudie*, Berlin: Akademie Verlag, pp 151-83.

Streib, G.F. (1985) 'Social stratification and aging', in R.H. Binstock and E. Shanas (eds) *Handbook of aging and the social sciences,* New York: Van Nostrand Reinhold Company, pp 339-68.

Tesch-Römer, C., von Kondratowitz, H.-J., Motel-Klingebiel, A. and Spangler, D (2000). *OASIS – Old age and autonomy: The role of service systems and intergenerational family solidarity. Ergebungsdesign und Instrumente des deutschen Survey* Discussion Paper no 32, Berlin: Deutsches Zentrum für Altersfragen.

Wagner, M. and Motel, A. (1998) 'Income dynamics in old age in Germany', in L. Leisering and R. Walker (eds) *The dynamics of modern society: Poverty, policy and welfare*, Bristol: The Policy Press, pp 125-42.

Ware, J.E. and Sherbourne, C.D. (1992) 'The MOS 36-item short-form health survey (SF-36)', *Medical Care*, vol 30, pp 473-83.

Weber, M. (1976) *Wirtschaft und Gesellschaft – Grundriß der verstehenden Soziologie [Economy and society: An outline of interpretive sociology]*, Tübingen: Mohr.

WHO (World Health Organisation) (1996) *WHOQOL-Bref – Introduction, administration, scoring and generic version of the assessment, Field trial version, December 1996*, Genf: World Health Organisation.

WHOQOL Group (World Health Organisation Quality of Life Group) (1994) 'Development of the WHOQOL: rationales and current status', *International Journal of Mental Health*, vol 23, pp 24-56.

WHOQOL Group (1998) 'Development of the World Health Organization WHOQOL-Bref quality of life assessment', *Psychological Medicine*, vol 28, pp 551-8.

FOURTEEN

Class, power and inequality in later life

Paul Higgs and Chris Gilleard

Key points

- The lifecycle theory of poverty has led to old age identified as a residual category of both the economy and social class.
- The post-war welfare state has decommodified later life, allowing for rising standards of living among retired people by creating a 'free-floating class' of non-producers.
- The successes of welfare states have led to changing expectations about how later life should be 'spent'. A new emphasis on reflexivity and choice marks out second modernity for all classes and age groups allowing greater individualisation of benefits and risks.
- In second modernity, the traditional conflicts between classes and gender are overlaid by conflicts over the distribution of resources in globalised capitalism. The ability of the nation state to continue to secure later life is increasingly constrained by these new sites of conflict.

Key readings

Beck, U. and Beck-Gernsheim, E. (2002) *Individualisation*, London: Sage Publications.

Blackburn, R. (2002) *Banking on death or investing in life: The history and future of pensions*, London: Verso.

Gilleard, C. and Higgs, P. (2000) *Cultures of ageing: Self, citizen and the body*, Harlow: Prentice Hall.

Vincent, J. (2003) *Old Age*, London: Routledge.

Introduction

Our aim in this chapter is to sketch out an argument that links the material well-being of the retired population in western Europe and North America with issues of power and social class. In the course of doing this, we challenge the continuing representation of older people as members of a residual class dependent on the rest of society and defined by the processes of poverty (Collins et al, 2001). We argue, instead, that later life must be viewed as a fragmented and complex formation fully connected to the dominant economic and cultural processes of late modernity as well as to its contradictions. The history of poverty among older people in industrialised societies has tended to marginalise the importance of later life in framing key aspects of the modern world. It has led to the assumption that issues relating to class and power are reflections of previous class locations rather than present ones with their own dynamics. Later life is no longer defined by its vulnerable position within the lifecycle theory of poverty. It has become secure because of the post-war welfare state. This transformation is creating dilemmas of its own, as policy success is represented as demographic crisis. This crisis is no longer at the margins of social policy. Through the operation of pension fund capitalism, it reaches the very core of social organisation. In this chapter, we chart the changes in later life from its initial residualisation as poverty, through its decommodification by the welfare state, to its current recommodification within second modernity. Throughout, we demonstrate that later life has been shaped by processes of social class and the drive to expand contemporary capitalism.

Industrialisation and the impoverishment of age

In Britain, the position of older people has long been associated with the Poor Laws that only disappeared with the creation of the post-war welfare state. This legislation formalised the responsibility of the local community to support those of its inhabitants who had fallen on hard times, recognising unemployment, as well as illness and infirmity, as potential causes of indigence. Within this framework, 'agedness' became a major category of need. As industrialisation led to increased demands on the productivity rather than the skill of older workers, late-life poverty grew more acute. These negative effects on later-life unemployment increased the strains on the parish-based model of Poor Law support. The Poor Law system became identified as a growing 'cost' to the state leading to attempts to reform the system, making its operation harsher and its 'beneficiaries' ever more immiserated (Brundage, 2002). By the end of the 19th century, there was broad recognition of the necessity for an old age pension so that those no longer able to work could live out the remaining part of their lives free from the stigma that had become attached to pauperism. When Lloyd George finally introduced legislation for old age pensions in 1908, it was an acknowledgement that:

> if a working man ... is able to keep himself from the Poor Law up to the age of 60, [one should not] attach any blame to him if, after 60, he finds it difficult to provide for himself. (Chamberlain, 1895, cited in Thane, 2000, p 185)

This first wave of pension legislation hardly transformed the material circumstances of later life. Although labour force participation rates among older men declined, this trend had been evident well before the legislation –

the result of a continuing decline in the size of the agricultural sector and a steady rise in heavy industry and manufacturing (Johnson, 1994). Wage labour still formed the economic mainstay for older men. While the state pension took some of the humiliation out of retirement, it offered few material benefits and was generally insufficient to fend off poverty. The new category of old age pensioner created by this legislation did little to reposition 'the aged' from the residual category they had occupied since the original 16th-century Poor Laws. The marginalisation of the old age pensioner gradually lessened after the establishment of the post-war welfare state.

The post-war welfare state

At the time the 1945 Labour government introduced universal pay-as-you-go old age pensions, 33% of the working population were already contributing to an occupational pension scheme (Hannah, 1986). This is not surprising given the previous history of state provision. What is surprising is that this tendency continued throughout the post-war period. A major reason was the limited scope of the reformers' vision. Flat-rate universal pensions were intended to establish solidarity between classes and generations but not any degree of affluence in retirement. As Beveridge himself put it:

> it is dangerous to be in any way lavish to old age. (Cited in Macnicol and Blaikie, 1989, p 36)

Although differing in their interpretation of subsistence, the Trades Union Congress (TUC) also supported the government's focus on improving opportunities for younger people and the conditions of those in work. Consequently, the unions were more concerned with negotiating higher wages and larger employer contributions to occupational pension schemes than improving the flat-rate system universal scheme (Thane, 2000, pp 380-1). Throughout this period, growth in occupational pension schemes was as significant as the growth in state pensions, although the consequences of this focus would not show through until the latter decades of the 20th century. What is more significant is that the route out of old age poverty was increasingly perceived by organised labour to be through sectional bargaining of occupational benefits rather than through social legislation.

This approach represents a paradox, most apparent in Britain, but with echoes elsewhere, namely that the articulation of class interests did not in practice lead to a focus on egalitarianism and flat-rate universalism. Certainly, the welfare state was a focus for social democratic politics within which most trade unions were immersed. However, beyond the corporatism that dominated national politics, British trade unions had to articulate the interests of their members through more localised and sectional arenas, based as much on maintaining as on minimising differential benefits (Cronin, 1979; Hyman, 1989). This contradiction between the sectional and the universal had its apogee in the conflicts between the trade unions and the 1974-79 Labour governments when incomes were supposed to be traded for the social wage. The hostility of skilled trade union members to pay freezes undermined the social compact. The notion that the interests of trade unions could be represented by the minimalisation of inequality at the expense of the better organised ignores the reality of workplace politics. The separation between such 'economism' and 'politics' has long been deplored, but it does represent the reality of class processes and the politics that emerge from them. This paradox is played out in the negotiations of trade union leaders, who must mediate between the interests of their members and the politics of social democracy. Sometimes this is in the form of gaining occupational pension entitlements for their members that are not available to all groups; other times it might be through universal social benefits such as equal pay.

The welfare state, as many have come to realise, is a contradictory phenomenon predicated on the ideology of equality in order to ensure that the inequalities of the market system can be maintained (Barbalet, 1993). As far as retirement income in the UK is concerned, the negotiation of occupational pensions has provided the most successful route out of an old age defined by poverty and not one that has been achieved through the rights of social citizenship. The downside is that groups with little leverage or that are outside the structures of the formal economy have not benefited to the same degree from the changes in the funding of later life. Occupational pensions have created differential outcomes in retirement and have fragmented later life, but rather than being a feature of the oppression of older people through the maintenance of inequality, they have been a product of the conflict between capital and labour under the conditions of wage labour. Pensions seen as deferred wages rather than as state benefits take us to the heart of the relationship between social class and later life in the advanced economies.

American exceptionalism?

Were things different in the US? We would argue not. The development of industrialisation created the same problems for the old. By the end of the 19th century, three quarters of men aged 65+ in the US were still working, the largest numbers employed as farmers. On farms, some 80% of older men were still working, while almost half of the urban working class had stopped work by the age of 65 (Costa, 1998, p 23). Poor law arrangements provided some relief for the indigent aged without alternative means of support, but such provision was much more limited than was the case in Britain (Orloff, 1993, pp 141-3). Veterans of the Civil War started to receive military pensions in the 1870s and this number increased significantly when the Dependent Pension Act of 1890 entitled Union veterans to claim a pension if they became unfit for manual labour (Orloff, 1993, p 135). This Veterans Pension began to function as a kind of federal old age pension and by 1910, nearly a quarter of the US population aged over 65 were reliant upon it.

Despite the absence of any central legislation on pensions, workforce participation rates of older men also declined throughout this period. By 1920, almost half were no longer working. There was little agitation for any national system of social insurance, while opposition to all forms of federal state provision was voiced regularly both by local politicians, labour organisations and employers. The Wall Street Crash and the economic depression that followed provided the spur for change. Unemployment, which had been a problem throughout the 1920s, rose dramatically from half a million in 1928 to more than eight million in 1931, reaching a peak of around 15 million men – one third of the male workforce (Piven and Cloward, 1993, pp 48-61). The impact of the Depression was much greater in the US. Manufacturing industry was severely affected. Since older workers were disproportionately concentrated in farming, the non-household service sector, crafts and the professions, the Depression affected younger workers more than older ones. Writing in *Vanity Fair* in 1931, Bruce Barton half jokingly suggested that as a potential solution "every man and woman in the United States be retired from work at the age of 45 on a pension amounting to one half of his or her average earnings in the preceding five years ... creat[ing] a special automatic class of consumers" (cited in Mitchell, 2000, p 85). Such ideas found a more serious expression in the Townsendite movement, which campaigned for a tax-funded old age pension of $150 per month for all US citizens aged 60+ (Mitchell, 2000).

Roosevelt's New Deal reflected some of this thinking by introducing an old age pension of $30 dollars per month aimed at enabling older workers to retire and free up jobs for younger men. Unlike the British old age pension legislation, the New Deal was not primarily concerned with preventing the pauperisation of older people. Rather it addressed the government's need to halt the social unrest created by the Depression (Piven and Cloward, 1993). Private charity and local state and municipal authorities had proved themselves unable to cope. The legislation sought to buy off the growing militancy of the workers and the unemployed, but in doing so Roosevelt was at pains to avoid treating social security as welfare payouts. Instead, he wanted to establish a federally run pension system that resembled a private pension plan. People would pay into a defined benefits scheme, earning an annuity that reflected the history of their contributions. Old age assistance continued as a means-tested benefit for the indigent aged and that was referred to as a pension. The new system of social security set itself a different goal – not the amelioration of indigence, but the maintenance in later life of "the distributional profile of incomes and benefits generated by the ... market" (Skocpol, 1995, p 137).

Bypassing the political institutions of the working class, the New Deal cemented the relationship between work and old age, ensuring that the latter was funded through the deferred wages of working life. Only those who had been marginal to the formal economy when younger would retain their marginal status in old age as 'welfare pension recipients'. Although the scheme soon turned effectively into a pay-as-you-go system, the idea that social security operates as a 'fund' into which employers and employees contribute has been retained. As in Britain, this difference in the formulation of retirement income is not a matter of detail, but has important implications for the relationship between working life and post-working life. Social security is seen as deferred income and as a fund to maintain a retirement that is as similar as possible to the lifestyle enjoyed while at work. As such, it neither precludes affluence nor seeks to define later life as poverty and when it is presented as a compact, it is as a compact between the generations, rather than between classes.

From welfare category to decommodified class

Further illumination of the connection between later life and social class can be gleaned from the work of Esping-Andersen, whose *The three worlds of welfare capitalism* (1990) divided the forms taken by the post-war welfare state on the basis of their differential capacity to introduce social rights and support decommodification. By decommodification, Esping-Andersen meant the ability of a person to maintain a livelihood without recourse to the market.

> [A] minimal definition must entail that citizens can freely, and without potential loss of job, income or general welfare, opt out of work when they themselves consider it necessary. (Esping-Andersen, 1990, p 23)

The neo-Marxist idea of individuals not being defined by their capacity to sell their labour power is one with profound consequences for the relations between classes. The degree to which decommodification can be realised is thus a political issue as much as it is one of social policy. The divisions between social assistance, social insurance and Beveridgian welfare states create different forms of social differentiation on top of that of social class. This is particularly important in relation to retirement pensions. The social assistance model designed as poor relief was (and is) clearly designed to stigmatise recipients through principles such as means-testing, while the social insurance model consolidates divisions between wage earners by giving different groups of employees their own set of rights and privileges corresponding to their social position. Esping-Andersen takes this further in his criticism of the Beveridge model, which, through its premise of universalism, seems to promote an equality of status. "But", as Esping-Andersen writes, "the solidarity of flat-rate universalism presumes a historically peculiar class structure, one in which the vast majority of the population are the 'little people' for whom a modest, albeit egalitarian, benefit may be considered adequate". The consequence of this 'modest equality' is that "the poor rely upon the state and the remainder on the market" (Esping-Andersen, 1990, p 25). It is not surprising, as we have seen in the case of the UK (and the US: Ghilarducci, 1992), that the middle class and affluent members of the working class turn to private schemes to escape this fate and effectively create a dual system of retirement income.

The welfare state and its social insurance programmes have been seen as representing a compromise between the interests of working people, employers and the state in creating a workable compact for national development in the aftermath of the Second World War. It can also be seen as an attempt to shift the position of retired people from that of a welfare class dependent upon 'assistance' to a 'free-floating class'[1] capable of participating in society without having to participate in the labour market. In continental Europe, this policy has been quite successful and many of the dilemmas now facing countries such as Germany, France and Italy relate to the public costs associated with maintaining an ageing population at the levels of replacement income that have become the norm (Casey and Yamada, 2002). In Britain, however, such policies were only ever partly successful, as a result of which they did little to inhibit the impetus for non-state solutions to the funding of later life that emerged in the inter-war years. The early post-war welfare state had insured against pauperism but it left the majority of pensioners close to the margins of poverty, reliant as they were on the state old age pension. This began to change as employment prospects in later life continued to shrink and state and occupational pensions rose in value. In Britain, by 1977, 58% of the male new retirees were recipients of both state and occupational (private) pensions and relative poverty levels among pensioners had dropped to 23% (authors' own calculations from the General Household Survey, 1977-78, supplied by the University of Essex). Despite its compromises, throughout Europe the welfare state system (in combination with the 'deferred income' of occupational pensions in countries such as Holland and the UK) had delivered a longer, healthier and richer later life than had been the experience of many pensioners during their earlier working lives. Increasingly, the retired had become a decommodified, 'free-floating class' removed from the exigencies of their earlier working lives and sharing in the growing affluence of the 'golden years' of welfare capitalism.

The contradictions of the mature welfare state

The success of the most developed nations in creating a longer, richer and healthier post-working life has paradoxically led to a reformulation of the role of the welfare state. In part, this has been a consequence of the de-institutionalisation of the modern lifecourse (Guillemard and Van Gunsteren, 1991) and the growing individualisation of what has been termed the 'postmodern' lifecourse (Featherstone and Hepworth, 1989). The equalisation of later life experience and its economic underpinning that was achieved in Britain between the 1950s and 1970s began to unravel during the 1980s (Johnson and Stears, 1995). During the 1980s and 1990s, growth in pensioner incomes has increasingly outpaced that of wage incomes. The consequence has been increasing material inequalities in later life, with, at the same time, increasing opportunities for later life to be lived beyond its institutionalised boundaries (Disney and Whitehouse, 2001, p 60). Patterns of income, wealth and expenditure mark out new categories of retired people whose lifestyles are ill defined by the social stratification created by welfare policy. Even in the relatively austere context of Britain, the idea that later life should be represented by the 'old age pensioner' no longer matches the reality. By the 1990s, income for the poorest 20% of UK pensioners was almost entirely made up from public transfers (old age pensions and supplementary benefits). At the same time, two thirds of the income of the richest 20% of retirees was derived from other, private sources (Johnson and Stears, 1995; DWP, 2003).

As stated earlier, this improvement in the standard of living of the retired, if funded by the state, always represented a drain on the resources of the economy. Considerable intellectual energy has been devoted to explaining this 'fiscal crisis' (Gough, 1979; Myles, 1984) and it is not surprising that the decades following the oil crisis saw a retrenchment of welfare throughout the major economies. To this has been added increasing anxiety about the impact of demographic ageing, prompting the World Bank to outline the need for urgent political action and structural reform of pay-go pension systems to forestall its impact (World Bank, 1994). The bank proposed its now famous 'three-pillar approach' of basic state pension, supplementary occupational pensions and individual voluntary arrangements in order to spread the risk of the 'age crisis'. Its main argument was that individuals needed to share responsibility by ensuring effective redistribution of their earnings over their working and non-working lifecourse. Effectively, the World Bank asked governments to reject the idea, dominant for much of the post-war period, that state-funded pensions alone could meet the demands for income replacement in retirement.

It is ironic that part of the reason for the 'crisis' in pensions is the success that social security has had in reducing the significance of age on relative poverty. As prosperity has become part of everyday experience, a larger proportion of revenue has to be spent by the state to ensure parity between workers and non-workers. The agenda is no longer about relieving poverty and want, but ensuring social inclusion within a consumer society. That such a scenario threatens the viability of even social democratic welfare states is evident in the collection of essays edited by Esping-Andersen, entitled *Why we need a new welfare state* (2002). This volume focuses on intergenerational equity and the need to encourage delayed exit from work in order to preserve the idea of the welfare state. While many continental European nations still wish to pursue their social insurance pension systems, this approach is a source of profound risk to the economic viability of both the nation state and the international financial order. A similar dilemma afflicts the discussion of social security in the US, where there are continued demands for its privatisation in order to release funds for the stock market (Aaron and Shoven, 1999). High incomes in retirement, according to the World Bank, should only emerge from an engagement with the market. They should not be based on flat-rate entitlements, nor should they be accrued solely through years of contributions. As a result, an increasing number of countries are attempting to reform their pensions and introduce the World Bank's 'second' and 'third pillar' to their existing pension arrangements. In this environment, pension funds have grown apace, representing an ever-larger share of total world assets and are fast becoming the dominant form of global capital (Blackburn, 1999, p 5).

In Britain, the impact of pension fund development on later life has been profound. Over the past quarter of a century, private sources of income in retirement have risen steadily, in part because of the widening population base that has been contributing to occupational pensions, and in part because of rising wages and increased contributions (DWP, 2003). The impact of the market has been to amplify income inequalities in later life while reducing the income differential between the retired and those still working. This is so even in countries operating contributory social insurance schemes, where earnings-related 'social transfers', rather than capital income, contribute positively to income inequalities (see Yamada, 2002, p 23). The retired have become more differentiated within themselves, while they have become less differentiated, materially, from people who are still in work[2]. Retirement is now constituted through a multiplicity of positions, each providing opportunities for, as well as obstacles to, a continuing increasingly individualised engagement with the market. The state no longer holds the ring, preferring instead to govern through the 'conduct of conduct'.

Old age uncontained? Reflexivity in 'second modernity'

The modern welfare state has sought to 'decommodify' old age, establishing what we have termed a 'free-floating class' of retirees able to enjoy a secure period at the end of their lives. For a 'glorious' 30 years after the Second World War, such a reality seemed close to being actualised. However, this success has run into longer-term difficulties as the affluence created by welfare capitalism has hit contradictions with both global capitalism and the transformation of social life. The turn to 'the market' that was first evident in Britain and the US, with the stimulation of personal occupational pensions, has effectively 're-commodified' retirement, shifting responsibility increasingly from the state to the individual (Bonoli, 1999). Given that this 'Anglo-Saxon model' is fast becoming the chosen solution to the economic problems created by demographic ageing, it is important to look at its implications for social inequalities and social class in the context of a changing society.

The UK experience would suggest that its main impact has been to enable more people to have retirement incomes similar to those of the working population. This has meant that inequalities in later life match those within the working population. Why then, as Beck et al (2003) have observed, has the growth of inequality over the past quarter century not been accompanied by a rise in class polarisation? Indeed, one of the principal concerns motivating the emergence of welfare states was the desire to overcome or marginalise inequality. In these circumstances, why has the effective abandonment of such an approach not created a 'legitimation crisis' among the populations of the most prosperous nations?

The answers to some of these questions may be found in Beck's theorisation of the individualisation of life in what he terms 'second modernity'. This social formation is as much based upon cultural as it is on structural change.

Using the idea of 'reflexive modernisation', Beck and his colleagues argue that a second modernity has emerged out of the first modernity of industrialisation and the nation state in which the modern welfare state was located (Beck et al, 2003). First modern societies were organised around 'full employment', where status, consumption and social security all flowed from participation in the economy. The culmination of first modernity was the realisation of universal social rights and social security in the context of equality of opportunity within a market economy.

Second modernity is a response to the challenges and dynamics of the first. Globalisation undermines the economic foundations of the nation state, while the intensification of individualisation through the successes of the welfare state (improved education, housing, healthcare and social security) has eroded the ascriptive patterns of collective life. A breakdown in the full-employment society leads instead to a decline in the significance of gainful employment: status, consumption and social security choices have – to some extent – become progressively independent of income, and thus of labour force participation (Beck et al, 2003, pp 6-7).

Second modernity is characterised by reflexivity, which is modernity's response to the unintended consequences of its own actions. The successful resolution of the conflicts that modernity has itself constructed (predominantly the conflicts of class and gender) has the effect of dissolving the boundaries of modern, corporate society. The dominance of the state and the nuclear family are challenged. The internal structure of classes and the characteristics of class society lose their salience in organising social identities. This is despite increasing social inequalities. The stability of individual subjectivity was presaged on the institutionalised modern lifecycle, but, in second modernity:

> the individual can no longer be conceived as a stable and unchangeable subject, but rather as a 'quasi subject', the result *as well as* the producer of its networks, situation, location and form. (Beck et al, 2003, p 25)

Hakim (2000), in a similar vein, has argued that "affluent and liberal modern societies provide opportunities for diverse lifestyle preferences to be fully realised". For her, this is most evident in the work–lifestyle preferences of women, who, because of equal opportunities and contraception, confront 'genuine choices' – whether to work, be home centred, or mix and modify the two. The general inference from Hakim is that the existence of preferences extends beyond the issue of women and paid employment. She argues more generally for the increasing importance of attitudes, values and preferences in shaping the modern lifecycle, which she sees as one of the main tenets of 'preference theory' whose underlying premise is individual agency – that is, social actors choosing to act. The individual life project, central to second modernity, requires the exercise of choice as a constant flow of action over the lifecourse. She is aware that these changes are taking place within the context of successive generations of men and women, and that increasingly they are extending across all sectors of society as exposure to the opportunities of preference has increased substantially since the cultural transformation of the 1960s (Hakim, 2000, pp 43-83). Later life, as we have argued in *Cultures of ageing* (Gilleard and Higgs, 2000), is equally affected by this cultural transformation. However, ageing in second modernity is also caught up in processes of power related to both the economy and social class.

Power and social class: what is different now?

Starting with the post-war affluence that has spread throughout the class structure of industrialised nations allows us to situate the potential, if not actual, re-commodification of later life. Such affluence, in part, is the redistribution of resources available to any society. Rising standards of living are a form of wealth redistribution, albeit one leading to unequal consequences. Starting from this assertion can cause problems for many class theorists, as it challenges a simple relationship between class and poverty. Even in Marx's *Wages, price and profit* of 1865 (1973 edn), there is recognition that working-class interests are served by trying to increase wages at the expense of profit. His argument was that such struggles could at best only temporarily halt the decline of living standards. The impact of trade unions, social reform and mass consumer society has ensured that the period of absolute immerisation has passed and that much of the population does live in relative affluence. This does not mean that the relations of class do not structure society. As a contemporary example, Scambler's triad of 'logics, relations and figurations' can be used to show how later life is being reconfigured (and is reconfiguring) class and power (Scambler, 2002). His argument, developed primarily in relation to health inequalities, is that we need to see the processes operating on social class as continually changing and that we should not confuse one set of figurations as representative of all. We also need to recognise that the logic of capitalist social relations determines a continuing power differential in the ability to obtain material and social advantage. It is this power differential that recreates the conflicts surrounding class, but in different circumstances from those normally connected to old age.

Applying this model to the funding of pensions, we can see an underlying logic at work. The operation of 'grey capitalism' is predicated on gaining large amounts of funds to fuel speculation. Minns (2000) argues that privatisation of public utilities and the emphasis upon 'third-pillar' private pensions are necessary conditions for market growth. These changes relate to the logics of globalised capitalism. The high returns initially available to pension funds made them attractive to national political elites eager to cut their responsibilities. As these returns have diminished, political elites face a difficulty in promoting reliance on returns that 'can go down as well as up'. The need for the nation state to appear competitive in terms of the world economy presents a further drive, forcing policy changes onto governments as the attempts to renegotiate pension entitlements in continental Europe demonstrate (Dang et al, 2001). Entry into the single European currency was conditional on reducing public spending to certain limits. The result was a wave of protest across France, Italy and Germany at attempts to change the social contract. The relations that emerge from these logics are ones that stress the necessity of individualisation in the pursuit of security in later life. The reliance on the social benefits of citizenship rights becomes one of differentiated outcomes of personal situation. Individuals need to invest both in pensions and in good jobs to be assured of resources in old age. This is only marginally less true in systems that pay out income-related social security pensions. The questions that then emerges are: will the pensioner of the second modernity fast become a latter day *rentier* dependent on the profits made by younger generations? Or is the late modern retiree expecting a good standard of living as a return on deferred 'surplus' income accumulated over the lifecourse? The answer to these question sets up the class relations of later life. Here, one of the neglected aspects of discussions on class inequality emerges; namely, how those in the very highest positions in the economy obtain benefit from these policies.

A major feature of global capitalism is the high levels of remuneration for those in charge (Haseler, 2000; Isles, 2003). Such benefit is closely connected to share value rather than profitability. This not only drives the economy, but it also sets up particular interests that often contradict the interests of those whose pensions they oversee. Similarly, the disputes over the closure of 'defined benefit' occupational pensions for employees but not for directors demonstrate how class interacts with retirement income in surprising ways. It is the case, as in classical Marxism, that the relation between classes is dictated by access to surplus, whether or not the economy is doing well. Indeed, contradictions are most exposed when there is a conflict over the distribution of a declining surplus.

The differential fates of state pensioner, holders of occupational pensions and those in receipt of private pensions are examples of how social position is dependent on individual and cohort histories. Expectations and conflicts emerge when returns are not what were expected, whether through the downsizing of citizenship benefits, or through poor returns from investments. Occupational pension holders are at risk of scheme failure as the impact of pensions holidays for employers in the past make their impact, while in the case of companies such as Enron, corporate failure wreaks devastation. These potential crises over pensions create new sites of conflict. While some of these are based upon traditional class relations, others draw upon generational and gender differences and the contrasting position of those in the public and private sectors of the economy. Those countries attempting to reform the benefits provided by national social insurance systems are witness to the lines of fracture of financial globalisation. The competing interests of a globally oriented capitalism and a nationally orientated population of retirees, or potential retirees, reflect the broader conflict between international and national capitals. By addressing the needs of one, the state may find itself in conflict with the other, with relative levels of elite integration into either global or national capitals serving as a critical variable in the articulation of power (see Sklair 2001). In second modernity, the increasingly deinstitutionalised relationship between working and post-working life has established new sites of inequality. In first modernity, the site for such conflicts was between a national working class and a national bourgeoisie, and its resolution lay in the modern welfare state. Old age was a residual location whose position improved as a function of the cumulative affluence of post-war adult cohorts. In second modernity, the sites of conflict have multiplied. Their resolution no longer seems to lie in the social compacts of the past. A 'free-floating class' of retirees is fragmenting in an increasingly marketised pensions 'free for all'.

Conclusion

Our argument is that the 20th century has seen the rise and fall of the notion that the old could be defined en masse as a 'decommodified' pensioner population. Through a variety of differing means, the retired population has become an increasingly socially differentiated group within society. In second modernity, the economic circumstances of all age groups before, during and after working life have become equally complex and equally less reducible to any single structure of power or dependency. In part, this reflects the success of post-war European societies and their social policies, but this is only part of the story. Old age is no longer a problem because of its poverty. There is still poverty in later life but poverty is no longer its defining condition. Rather, the contemporary crisis is about the contradictions that have emerged from a new image of later life – the third age. Establishing and maintaining a comfortable income in later life is now the major consideration affecting not only those in retirement but all those younger cohorts struggling to maintain the presence of a third age in their own lifetimes.

Examining the circumstances by which the economic basis for later life is funded helps clarify the linkages between class, power and later life and identifies the sites of conflict around the third age. Consumerism pervades all age groups and all social classes. The desire and expectation of people to continue to be included in consumer society before and after their working life ends explains why the arguments for maintaining post-work incomes are so acute. Stimulation of consumption is not intended to liberate people from their ties to the market; rather, it helps maintain the reproduction of capital. However, as markets expand and mass consumption moves well beyond the reproduction of mass labour (Marx, 1978, p 457) the figurations of capitalist relations change. Time freed from the necessity of labour increases. The conflict over where the money will come from to sustain this 'surplus' time continues the argument between capital and labour. But class is now only one site of this conflict, and is arguably losing some of its salience. New sites have emerged, between the interests of global and national capital, between the lifecourses of men and women, between the need for economic prosperity and the need for social legitimation, and between the responsibilities of the state and the duties of its citizens.

Leon Trotsky once wrote that old age is "the most unexpected thing" that could happen to an individual[3]. We would extend this view by suggesting that it is the prospect of circumventing old age that is now throwing up unexpected challenges that stretch our understanding of ageing and demand a new focus on the changing contexts of later life.

Notes

[1] We use this term in the sense of Mannheim's ascription of intellectuals to membership of an unanchored, classless stratum or 'free-floating class' within modern society, relatively distanced from the polarities of the productive process (see Mannheim, 1960, pp 136 ff).

[2] Trends over the latter decades of the 20th century indicate that "income inequality among the retirement-age population was not significantly different from income inequality among the working age population", reflecting a general increase in income inequalities across the lifecourse. At the same time, older people are becoming relatively better off compared with younger people (Yamada, 2002, pp 9, 15).

[3] The aphorism attributed to Leon Trotsky is "old age is the most unexpected of all things that happen to a man", and is a diary entry for 8 May 1935 (Trotsky, 1958).

References

Aaron, H. and Shoven, J. (1999) *Should the United States privatize social security?*, Cambridge, MA: MIT Press.

Barbalet, J. (1993) 'Citizenship, class, inequality and resentment', in B. Turner (ed) *Citizenship and social theory*, London: Sage Publications, pp 36-56.

Beck, U., Bonss, W. and Lau, C. (2003) 'The theory of reflexive modernisation: problematic, hypotheses and research programme', *Theory, Culture and Society*, vol 20, pp 1-33.

Blackburn, R. (1999) 'Grey capitalism and pension reform', *New Left Review*, vol 233, pp 3-66.

Bonoli, G. (1999) *Globalisation, the welfare state and recommodification*, Paper, Bath: Department of Social and Policy Sciences, University of Bath.

Brundage, A. (2002) *The English Poor Laws 1700-1930*, London: Palgrave.

Casey, B. and Yamada, A. (2002) *Getting older, getting poorer? A study of the earnings, pensions, assets and living arrangements of older people in nine countries*, Labour Market and Social Policy – Occasional Paper, Paris: OECD.

Collins, A., Estes, C. and Bradsher, J. (2001) 'Inequality and aging: the creation of dependency', in C. Estes and associates (eds) *Social policy and aging*, Thousand Oaks, CA: Sage Publications, pp 137-63.

Costa, D.L. (1998) *The evolution of retirement: An American economic history*, Chicago, IL: University of Chicago Press.

Cronin, J. (1979) *Labour and society in Britain 1918-1979*, London: Batsford.

Dang, T., Antolin, A. and Oxley, H. (2001) *Fiscal implications of ageing: Projections of age related spending*, Economics Department Working Papers, no 305, Brussels: OECD.

Disney, R. and Whitehouse. E. (2001) *Cross-country comparisons of pensioners' incomes*, Research Report 142, Department of Social Security, Leeds: The Stationery Office.

DWP (Department for Work and Pensions) (2003) *Pensioner Income Series, 2001/2*, London: The Stationery Office.

Esping-Andersen, G. (1990) *The three worlds of welfare capitalism*, Oxford: Polity Press.

Esping-Andersen, G. (ed) (2002) *Why we need a new welfare state*, Oxford: Oxford University Press.

Featherstone, M. and Hepworth, M. (1989) 'Ageing and old age: reflections on the post-modern lifecourse', in B. Bytheway, T. Keil, P. Allat and A. Bryman (eds) *Being and becoming old*, London: Sage Publications, pp 143-57.

Ghilarducci, T. (1992) *Labor's capital: The economics and politics of private pensions*, Cambridge, MA: MIT Press.

Gilleard, C. and Higgs, P. (2000) *Cultures of ageing: Self, citizen and the body*, Harlow: Prentice Hall.

Gough, I. (1979) *The political economy of the welfare state*, London: Macmillan.

Guillemard, A. and Van Gunsteren, H. (1991) 'Pathways and their prospects: a comparative interpretation of the meaning of early exit', in M. Kohli et al (eds) *Time for retirement: Comparative studies of early exit from the labour force*, Cambridge: Cambridge University Press, pp 362-87.

Hakim, C. (2000) *Work–lifestyle choices in the 21st century: Preference theory*, Oxford: Oxford University Press.

Hannah, L. (1986) *Inventing retirement: The development of occupational pensions in Britain*, Cambridge: Cambridge University Press.

Haseler, S. (2000) *The super-rich: The unjust new world of global capitalism*, London: Macmillan.

Hyman, R. (1989) *The political economy of industrial relations*, London: Macmillan.

Isles, S. (2003) *Life at the top: The labour market for FTSE −250 chief executives*, London: The Work Foundation.

Johnson, P (1994) 'The employment and retirement of older men in England and Wales, 1881-1981', *The Economic History Review*, vol 47, pp 106-28.

Johnson, P. and Stears, G. (1995) 'Pensioner income inequality', *Fiscal Studies*, vol 16, pp 69-93.

Macnicol, J. and Blaikie, A. (1989) 'The politics of retirement 1908-1948', in M. Jeffreys (ed) *Growing old in the twentieth century*, London: Routledge, pp 21-42.

Mannheim, K. (1960) *Ideology and utopia: An introduction to the sociology of knowledge*, London: Routledge and Kegan Paul.

Marx, K. (1973) *Wages, price and profit*, Peking: Foreign Languages Press.

Marx, K. (1978) *Capital: Volume II*, Harmondsworth: Penguin.

Minns, S. (2000) *The cold war against welfare*, London: Verso.

Mitchell, D. (2000) *Pensions, politics and the elderly: Historic social movements and their lessons for our aging society*, Armont, NY: M.E. Sharpe.

Myles, J. (1984) *Old age and the welfare state*, Boston, MA: Little, Brown & Co.

Orloff, A. (1993) *The politics of pensions: a comparative analysis of Britain, Canada and the United States, 1880-1940*, Madison, WI: University of Wisconsin Press.

Piven, F.F. and Cloward, R.A. (1993) *Regulating the poor: The functions of public welfare*, New York, NY: Vintage Books.

Scambler, G. (2002) *Health and social change: A critical theory*, Buckingham: Open University Press.

Sklair, L. (2001) *The transnational capitalist class*, Oxford: Blackwell.

Skocpol, T. (1995) *Social policy in the United States: Future possibilities in historical perspective*, Princeton, NJ: Princeton University Press.

Thane, P. (2000) *Old age in English history*, Oxford: Oxford University Press.

Trotsky, L. (1958) *Trotsky's diaries in exile 1935*, London: Faber and Faber.

World Bank (1994) *Averting the old-age crisis: Policies to protect the old and promote growth*, Washington, DC: World Bank.

Yamada, A. (2002) *The evolving retirement income package: Trends in adequacy and equality in nine OECD countries*, Labour Market and Social Policy Occasional Papers 63, Paris: OECD.

FIFTEEN

Ageing and diversity, what next?

Svein Olav Daatland and Simon Biggs

Three reasons to insist on diversity

If people are in fact ageing differently, and if old age is better characterised by variation than by some general order, then we need to address these diversities, test out their empirical validity, and theorise about how they are produced and played out. This volume has contributed to this effort, and represents a contrast to the prevailing obsession with similarities and central tendencies. Gerontologists may have observed and documented that there are divergent pathways of ageing and substantial differences among older persons, but they have also tended to retreat to normative models as templates for theorising. Empirical observations may not have been taken seriously, or may have been lost in paradigms that give attention to means, and thereby lose sensitivity to variation.

There are then good reasons for a continued insistence on diversity. Let us point to three such reasons. The first is the need to counteract stereotypes about ageing and older people. Why such stereotypes are still widespread when gerontologists have long insisted otherwise may be an indication of the impotence of gerontological theorising. People in general seem to be more attracted to stereotypical attributions, perhaps in a need to distance themselves from the fear and unpleasantness associated with adult ageing. We all do this by accentuating the differences between 'us' and 'them', and in so doing denying the other the individuality and differentiation that we so generously attribute to ourselves, maybe in some vain hope that this may help us avoid the same destiny. We need to develop a better understanding of the nature, sources and mechanisms of the multiple pathways in later life as a contrast to the stereotyping of ageing and older people.

A second reason is the bias towards the mean in observations and theorising. Attention is then directed towards whatever general tendency that may be extracted from empirical observation. Variations around the mean are treated as deviations or idiosyncrasies or, in what is even more likely, as random error or 'noice'. We know more about the average trend of selected outcome variables, be they health or class, intelligence or well-being, than what individual trajectories look like. However, if 50% fall into a plus (+) category and the other 50 into minus (–), it makes little sense to conclude with an average of zero. In this context, we need to move from variables to lives, and study the different trajectories and pathways of ageing, in addition to more global trends. Perhaps then insight would be gained more readily into how variation and inequality are produced among older people. This is, after all, what critical research should be about – about people, their problems, hopes, opportunities and remedies. We need to ask what types of pathways which are masked behind the aggregate trends or, to quote Binstock (2000, p 372):

> Rather than theorise [the] average experiences, how can we better understand the full range of experiences and their outcomes?

A third reason is that a focus on diversity and differentiation brings us into one of the central controversies in gerontology, that between continuity and change over the lifecourse. Many writers on ageing have explicitly or implicitly taken a position on this issue. The *continuity position* was in the formative years of gerontology represented by activity and continuity theory (Havighurst et al, 1968; Atchley, 1989), and is later represented for example by the ageless self model (Kaufman, 1986). The *change position* has been advocated by disengagement theory (Cumming and Henry, 1961), by developmental models (Erikson, 1959), and by maturation theories (Tornstam, 1989; Biggs, 1999). Selectivity models (Baltes and Baltes, 1990) assume an intermediate position with an emphasis on change as adaptation in the service of maintaining self-esteem. Age stratification theory (Riley, 1985) has from a sociological perspective theorised how cohort flow and social structure combine to change the status and role of older people. In general, role theory and other variants of functionalism are inclined towards explaining and supporting stability, while more critical perspectives, as in the political economy tradition (Estes et al, 1995; Phillipson, 1998), have focused on changes and new directions.

Ageing as diversity

Dannefer (1988) has criticised gerontology for the surprisingly little theorising about the heterogeneity of ageing, as have Calasanti (1996) and McMullin (2000). Dannefer sees the reason for this neglect in a poor fit between the heterogeneity of lived experience and dominating theoretical traditions that are insensitive to diversity in later life. For example, both 'development' and 'socialisation' – two of the most central concepts that capture the mechanisms of age-related changes – tend to obscure the question of heterogeneity, as they both build on ideas of normativity and consensus. Development is supposed to lead to a standardised end-state, while socialisation assumes that individuals are shaped to a common, social norm. Both concepts, according to Dannefer, are unable to deal with human ageing, which is not only a biological, but also a dialectical phenomenon. He suggests that these two constructs be replaced by 'habituation' and 'social reproduction', which are less contaminated by a bias towards convergence and normative expected outcomes. The means by which personal agency and choice may alter trends and directions should also be included in such models and as indeed done in Section IV of this volume.

We do, however, also need to examine critically the ageing and diversity issue itself. Questions need to be asked about whether divergence and diversity are empirically valid descriptions of adult ageing and older people, and for example, what the meaning of diversity is, and what the implications for social solidarity are.

It should be clear by the range of themes and approaches in the present volume that diversity is a perspective, more than an analytical concept. Diversity may refer to different levels and characteristics, and to processes as well as outcomes. Focus may be on intra-individual or on interpersonal variation, with both shedding light upon how different people experience ageing are and how differences have come about. There is no reason to assume that all these patterns and processes have a common logic or explanation. They do, however, have common themes and questions, like the extent to which diversity is expanding or declining over the lifecourse, and what the influences of race, class, culture, gender, sexual orientation and other forms of inequality are.

As for *intra-individual diversity,* there seems to be solid empirical evidence for a considerable variation in the age-related trajectories of sub-functions and capacities. Some domains are seemingly more sensitive to age than are others; for example fluid intelligence more so than crystallised intelligence, and memory more so than self-esteem, as shown in Section One of this volume. We know less about why this is so, and whether certain phases of the lifecourse are formative for negative or positive change in old age. Nor do we have sufficient knowledge about when variation peaks, and how general patterns are across domains. Some findings indicate an expansion of intra-personal variation with age, possibly with a contraction if and when functional systems break down in the fourth age, or in a short period of anticipation of death or 'terminal drop'. We need also to know more about the impact of intra-personal variation on interpersonal differences. Whether, for example, increases and contractions of intra-personal heterogeneity would accentuate or reduce intergroup differences.

There is also evidence for considerable *interpersonal variation* in old age, as documented in Sections II to IV of this volume. Older people differ in a number of characteristics (as do younger people), be it in health or habits, class or contacts, power or happiness. There is less consensus about what age has to do with it. Are these differences stable over the lifecourse and thereby unrelated to age? Are they expanding or are they levelling out in response to ageing or age-related factors and processes? Here our understanding needs to be refined to differentiate inter-individual variation and the effects of cumulative social inequalities – the relationship between social location and social privilege.

Divergence over time may be produced by social structures if, for example, attractive positions are scarce, and some selection is needed to give access to these positions. This should in particular be the case in what Sørensen (1986) calls 'closed systems', where access is controlled by others and only available when vacancies arise. Access to the advantages of 'open systems' where social constraint is less, should allow personal factors and identifications to be expressed more freely. Dannefer (2003) suggests that a cohort may function as a closed system in this respect, as inter-individual differences *within a cohort* tend to increase with age, and tend to do so with considerable regularity from cohort to cohort. When this is the case, he argues that it need be theorised and explained on a macro level, not as a product of individual differentiation or personal agency. Cumulative advantage theory may contribute here – the tendency of initial advantages and disadvantages to accumulate with time, and then to widen the gaps between more and less priviledged people and social groups. Further empirical study is needed that includes both macro and micro factors, and how the two may interact to produce divergence or convergence of different domains and circumstances. In short, we need to know more about the kind of mechanisms that influence such accumulation with specific reference to ageing and old age.

'Social reproduction' and 'social allocation' would be two such macro-level mechanisms. Institutions tend to preserve and reproduce themselves, and socialise individuals for that purpose, implying differential access to opportunities and benefits which they tend to cumulate over time. Social allocation refers to the regulation of access to roles and statuses. As the more attractive positions are scarce, selection will tend to favour those already privileged. However, when ageing is considered, far more clarity is needed to explain the role of time within a lifecourse perspective. Also missing is the interaction between social structure, ageing and individual agency. Among the individual-level mechanisms that may produce divergence over time are, for example, 'personal differentiation' and 'human capital investment'. The former implies that people tend to unfold over time, as both genes and experiences are given more time to be expressed. The latter refers to how different types of resources (social, economic and cultural) may be invested earlier in life, and pay off later, and the more so the more you have invested (O'Rand, 2001).

We need also to locate interpersonal variation in historical time and space, exploring differences *between cohorts*, and then the degree of regularity between trends from one cohort to another. Among the more cohort-specific factors are the effects of age norms and social policy. Age norms may have become looser over time, implying fewer constraints on the individual and allowing people to live out their individuality and uniqueness. Whether or not social policy tends to reproduce, increase or decrease such differences is a matter of dispute.

Implications

Among the benefits of including diversity more centrally within gerontology would be to sharpen attention to individuality and pluralism, and in so doing help us integrate old age into mainstream life, and older people into mainstream society. The recognition of differences also helps us identify the barriers and constraints to differentiation between groups of all locations and identifications. Forefronting diversity, in this sense, is a humanistic – even a democratic – project.

A focus on how differentiation and inequality develop over the lifecourse also helps us evaluate the impact of ageing relative to the more established stratification factors like class, gender and ethnicity. Ageing research would thereby feed into mainstream sociology and psychology and help raise the awareness of age and ageing in social research more generally.

More attention to diversity and differences should also be reflected in policy and practice, and contribute to preventing the standardisation of services and treatments that are often imposed on older people. Globalisation and individualisation, migration and transnationalism will add to these diversities and demand further adaptations between structures and individuals as pointed out in Section Three of this volume.

Yet, an ageing and diversity paradigm may still fall victim to the same fallacy as more traditional approaches in imposing some standard and convergent order on reality. The tendency to assume linear trends and relationships is strong, be it in the form of divergence or convergence over time. We should also study the breaks in these developments, discontinuities as things turn, take new directions and forms. People are not positions. Given the right circumstances, we respond actively to constraints as well as to possibilities, engage in personal and collective agency, and it is perhaps here that the impact of understanding multiple pathways and cultural migrations will lie.

References

Atchley, R. (1989) 'A continuity theory of normal aging', *The Gerontologist*, vol 29, no 2, pp 183-90.

Baltes, P.B. and Baltes, M.M. (1990) 'Psychological perspectives on successful aging: the model of selective optimization with compensation', in P.B. Baltes and M.M. Baltes (eds) *Successful aging: Perspectives from the behavioral sciences*, New York, NY: Cambridge University Press, pp 1-34.

Biggs, S. (1999) *The mature imagination: Dynamics of identity in midlife and beyond*, Buckingham: Open University Press.

Binstock, R.H. (2000) 'On the unbearable lightness of theory in gerontology: review of V.L. Bengtson and K.W. Schaie (eds) *Handbook of theories of aging*, New York: Springer, 1999', *The Gerontologist*, vol 40, no 3, pp 367-73.

Calasanti, T.M. (1996) 'Incorporating diversity: meaning, levels of research, and implications for theory', *The Gerontologist*, vol 36, no 2, pp 147-56.

Cumming, E. and Henry, W. (1961) *Growing old*, New York, NY: Basic Books.

Dannefer, D. (1988) 'What's in a name? An account of the neglect of variability in the study of aging', in J.E. Birren and V.L. Bengtson (eds) *Emergent theories of aging*, New York, NY: Springer, pp 356-84.

Dannefer, D. (2003) 'Cumulative advantage/disadvantage and the life course: cross-fertilizing age and social science theory', *Journal of Gerontology: Social Sciences*, 58B, vol 6, S327-37.

Erikson, E. (1959) *Identity and the life cycle*, New York, NY: W.W. Norton.

Estes, C.L., Linkins, K.W. and Binney, E.A. (1995) 'The political economy of aging', in R.H. Binstock and L.K. George (eds) *Handbook of aging and the social sciences*, San Diego, CA: Academic Press, pp 346-61.

Havighurst, R.J., Neugarten, B.L. and Tobin, S.S. (1968) 'Disengagement and patterns of aging', in B.L. Neugarten (ed) *Middle age and aging: A reader in social psychology*, Chicago, IL: University of Chicago Press, pp 161-72.

Kaufman, S. (1986) *The ageless self*, Madison, WI: University of Wisconsin Press.

McMullin, J.A. (2000) 'Diversity and the state of sociological aging theory', *The Gerontologist*, vol 40, no 5, pp 517-30.

O'Rand, A.M. (2001) 'Stratification and the life course. The forms of life-course capital and their interrelationships', in R.H. Binstock and L.K. George (eds) *Handbook of aging and the social sciences*, San Diego, CA: Academic Press, pp 197-231.

Phillipson, C. (1998) *Reconstructing old age: New agendas in social theory and practice*, London: Sage Publications.

Riley, M.W. (1985) 'Age strata in social systems', in R.H. Binstock and E. Shanas (eds) *Handbook of aging and the social sciences*, New York, NY: Van Nostrand Reinhold, pp 369-411.

Sørensen, A.B. (1986) 'Social structure and mechanisms of life course processes', in A.B. Sørensen, F.E. Weinert and L.R. Sherrod (eds) *Human development and the life course*, Hillsdale, NJ: Lawrence Erlbaum Associated Publishing, pp 177-97.

Tornstam, L. (1989) 'Gero-transcendence: a meta-theoretical reformulation of the disengagement theory', *Aging*, vol 1, pp 55-63.

Index

A

Activities of Daily Living (ADL) 70
activity theory 100-1, 224
adaptive potential in very old 20-2
adult stability model 15
age cohorts 226
  and culture 4
  size of cohort and inter-individual
    heterogeneity 15-16
Age Concern 108
age differences: individuality and
    relatedness 34-41
age imperialism 103-4
age norms 226
age stratification theory 52, 224
age-dependent inequalities 191-2
ageing differently *see* differential ageing
ageing population 1, 81, 143
ageing process 3-4
  as 'absent presence' 89
  see also multiple pathways
'ageing well' *see* 'positive ageing'
ageism
  and elderly migrants 169
  history of 2
  productive ageing policies 96-104
ageless self model 224
agency 55
Albrow, M. 169
alterity *see* otherness
'amenity-seeking' migration 144, 146,
    148-9, 152, 153
America *see* United States
Andersson, L. 48
androgyny 32, 40
Angel, J.L. 127
Angel, R.J. 127

B

Bach, R. 159
Baltes, M.M. 130
Baltes, P.B. 16, 129, 130
  see also Berlin Aging Study
Bangladeshi migrants 161-8
Barrett, A.E. 47-8
Barton, Bruce 211
Basch, L. 158-9
BASE *see* Berlin Aging Study
Bass, S.A. 101

Bauer, E. 165
Bauman, Z. 85, 158
Beauvoir, Simone de 8
Beck, U. 158, 169, 215-16
Belle, D. 116
Bengtson, V.L. 46
Berger, R.M. 117
Berlin Aging Study (BASE) 18-24, 197
Berlusconi, Silvio 143
Beveridge, W.H. 209
  welfare model 212
Binstock, R.H. 224
biographies 88
  choice biographies 177-8
  standard biographies 177
  see also lifespan theory
Birren, J.E. 18
Blakemore, K. 134
Bode, C. 39
body
  and identity 80, 97-8
  and productive ageing policies 103-4
  sexuality and old age 110-11
  strategies of denial 84-5
Bolzman, C. 152
Brandtstädter, J. 130
Brecher, E. 112-13, 114, 115
British General Household Survey 63,
    64-8
British migrants 149, 150
Burgess, E.O. 46
Butler, R. 101

C

Calasanti, T.M. 109, 110, 111, 116, 224
car ownership and gender 65, 67, 68, 69
cardiovascular health 20
care homes *see* residential care
caring
  family as carers 71, 73
  women migrants 159, 162-4
  see also dependency
Caro, F. 101
Carstensen, L.L. 129, 130
Castles, S. 126
categories of ageing 51-3, 79-80
  and identity 81-3, 89-90
  sexual categories 115
  subjective views of 85-7

tenuous nature of 53-4
change theory 224
children
  interconnectedness with 180-1, 182-3,
    184-5
  see also family
choice *see* lifestyle choice
choice biographies 177-8
'closed systems' 225-6
cohabitation *see* partner history;
    unmarried cohabitation
Cohen, A.P. 83
cohorts *see* age cohorts
collective identities 51-3
commodification of old age 99
communitarianism 102
complexity 16
constructivist perspective on diversity 46
continuity
  as given for successful old age 5, 224
  in lifecourse models 168
  and migrant experience 126, 128, 168
  and social inequality 191
contraception 178
Cooper, H. 115, 116
crystallised intelligence 225
Cuellar, L. 127
cultural adaptation: migrant experience 4,
    132-3
cultural diversity 1, 2-3
cumulative advantage theory 226
cumulative stress models 17-18
Cunningham, W. 18

D

Dannefer, D. 54, 55, 109, 224, 226
De Beauvoir, Simone 8
Deacon, S. 110
decommodification of welfare 212-13,
    215, 219
deconstructed self 83-5
'deinstitutionalisation of life course' 53,
    54, 213
DeLaet, D. 159
dependency
  Iranian immigrants 132
  physical dependency and emotional
    well-being 21-2
  structured dependency 160-1
  see also caring
Depression, The: welfare impact 211
destructuring and social inequality 191,
    202

developmental models 224
Die, A.H. 127
differential ageing 13-24
  as concept 14-16
  and social inequality 191
dimension specificity 17
disability: gender effects 65, 67, 70-1, 74
discontinuity
  migrant experience 126, 128, 168
  positive value 5
disengagement theory 100, 224
  Iranian immigrants 131-2
diversity and ageing 1-3, 5, 223-7
  in health 46-51
  heterogeneity approaches 45-6, 53-6
  neglected by gerontology 224-6
  sexual diversity 107-19
divorce
  gender effects 64, 66-7, 68, 69, 70, 108
  as life event 176
  partner history and societal trends 179,
    180-5
Dorfman, R. 116
Dutch Aging Survey 32-41
Dykstra, P.A. 178

E

Elder, G.H., Jr 175
emotional well-being 21-2
employment *see* paid work; pension
    provision; retirement
environment: quality of life survey 195,
    196-7, 198-202
Erikson, Erik 97
Esping-Andersen, G. 212, 214
Estes, C. 159-60
Europe
  migration in 141-53
  welfare systems 212-13
Europe's response to World Ageing (EC) 101-
    2
extraversion 22

F

Faist, T. 128
family
  as carers 71, 73
  interconnectedness with children 180-1,
    182-3, 184-5
  lesbian and gay social support 116, 117
  and migration
    dependency factor 132

as reason for migration 149-50
support networks 148, 163-8
'fate': role of 168
Featherstone, M. 97
financial well-being
gender effects and marital status 64-8,
73-4
retirement migrants 149, 152
women migrants 165, 166-7
see also income in later life; poverty
fluid intelligence 225
Foucault, Michel 81-2
'fourth age' category 52
'free-floating class' 213, 215, 219, 220*n*
Friend, R.A. 116-17
friendship: lesbian and gay experience
116, 117-18
'friendship families' 116
functioning profiles 22-4

G

Gardner, K. 161, 166
gay older people *see* lesbian and gay older
people
gender
individuality and relatedness 31, 35-9,
40-1
and life expectancy 47, 62
and marital status 61-74, 108
'normal' model 109-10
and partner status in later life 179,
181-2, 185
sexual expectations 111
and structured dependency 160-1
gender crossover theory 40
'generation' concept 52
George, L.K. 53
Germany: migrants from 149-50
gerontology 4-5
categories of ageing 51-3
heteronormative model of sexuality
109-15, 116, 119
'inner perspective' studies 50-1
migrant experience
discontinuities in models 168-9
as research source 125-6, 133-5
neglect of diversity 224-6
normative model 223-4
see also lifespan theory
Giddens, A. 55
GLAMS 84
globalisation 3, 86
and social inequality 217-19

transnational communities 127-8,
157-170
Goffman, E. 85
governance in Europe 142-3
Gulati, L. 161

H

Hagestad, G.O. 55
Hakim, C. 216-17
Hall, A. 110
Hall, S. 87
health
diversity and ageing 46-51
gender effects 65, 67, 69-71, 74
and intellectual functioning 20
quality of life survey 195, 196, 198-202
see also mental health; welfare
Hepworth, M. 97
Hertzman, C. 46
heterogeneity *see* diversity and ageing;
inter-individual heterogeneity
heteronormativity 109-12
social constructions 112-15
and social support research 116
Hinterlong, J. 100
historical attitudes to ageing 2
historical time 176, 226
Hochschild, A. 159, 160
Hockey, J. 79, 80, 89
Hodson, D. 110-11
Hoerder, D. 168
holistic interactionist models 16
home ownership and gender 65, 67, 68
homogenisation and social inequality 191,
202
homosexuality *see* lesbian and gay older
people
House, J.S. 115-16
household objects: value of 86-7
human capital 226

I

ideal age surveys 55-6, 57, 58
identity
ageing identities 79-90
collective identities 51-3
inner and outer logic of ageing 96-9,
104-5
self-identity and diversity 55
sexual identity 112-15, 116-17
subjective views of 85-7
illegal migrant workers 151-2

imagination 87
income in later life
    gender differences 64-8, 73-4
    retirement migrants 149, 152
    and social inequality 213-15, 219, 220*n*
    see also inequalities; pension provision;
        poverty
individualistic lifestyles 178
individuality
    and diversity 55
    and identity 84
    reflexive modernity 215-17, 218-19
    and relatedness 29-41
        see also social support
    see also self
inequalities 227
    in health 46-7
    and power and social class 207-20
    social inequality 189-202
inner and outer logic of ageing 96-9,
    104-5
'inner perspective' studies 50-1
institutional care *see* residential care
'institutionalisation of life course' 52, 54,
    89
intellectual functioning
    domain differences 17
    and physical health 20
    trajectories of decline 20
    see also mental health; psychological
        functioning
inter-individual heterogeneity 14-16,
    191, 225
    and size of age cohort 15-16
international migration
    multiple pathways 141-53
        labour migration 143-4, 145, 147-8,
            151-2
        retirement migration 142, 148-9, 152,
            153
    and successful ageing 4, 125-35
    transnational communities 157-170
Internet: lesbian social networks 117, 118
intra-individual change 14-15, 16, 225
    variable-centred approach 17-18
Iranian immigrants survey 130-5

J

James, A. 79, 80, 89
Jenkins, R. 88
Jensen, K.L. 113
Jylhä, M. 50-1

K

Kahn, R. 115-16
Karisto, A. 52
Katz, S. 101
Kelly, J. 117
Khanum, S.M. 159
Kimmel, D.C. 117
Klein Ikkink, K. 184
Kohli, M. 52, 89
Kunzmann, U. 21

L

labour migration 143-4, 145, 147-8, 160
    and disadvantage 151-2
Laslett, P. 52
LAT (living apart together) 179
latency in health status 48
lesbian and gay older people 107-19
Levitt, Peggy 158
Liefbroer, A.C. 178
life events 176
life expectancy
    dominance of women in later life 62
    novel experience of modernity 81
    see also mortality
lifecourse as concept 52-3
lifespan theory
    and categorical identities 82-3
    heterogeneity of lifecourse 14-16, 53-6
    and societal trends 175-85
    and successful ageing 129-30
    see also gerontology; theories of ageing
lifestyle choice 2, 55, 216-17
    choice biographies 177-8
    and identity 84
linear models of ageing 45-6, 168
living apart together (LAT) 179
living arrangements 179, 180-85
living conditions: quality of life survey
    195, 196, 197
living systems perspectives 16
Lloyd George, David 208
loneliness and partner history 181, 183,
    185
loss-related decline 17-18

M

McAdams, Dan 97
McCrae, R.R. 22
McMullin, J.A. 224
magnification model 15

Malta: British migrants in 149
marital status
  and gender inequality in later life 61–74, 108
  and heteronormativity 110, 112
  and lesbian and gay identities 114
  and mental health 47–8
  partner history and societal trends 176, 178–85
  and social support 116
Marx, Karl 217
'mask of age' 85, 97, 98–9
masquerade 96, 98, 105
Massey, Douglas 158
master-nature mentality 131
material well-being 65, 67, 68–9, 73–4
maturation theory 224
Mayer, K.U. *see* Berlin Aging Study
Mead, G.H. 88
mean: bias towards 223–4
medical model of old age 80, 87
medico-technical advances 3
memory 225
men
  marital status in later life 63–4
  see also gender
mental health
  and marital status 47–8
  quality of life survey 195, 196, 198–202
  see also psychological functioning
migration *see* international migration
Miller, M.J. 126
Mills, C. Wright 86
Minns, S. 217
Mirowsky, J. 116
modernisation theories 55
modernity
  novel experiences of old age 81
  second modernity 215–17, 218–19
  and social status of old 82
Moody, H.R. 4, 103
Moon, J.H. 127
mortality
  selective mortality and diversity 15
  and socioeconomic status 46–7, 48
  see also life expectancy
multiple pathways 3–4, 227
  migrant experience 141–53

N

Nederveen-Pieterse, J. 128, 135
Netherlands: partner history research 180–5

Neugarten, B.L. 51–2, 53
neuroticism 22
never marrieds
  gender effects 64, 67–8, 69, 71
  lesbian and gay older people 112
New Deal 211–12
New Labour
  heteronormativity 110
  productive ageing policies 102
normative lifecourses 53–4
Norway: migrant population 146–7

O

OASIS project 193–4
Öberg, P. 55
occupational pension schemes 209, 210, 215, 218
O'Connor, P. 116
one-person households 178
'open systems' 226
openness 22
otherness 2, 87

P

Pahl, R. 129
paid work
  in lifecourse models 168
  positive ageing policies 100, 102
  and social status 81, 82, 102, 103, 216
  and welfare status *see* pension provision
Papastergiadis, N. 159, 168
partner history
  and societal trends 176, 178–85
  see also marital status
pathways 2
  see also multiple pathways
Pearl, J. 127
Peate, I. 111
pension provision
  gender effects and marital status 64–5
  historical background 208–10
    American experience 210–12
  for migrants 150–1
  pension funds as global capital 214–15
  and social inequality 212–20
'performing self' 84–5, 98
person-centred approach to differential ageing 16, 18
personal differentiation 226
personality
  age-related trends 22
  domain differences 17

and identity 84-5
personality structures 15
Phillipson, C. 128, 134, 161
Phizacklea, A. 159
physical health
  and intellectual functioning 20
  quality of life survey 195, 196, 198-202
policy *see* social policy and ageing
Poor Law system 208, 210
popular culture and identity 87-8
population ageing 1, 81, 143
Portes, A. 159
'positive ageing' 87, 95-6
  and social policy 99-102, 104
  see also successful ageing
possessions: value of 86-7
postmodernity
  and diversity 97
  and social status of old 82
poverty
  gender effects and marital status 65-6,
    66-7
  and power and social class 207-9, 213,
    217, 219
  see also social exclusion
power and inequality 217-19
'preference theory' 216-17
process-oriented approach to successful
    ageing 129-30
productive ageing 99-104
  definitions 101
psychological ageing theories 30-1
psychological functioning 17-18
  adaptive potential in very old age 20-2
  functioning profiles 22-4
  see also intellectual functioning; mental
    health

Q
quality of life 189-202

R
racism 170
realist perspective on diversity 45-6
reflexive modernity 215-17, 218-19
relatedness *see* individuality and
    relatedness; social support
remarriage 179
Renner, G. 130
renting accommodation and marital
    status 68
repartnering 176, 179, 180-5

residential care: gender effects 71-3, 74
retirement
  and age categories 53-4
  and health diversities 48-50
  as lifecourse marker 62-3
  migration on 142, 148-9, 152, 153
  see also pension provision
Rich, A. 114, 116
Riley, M.W. 52
Rindfuss: high-school study 54-5
risk society 169
role theory 224
Roosevelt, F.D.: New Deal 211-12
Rose, S. 116
Rosenfeld, D. 113-14
Ross, C.E. 116
Ryff, C.D. 30

S
Sanders, A. 111
Scambler, G. 217
Schechter, M. 101
Schneewind, K.A. 30
Schultz, H.J. 103
second modernity 215-17, 218-19
Seelbach, W.C. 127
SELE instrument 33
selection, optimisation and compensation
    (SOC) model 16, 130
selective mortality 15
selectivity models 224
self
  adaptive potential in very old 20-2
  deconstruction of 83-5
  domain differences 17
  see also identity; individuality;
    personality
self-conception 29-41
self-esteem 225
self-identity and diversity 55
senescence: differential ageing 14
sexual diversity 107-19
  heteronormativity 109-12
Singer, T. 20
Skeen, P. 110-11
Slevin, K.F. 110, 111
social allocation 226
social assistance welfare model 212
social class *see* social stratification
social clocks 53
social construction of sexual identity
    112-15
social exclusion

migrants 151-2, 169-70
  see also inequalities; poverty; social
    inequality
social groups 3-4
social identity 88
social inequality 189-202
  power and social class 207-20
  theoretical assumptions 191-2
social insurance welfare model 212, 215
social model of old age 82-3
social networks
  lesbian and gay experience 117, 118
  see also social support
social pathways 54
social policy and ageing 96-104, 226, 227
  age imperialism 103-4
  migrant experience 169-70
social relationships: quality of life survey
    195, 196, 197, 198-202
social reproduction 226
social roles 54-5
social security *see* pension provision;
    welfare state
social status and paid work 81, 82, 102,
    103
social stratification
  BASE study 19
  and inequality 207-20
  socioeconomic status and diversity in
    health 46-50
social support
  lesbian and gay experience 108, 115-19
  and marital status 116
  migrant experience 127-8, 149, 160-8
  and partner history in later life 180-1,
    182-3, 184-5
  see also individuality: and relatedness
socialisation 224
societal trends and diversity 175-85
Sørensen, A.B. 225-6
Spain: migrants in 148, 149
Spence, S.H. 111
state-oriented approach to successful
    ageing 129
stereotyping 2, 14, 87, 223
  and categories of ageing 51-2
  sexuality in later life 111, 116
stigmatisation 84
stochastic stress models 17-18
structural determination 80-1, 89
structured dependency 160-1
subjective health
  gender effects and marital status 70-1
  and measurement methods 50-1

successful ageing
  as construct 128-30
  continuity and 5, 126
  migrant experience 125-35
  psychological ageing theories 30
  see also positive ageing
support systems *see* social support
surveys: impact of measurement method
    50-1
survival curves 23-4
survivor model of old age 99
Sweden
  inequalities in health 46-7
  Iranian immigrants survey 130-5
systemic loss: functioning profiles 22-4

T

television 178
terminal decline 17, 18
theories of ageing 30-1
  see also lifespan theory
'third age' category 52
Thompson, P. 82, 165
time *see* historical time
Tornstam, L. 55
Townsendite movement 211
trades unions and welfare state 209-10
trajectories of ageing
  differential ageing 14
  and health diversities 47-50
  trajectories of decline 20
Tran, T.V. 127
transnational communities 157-170
  definition 158-9
trends *see* societal trends
Trotsky, Leon 219-20
Twenge, J.M. 31, 40

U

UN World Assembly on Ageing 100
unemployment 211
United States: welfare and inequality
    210-12
universal welfare model 212
unmarried cohabitation 179

V

VanEvery, J. 110
variable-centred approach to differential
    ageing 16, 17-18
Verhaeghen, P. 20

Veterans Pension 210
Vincent, J. 160

W

Warnes, A.M. 169–70
Weeks, J. 127
welfare services: position of migrants 142,
    149, 152, 169–70
welfare state and inequality 208–20
  historical background 209–10
    American experience 210–12
  pensions crisis 214–15
well-being *see* emotional well-being;
    health
Westwood, S. 159
WHOQOL-Bref measure 193–201
widowhood
  gender effects 63–4, 64–5, 66, 67, 68, 69,
    71
  as life event 176
  partner history and societal trends 178,
    179, 180–5
Wolf, D.A. 179
women
  effects of marital status in later life
    61–74
    on income 64–8
    lesbian experience 108
  effects of societal trends 177
  lifestyle choices 216–17
  and migration experience 159, 160–8
    disadvantaged women 151
  see also gender
WOOPIES 84
work *see* paid work
World Bank: pension proposals 214

Y

Yee, D. 109
youth
  and ideal age 55–6, 57, 58
  staying young 3
youthful self 97, 98

The health and social care divide (Revised 2nd Edition)
The experiences of older people
Jon Glasby and Rosemary Littlechild
Consultant Editor: Jo Campling

"... achieves what it sets out to do: it is accessible to a wide range of readers. For consumers of services it provides knowledge and powerful insights; for students, practitioners, managers and teachers in health and social care it is an invaluable textbook in a complicated area of policy and practice; for researchers and policy makers it brings together and synthesizes definitive polices and research. It's also a good read." *Journal of Interprofessional Care*

Paperback £18.99 US$29.95 ISBN-10 1 86134 525 9 • ISBN-13 978 1 86134 525 7
Hardback £50.00 US$75.00 ISBN-10 1 86134 526 7 • ISBN-13 978 1 86134 526 4
240 x 172mm 176 pages May 2004

Depression and older people
Towards securing well-being in later life
Mary Godfrey and Tracy Denby

"We know too little about depression in later life. It hasn't been taken seriously enough. Here is a report that sets out the issues clearly and makes recommendations that are realisable." *Heather Clark, School of Social Studies, University College Chichester*

The literature on depression in old age has tended to be dominated by the medical model with its focus on symptoms and treatment. This report breaks new ground by adopting a psycho-social approach – one that explores depression in the context of the everyday lives of older people.

Paperback £14.99 US$25.00 ISBN-10 1 86134 642 5 • ISBN-13 9781 86134 642 1
A4 REPORT (297 x 210mm) 64 pages November 2004
Published in association with the Help the Aged

Happy retirement?
The impact of employers' policies and practice on the process of retirement
Sarah Vickerstaff, John Baldock, Jennifer Cox and Linda Keen

"... immensely helpful for researchers and practitioners alike ... a valuable picture of the complex and changing face of retirement."
Ageing & Society

Any attempt by governments to stem the tide of early retirement will need to focus as much on employers' management of human resources as on the impacts of social policy. This report focuses on this previously neglected area: employers' policies and practice as a dynamic force in retirement decisions.

Drawing on data from a series of organisational case studies that situate the individual's decisions and experience in the context of employers' age management policies, the report:

- examines how the retirement process is currently managed in a range of organisations;
- identifies barriers to effective planning for retirement;
- considers whether individuals feel there is enough choice when facing decisions about retirement;
- addresses the concerns of both researchers and academics in the fields of human resource management and social policy.

Paperback £13.95 US$23.95 ISBN-10 1 86134 584 4 • ISBN-13 978 1 86134 584 4
297 x 210mm 52 pages July 2004

To order further copies of this publication or any other Policy Press titles please contact:

In the UK and Europe:
Marston Book Services, PO Box 269,
Abingdon, Oxon, OX14 4YN, UK
Tel: +44 (0)1235 465500
Fax: +44 (0)1235 465556
Email: direct.orders@marston.co.uk

In the USA and Canada:
ISBS, 920 NE 58th Street, Suite 300,
Portland, OR 97213-3786, USA
Tel: +1 800 944 6190 (toll free)
Fax: +1 503 280 8832
Email: info@isbs.com

In Australia and New Zealand:
DA Information Services, 648 Whitehorse
Road Mitcham, Victoria 3132, Australia
Tel: +61 (3) 9210 7777
Fax: +61 (3) 9210 7788
E-mail: service@dadirect.com.au

Further information about all of our titles can be found on our website:

www.policypress.org.uk

Evidence & Policy
A Journal of Research, Debate and Practice
Managing Editor: Ken Young, School of Social Science and Public Policy, King's College London, UK

"Academics and policy makers now have a place to share data, ideas and arguments about the promises and pitfalls of basing policy on hard evidence – or even the possibility of doing so. *Evidence & Policy* will be a great addition to the international conversation."
Carol Weiss, Harvard University, USA

Aims and scope:
Evidence & Policy is the first peer-reviewed journal dedicated to comprehensive and critical treatment of the relationship between research evidence and the concerns of policy makers and practitioners. International in scope and interdisciplinary in focus, it addresses the needs of those who provide public services, and those who provide the research base for evaluation and development across a wide range of social and public policy issues – from social care to education, from public health to criminal justice.

Policy & Politics
An International Journal
Joint Editors: Misa Izuhara, School for Policy Studies, University of Bristol, UK
Adrian Kay, Department of Politics and Public Policy, Griffith University, Australia

The multidisciplinary journal analyzing the origin, impact and evaluation of public policy

Aims and scope
Policy & Politics is a leading peer-reviewed journal in the field of public policy with a reputation for publishing papers of the highest quality. The journal is unique in focusing on cross-cutting themes across a wide range of policy areas. Themes include:

* accountability and regulation
* theorising the policy process
* human rights and discrimination
* evaluation
* policy making and implementation
* globalisation and internationalisation

The journal also explores the match between theory and empirical applications and links macro-scale political economy debates with micro-scale policy studies.